Learn Computer Forensics

A beginner's guide to searching, analyzing, and securing digital evidence

William Oettinger

BIRMINGHAM—MUMBAI

Learn Computer Forensics

Commissioning Editor: Vijin Boricha
Acquisition Editor: Shrilekha Inani
Senior Editor: Rahul D'souza
Content Development Editor: Ronn Kurien
Technical Editor: Dinesh Pawar
Copy Editor: Safis Editing
Project Coordinator: Neil D'mello
Proofreader: Safis Editing
Indexer: Priyanka Dhadke
Production Designer: Nilesh Mohite

First published: April 2020

Production reference: 2110620

Published by Packt Publishing Ltd.
Livery Place
35 Livery Street
Birmingham
B3 2PB, UK.

ISBN 978-1-83864-817-6

www.packt.com

This book is dedicated to IACIS and the pioneers of this field whom I have had the privilege of meeting and learning from. Mike Anderson and Will Docken were some of the first professionals I met and they had a significant impact on me as I started in this field. I want to thank Eric Zimmerman, Harlan Carvey, Brett Shavers, and Steve Whalen for all of the work they do for the forensics community. Your information sharing and work have impacted me and helped me grow as an examiner. There is a long list of people who contributed to my success that I want to thank: Larry Smith, David Papargiris, Tom Keller, Dave McCain, Steve Williams, Scott Pearson, Scot Bradeen, Matt Presser, Mike Webber, and everyone else who has helped me along the way.

Contributors

About the author

William Oettinger is a veteran technical trainer and investigator. He is a retired police officer with the Las Vegas Metropolitan Police Department and a retired CID agent with the United States Marine Corps. He is a professional with over 20 years' experience in academic, local, military, federal, and international law enforcement organizations, where he acquired his multifaceted experience in IT, digital forensics, security operations, law enforcement, criminal investigations, policy, and procedure development. He has earned an MSc from Tiffin University, Ohio. He works for Bilecki and Tipon LLLC and the University of Maryland Global Campus (UMGC). When not working, he likes to spend time with his wife and his two miniature schnauzers.

About the reviewer

Peter Phurchpean is an investigator with the Computer Crimes Investigation Unit, California Highway Patrol. He has been with the California Highway Patrol (CHP) since 2002. He has been a member of the CHP's Computer Crimes Investigation Unit for the past 7 years as a digital forensic analyst and investigator. During his time with the unit, he has been responsible for investigating computer crimes against the State of California, ranging from network intrusions against State agencies to child exploitation cases. He is experienced in the analysis of computers, smartphones, and network systems. He has also successfully obtained computer forensic certifications through the California Department of Justice and many other institutions besides.

Packt is searching for authors like you

If you're interested in becoming an author for Packt, please visit `authors.packtpub.com` and apply today. We have worked with thousands of developers and tech professionals, just like you, to help them share their insight with the global tech community. You can make a general application, apply for a specific hot topic that we are recruiting an author for, or submit your own idea.

Table of Contents

3

Acquisition of Evidence

4

Computer Systems

Section 2: Investigation

5

Computer Investigation Process

6

Windows Artifact Analysis

7

RAM Memory Forensic Analysis

8

Email Forensics – Investigation Techniques

9

Internet Artifacts

Section 3: Reporting

10

Report Writing

Preface

Welcome to the world of digital forensics! In this book, you will be going into the depths of the Windows operating system to determine the user's actions on the system. You will also learn about the different filesystems used by the Windows operating system. The role of the examiner is not only about the examination, but also about the report you generate and how you explain your findings. You will learn how to prepare for the digital investigation, including equipment selection, training, and planning a response to the crime scene. It is my hope this book will be your resource if you are a novice examiner or an experienced examiner.

Who this book is for

This book is for the novice and experienced examiner. While an understanding of operating systems and filesystems would be helpful, it is not required.

What this book covers

Chapter 1, Types of Computer-Based Investigations, introduces to the reader the different topics of computer-based investigations, from criminal acts investigated by the police to potentially illegal actions performed by an employee or third parties and examined by a non-governmental investigator. While the goal is the same—to present evidence about an incident—the methods of the two slightly differ. It is essential for the reader to understand the similarities, that is, being able to present evidence in judicial proceedings, and recognize the differences, that is, search warrant requirements for a government agent.

Chapter 2, The Forensic Analysis Process, details the critical thinking in the planning of providing digital investigative services. This topic will allow the reader to create a strategy to conduct an efficient investigation. The reader will learn to offer different approaches to conduct the investigation depending on the unique set of circumstances for each matter.

Chapter 3, Acquisition of Evidence, explains that digital evidence is one of the most volatile pieces of evidence an investigator can handle. Mishandling of digital evidence can severely impact the investigation. Additionally, you may destroy the entire dataset. This chapter will address how to minimize or eliminate these issues when using a validation process to create a forensic image.

Chapter 4, Computer Systems, explains that the investigator must control the computer processes while acquiring digital evidence. When dealing with the many combinations of operating systems and hardware, you must implement controls to protect the integrity of the evidence. This chapter will discuss the boot process in detail and identify the most commonly used filesystems.

Chapter 5, Computer Investigation Process, explains that being a forensic examiner is much more than pushing a button. Once the evidence has been collected, you have to analyze the dataset. It is not about finding artifacts but rather examining the data and putting it into a context that will either support or not support the hypothesis about the user's actions on the system.

Chapter 6, Windows Artifact Analysis, explains that Microsoft Windows is by far the most common operating system today. In this chapter, we will look at the different versions of Windows and will show the reader how to identify and recover common artifacts based on the release of Windows being examined.

Chapter 7, RAM Memory Forensic Analysis, covers the analysis of RAM, which is a source of evidence that has recently been recognized to contain vital information about the user's actions on the system. RAM is very volatile evidence and can provide data that cannot be found anywhere else on the computer system.

Chapter 8, Email Forensics — Investigation Techniques, discusses email, which is a part of everyday life. This communication vector can be one of the primary communication tools for the majority of the population. These communications can contain incredible amounts of data related to an investigation. The investigator must be able to reconstruct the path that email took from the source to the destination to determine its validity.

Chapter 9, Internet Artifacts, explains that using the internet is a daily activity for the majority of the population. Like any other activity, the internet can be used for legal, law-abiding business, or for criminal activity. The internet can be accessed in a variety of ways. The forensic investigator must be able to analyze all these different aspects of the internet to get to the truth of the matter.

Chapter 10, Report Writing, covers report writing, which is not the most exciting portion of the forensic exam process. The forensic examiner must be able to explain a technical topic to a non-technical user. As a forensic examiner, you must be able to place that artifact into a context that the audience understands. This ability is a critical skill that you need to master to be a competent forensic examiner.

Chapter 11, Expert Witness Ethics, explains that a forensic examiner must be objective, truthful, honest, and perform their due diligence when conducting an examination. The examiner will be providing testimony that may result in someone losing their freedom. The ultimate goal of the investigation conducted by the forensic examiner is to provide testimony or evidence in a judicial or administrative proceeding to stop the cybercriminal's activity.

To get the most out of this book

It will be helpful if you have access to a computer and the commercial and open source forensic tools, such as X-Ways Forensics or Paladin, described in this book. It is not required. If you have access to any of the commonly available forensic (open source or commercial) tools you will be able to follow along as you are reading the different chapters.

If you are using the digital version of this book, we advise you to type the code yourself. Doing so will help you avoid any potential errors related to copy/pasting of code.

Download the color images

We also provide a PDF file that has color images of the screenshots/diagrams used in this book. You can download it here: `http://www.packtpub.com/sites/default/files/downloads/9781838648176_ColorImages.pdf`

Conventions used

There are a number of text conventions used throughout this book.

`Code in text`: Indicates code words in text, database table names, folder names, filenames, file extensions, pathnames, dummy URLs, user input, and Twitter handles. Here is an example: "Mount the downloaded `WebStorm-10*.dmg` disk image file as another disk in your system."

A block of code is set as follows:

```
html, body, #map {
  height: 100%;
  margin: 0;
  padding: 0
}
```

When we wish to draw your attention to a particular part of a code block, the relevant lines or items are set in bold:

```
[default]
exten => s,1,Dial(Zap/1|30)
exten => s,2,Voicemail(u100)
exten => s,102,Voicemail(b100)
exten => i,1,Voicemail(s0)
```

Any command-line input or output is written as follows:

```
$ mkdir css
$ cd css
```

Bold: Indicates a new term, an important word, or words that you see onscreen. For example, words in menus or dialog boxes appear in the text like this. Here is an example: "Select **System info** from the **Administration** panel."

> **Tips or important notes**
> Appear like this.

Get in touch

Feedback from our readers is always welcome.

General feedback: If you have questions about any aspect of this book, mention the book title in the subject of your message and email us at customercare@packtpub.com.

Errata: Although we have taken every care to ensure the accuracy of our content, mistakes do happen. If you have found a mistake in this book, we would be grateful if you would report this to us. Please visit www.packtpub.com/support/errata, selecting your book, clicking on the Errata Submission Form link, and entering the details.

Piracy: If you come across any illegal copies of our works in any form on the Internet, we would be grateful if you would provide us with the location address or website name. Please contact us at copyright@packt.com with a link to the material.

If you are interested in becoming an author: If there is a topic that you have expertise in and you are interested in either writing or contributing to a book, please visit authors.packtpub.com.

Reviews

Please leave a review. Once you have read and used this book, why not leave a review on the site that you purchased it from? Potential readers can then see and use your unbiased opinion to make purchase decisions, we at Packt can understand what you think about our products, and our authors can see your feedback on their book. Thank you!

For more information about Packt, please visit packt.com.

Section 1: Acquiring Evidence

You will learn about the forensic process and the importance of obtaining forensically sound data and the procedures to achieve that goal.

The following chapters are in the section:

1
Types of Computer-Based Investigations

Welcome to the 21st century, where almost everything in life is connected to an electronic device. There are digital cameras inside doorbells; your smartphone tracks your daily progress from work to home and back again; you get social media updates when you go to the gym, a show, or travel to a new city.

Your phone calls, bank access, and medical appointments are all tracked via digital technology. If it tracks your mundane daily activity, what about criminal or unethical behavior? That activity is also followed, and if you are a digital forensic investigator, you must know the repositories of the digital evidence and how to analyze it. There is almost no criminal activity that will not have digital evidence associated with it and, as an investigator, it is your job to find all available evidence, process it, and present findings to the finder of fact.

This chapter will introduce you to the different topics of computer-based investigations, from criminal acts investigated by the police to civil and potentially illegal actions performed by an employee or external third party that are examined by a nongovernmental investigator.

While the goal is the same, to present evidence about an incident, the methods for each are slightly different. It is essential for you to understand the similarities between the investigations; being able to present evidence in a judicial proceeding and recognize the differences.

The topics that will be covered in this chapter are as follows:

- Differences in computer-based investigations

- Criminal investigations

- Corporate investigations

Differences in computer-based investigations

This book is all about introducing a beginner to the realm of digital forensics. What is digital forensics? It is a division of forensics involving the recovery and analysis of data that has been recovered from digital devices. At one time, the term *digital forensics* was treated as a synonym for computer forensics, but now it involves all devices capable of storing digital data. No matter what term is used, the goal is to identify, collect, and examine/analyze digital data while preserving its integrity. Digital forensics is not only about finding the artifact, it is a formal examination/analysis of the digital evidence to prove or to disprove whether the accused committed the violation.

It is not always about demonstrating that the suspect is guilty; as a forensic examiner, you also have that ethical obligation to find exculpatory evidence that will prove the subject's innocence. Your duty is to be an unbiased third party in presenting the findings of the investigation. In a criminal examination, your findings could deprive someone of their liberty, and in a corporate investigation, your findings may lead to a criminal investigation or cost someone their livelihood. As a digital forensic examiner, your conclusions can have an extraordinary impact on the subjects of the investigation.

To be a digital forensic examiner, you need to have a desire to ask questions, have specialized equipment, and have the required training. From teaching people interested in the field, I have found the best students can critically examine the facts and circumstances being presented and, using that ability, can focus their efforts on efficiently reaching an accurate conclusion. Unfortunately, I find many students want to use a "find evidence" button, find all the artifacts, and print up a thousand-page report and call it a day. That is not digital forensics.

Digital forensics is not finding the artifact. By artifact, I am talking about an incriminating Google search in browser history, an incriminating email between the subject and a co-conspirator, and illicit images found in the filesystem. Artifacts are breadcrumbs leading to the identity of the person conducting the illegal activity. However, on their own, they do not identify the user who created these artifacts or the one who is responsible for their creation indirectly. One of the biggest challenges in this field is to determine what is colloquially known as the "idiot behind the keyboard." You want to tie the user to the specific subject and to do that, you have to analyze – that is the key word–the digital evidence to associate it with a particular user.

If you are in the IT field, you will understand networking and computer operating systems, but you will lack knowledge of how to preserve evidence, maintain a chain of custody, and present it in a criminal/administrative proceeding.

If you are an investigator, you will understand the chain of custody, evidence preservation, and testifying in a criminal/administrative proceeding. However, you may lack experience in the digital field. To be an effective digital forensic examiner, you have to be part of both those worlds. You have to understand how data is created, shared, and saved in the digital realm and be able to preserve that evidence in a forensically sound manner and testify in proceedings. Sometimes, the ability to talk in front of a large group while answering hard questions posed to you by attorneys from both sides is the hardest part of the field.

As with any field, the way you get better and more effective is to practice, to conduct real and mock examinations, to receive training, and have the willingness to reach out to your peers for advice. Since you are reading this book, you are taking that first step. You could be reading the text on your own, using it as a textbook for a college course you are taking, or using it in a corporate training session. The reason does not matter. Reading this book will put you on the road to be a more effective digital forensic examiner.

What is cybercrime? What crimes does a digital forensic examiner investigate? A digital forensic examiner may investigate any alleged wrongdoing that touches on the digital world. Nearly everyone possesses a mobile device. Sometimes, a person owns or uses multiple mobile devices and laptops and the traditional desktop. All of these sources have the ability to maintain a significant amount of information as it relates to the investigation. For example, I investigated a crime against a person where the victim was physically unable to communicate with the police. How does that become a crime that requires the use of a digital forensic examiner?

Well, in this case, she had maintained communication with the suspect of that crime via a website and instant messaging on her mobile device. While they did not directly have evidence relating to the crime being investigated, they had evidence about the relationship between the victim and the suspect. In the 21st century, almost any crime may have evidence stored in a digital format. Now, there are some crimes where someone will have used their computer as a tool to commit the crime, such as sending harassing emails, fraud and forgery, hacking, corporate espionage, or the trafficking of illicit images.

Your occupation will dictate your response to a situation; if you are law enforcement, you will have one set of procedures to follow, while if you are in the corporate world, you will have a different set of procedures to follow. While some processes may overlap in different fields, each one has its unique differences, which is what we will discuss next.

Criminal investigations

As a law enforcement professional, your first consideration will be officer safety. Is the scene secure to process and secure evidence? When the investigation starts, you may take part in one or more roles. The most basic positions are as follows:

- The first responder
- The investigator
- Crime scene technician

Depending on the size of your agency, you may fill one position or all three, and you may report to one or more supervisors. Now, in the matter of digital evidence, it is preferable that the person in charge of the crime scene has some knowledge of the fragility of digital evidence. That allows personnel to enact the proper procedures to ensure that the evidence is not corrupted.

Let's talk about what each role does.

First responders

The first responders are the first ones on the scene. They secure what may be a chaotic scene. They will identify the following:

- Potential victims
- Witnesses
- Potential suspects
- How best to maintain control

They will do this until the investigator arrives. The first responder's primary mission is to make the scene safe and secure and ensure that no one can contaminate the evidence. As you can imagine, crime scenes can vary from a dynamic crime scene to the relatively static crime scene, depending on the nature of the crime. In both scenarios, the first responder must have basic knowledge of what items could contain digital evidence when they secure the scene. We would not want to have subjects grabbing cell phones or laptops and using them for any activity.

So, how does a first responder protect the crime scene? Just like you see in TV shows and movies, yellow crime scene tape is the most common method. It is the most straightforward visible sign of a crime scene barrier, and in our culture, people recognize the barrier being presented by that thin piece of yellow plastic. One or more personnel will have to monitor the crime scene to regulate who can cross that line and enter the scene.

Investigators

The investigator will respond to the scene after being requested by the first responder. Upon arriving at the scene, the first responder and the investigator will coordinate, and information sharing will now start. The first responder will provide the basic information, which typically involves the five Ws and one H, specifically the who, what, when, where, why, and how, about the incident.

The first responder will also provide information about any actions they or anyone else had taken before the arrival of the investigator. For example, the investigator will want to know whether the first responder(s) touched anything, moved anything, or changed anything within the crime scene. This could be a physical action such as applying first aid to a victim or turning a computer on or off. I remember an examination I did where the first responders did not reveal that they had accessed the victim's computer. While conducting my examination, I did a timeline analysis and saw an abnormality in the activity after the victim had died. The abnormality was caused by the unreported actions of the first responders. What's important to understand here is that the first responders' actions were not wrong. What created complications is that they did not report the actions, which led to additional work and explanations.

The investigator takes charge of the scene and directs all activity. They will direct the other team members' investigative efforts to ensure the proper documentation is completed regarding the seizure of evidence. Sometimes, the first responder will seize evidence and turn it over to the investigator. A chain of custody document must be completed and maintained showing who found the item and who maintained control until the completion of the judicial or administrative proceeding.

Crime scene technician

Finally, we come to the crime scene technician. This can be a sworn or unsworn position within the law enforcement agency. They have specialized training in the collection of evidence. This could be physical evidence, such as fingerprints, tool comparison, the collection of biological fluids, and crime scene photography, all of which require specialized training and equipment. The collection of digital evidence requires the same level of expertise that the collection of physical evidence does.

> **Note**
>
> We can put law enforcement jobs into two basic groups:
>
> **Sworn**: May take an oath to support the laws in their jurisdiction; they have the power to make arrests and carry firearms.
>
> **Non-sworn**: May take an oath but do not have powers to arrest. These positions are typically crime scene analyst or law enforcement support technicians.

The crime scene technician is responsible for the preservation of evidence and starting the chain of custody. Some actions they could carry out include the acquisition of volatile memory of a computer system, creating forensic images of the storage devices, or creating the logical forensic image of logical files from a server. The evidence will be bagged and tagged and transported to a secure location. What do I mean by *bagged and tagged*? They will place all the evidence or the containers holding the digital evidence in the appropriate storage container. A tag will then be filled out with the identifiers to specify which investigation the evidence belongs to, who collected it, and what evidence is contained within the container.

As we go through the rest of this book, we will cover the duties of the crime scene technician in greater detail.

A law enforcement officer may be a first responder, investigator, or crime scene technician and, in all roles, is an agent of the government. Depending on your jurisdiction, the government may restrict how and when the property can be seized and searched. I will discuss the judicial process in the United States; your locality may have different laws and procedures.

In the United States, a citizen's rights to privacy are protected by the fourth amendment of the US Constitution, which states the following:

> *"The right of the people to be secure in their persons, houses, papers, and effects, against unreasonable searches and seizures, shall not be violated, and no Warrants shall issue, but upon probable cause, supported by oath or affirmation, and particularly describing the place to be searched, and the persons or things to be seized."*

At a basic level, this means that before the government can seize any evidence, there must be (a) a search warrant based upon probable cause or (b) the consent of the owner. The consent given by the owner must be willingly given and must be able to be revoked, which can create an issue in some jurisdictions where the processing of digital evidence can take months, and in some jurisdictions, years. If the owner revokes their consent or refuses to give it, what options does law enforcement have? A search warrant.

How does a member of law enforcement get a warrant? As we learned from the preceding passage, it must be based on probable cause. The definition of probable cause is a reasonable standard that the applicant must reasonably believe that the items being searched for are at that location. Who determines what is reasonable? This would be the judicial official, such as a judge, Justice of the Peace, and so on.

The law enforcement officer makes the written request, while the judge reviews it and will either approve/disapprove it. If approved, then the law enforcement officer can then seize and search the property within the guidelines specified by the judicial official. The law requires only agents of the government to get a search warrant to seize and search property. If you work in the corporate world, this process will not pertain to you.

Now, let's talk about some potential crimes someone might call you to investigate. This will be a high-level overview of the crime itself, and later on in this book, we will address the specific artifacts we should analyze to determine whether criminal actions occurred.

Illicit images

Nearly everyone is connected to the many different forms of digital networks via our mobile devices, tablets, laptops, and computers–we are always connected in one manner or another. Depending on who you ask, it is either the best thing in the world or the worst. There are some excellent aspects; social media allows people/family members to stay in contact, no matter where they are in the world. The totality of the world's knowledge is just a few clicks away. You can read news reports from portions of the world that you previously did not know existed. It is an adventure waiting to happen. Now, it is not all unicorns and rainbows out there. Like any society, there are dark and dangerous portions of the internet where you should be hesitant to travel. That includes the sourcing and sharing of illicit images. For our purposes, an illicit image is an image whose subject matter is offensive or illegal, depending on your cultural or legal landscape.

Before the advent and widespread use of the internet, trafficking in illicit images was almost eradicated, so what changed? The consumer of illicit images no longer had to be physically present to pick up the physical images. The internet allows the user to be relatively anonymous and to access the illicit images with minimal exposure. I have read reports that state that the high-speed data network that most of us enjoy is because of the consumer wanting faster throughput speeds to download illicit images.

Consumers of illicit images have free access to terabytes of data with simple clicks of the mouse. If the consumer wants higher quality or a specific subject matter, then it is not a complicated process to find a vendor to meet the needs of the consumer for a price.

Your jurisdiction will determine what is or is not an illicit image and the level of criminality associated with the possession and/or distribution of the contraband images. I will not differentiate or specify a subject to define illicit images. I will discuss them using the generic title of illicit images or contraband images. You can use either phrase depending on what may be legal/illegal in your jurisdiction.

How do people share contraband images? At a basic level, a file is a file. A JPEG image of a sunset does not differ from a JPEG image of a contraband subject. Anyone can use any aspect of the internet to share files–the content of the files is irrelevant. If the system allows the user to share data, then the contents of those shared files can be legal or illegal content. Let's look at some media through which illicit images could be exchanged.

Email-based communications

Email is one of the easiest ways to share information through files between two or more people. An email address does not automatically point to a specific user. There are service providers who actively advertise anonymity for users of their email accounts. The service provider states that they do not save users' transactional information, such as source IP, dates and times of connection, or billing information. The service provider may be located outside of the jurisdiction investigating the contraband, which will allow the service provider to ignore the judicial paperwork requesting the subscriber information.

Newsgroups/USENET

This is one of the first components of the internet, and one that has fallen off the radar for the everyday user. Initially, the internet comprised the World Wide Web, with components such as web browsing, email, and USENET. Web browsing and email are known by nearly every user of the internet, while USENET has faded out of public perception. This does not mean it is not being used. USENET is like the old bulletin board system, where you had specific groups, and users could post messages, attach files, and other users could download the files and comments. The user can post just a text message or attach a file to the message. This file is known as a binary.

A binary is a file type–digital images, video, audio software, or any other file type. The user has to use a newsreader to access USENET. There are free and paid versions of newsreaders available in which the user can subscribe to a USENET service. Just like the email service providers that we discussed earlier, one selling point for USENET service providers is anonymity, where they explicitly state that they maintain no user transactional data or billing records or they are in jurisdictions whose laws may not adequately address the contraband contained on the server:

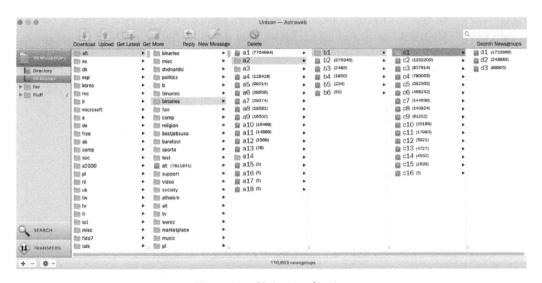

Figure 1.1 – Unison application

The preceding screenshot shows you the Unison program running on macOS and accessing the service provider Astraweb.

Looking from left to right, you can see the hierarchical system used by USENET. At the far-left column, I have selected `alt`, which then populates the next column with many named folders. The folders' naming convention shows the subject of the group. I have selected `binaries`, which means I am looking for attached files to the postings. In the third column, we can see folder icons and a brown folder icon with papers coming out the top. The folder icon shows that there are additional groups contained within, while the brown folder icon shows that this is a newsgroup.

As you can see from the preceding screenshot, there are a variety of subjects for the user to explore; some groups may or may not contain contraband images/files. Your jurisdiction will determine what is legal or not as you conduct your investigation.

Peer-to-Peer file sharing

Peer-to-Peer (P2P) file sharing is a decentralized method of file sharing. In traditional file sharing, a server hosts the file and the client accesses the server to download the file. In the early days of Napster and music sharing, this became a liability for copyright violations. The service provider was served with judicial processes and was found to be liable for hosting a directory of copyrighted files.

In response, the P2P method was changed; no longer was a centralized database created, but rather users were able to directly search for other users' shared folders on the network. Users connected to a shared network and acted as both a server and a client. In P2P file sharing, when a user identifies a file they want to download, the software reaches out to the other users who possess the desired file. Each user then provides a piece of the file to the recipient. When all the pieces are collected, the software puts them back to the original configuration. The user could then participate as a node and start sharing the file they just downloaded:

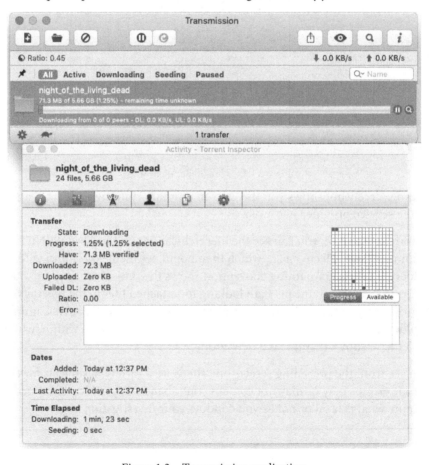

Figure 1.2 – Transmission application

The preceding screenshot shows the **Transmission** program running on macOS. I am downloading a movie from the public domain (`archive.org`), and in the bottom portion of the preceding screenshot, you can see that the file has been broken into much smaller bits. The highlighted bits show which parts of the file I have downloaded. Later, we will go into much greater detail about P2P file sharing and the artifacts that will be left in the filesystem.

The crime of stalking

For all of the good that the internet provides, it also provides a conduit for people to exploit, harass, and bully other people. The victim could be known to the subject or could have interacted with the victim's online persona in some manner and felt the victim had wronged them. A lot of the bad behavior we see with online activities is because of the anonymity that the internet provides the attacker/subject. When eyes are watching or when we know the true identity of the attacker, they change their behavior to conform to societal norms. Unfortunately, it takes time for society to recognize the criminality of specific actions via the digital medium.

Cyberstalking or cyberbullying is now being regulated and is now considered an actual crime. Depending on your jurisdiction, the definition will vary, and what resources the government will spend in the prosecution of these crimes will vary too. Remember, the identity of the user at the other end of the digital world can be challenging to prove to the high standard required by a court of law.

According to the National Center for Victims of Crime, `https://members.victimsofcrime.org/our-programs/past-programs/stalking-resource-center/stalking-information`, historically, in the United States, almost 1,500,000 people, the majority of them women, have been victimized, harassed, and bullied via the digital medium, with the attacks lasting in excess of 2 years. The attacks increased in length if the participants had been intimate partners.

The impact of this criminal behavior is immense; the victim will lose time from work, have to move residences (several times, sometimes), and suffer from the physical and mental effects such as the anxiety and depression that comes from being targeted. The ability to stalk a former intimate partner in the digital world opens the door to the ability to inflict significant violence on a former partner and, in some cases, bring about their death.

What behaviors make up cyberstalking? There have been documented incidents where a terminated employee has sent manipulated, compromising images of their supervisor to members of the organization and to the general public. This activity continued for months before it was stopped. Despite the harassment ending and the perpetrator being identified, the supervisor still felt the need to leave their job, change their name, and move to another community.

So, where do we begin in our attempts to investigate this crime? The interview will be the best starting place. Asking the victim if they know or suspect who may be behind the harassment is the first question asked. In my experience and most of the time, the victim will have a general idea of who the harasser is, especially if it is a former intimate partner. Now, there will be some victims who may suffer from mental health issues that could complicate the assessment. As an investigator, you have to listen to the whole story to understand the totality of events. Just because someone is paranoid does not mean someone is not out to get them. As an investigator, you have to have an open mind and not allow your preconceptions to make you miss evidence or indicators that may be visible.

If the victim has an idea of who the harasser may be, make sure you record all the pertinent information they can provide you with. Names, addresses, usernames, email addresses, screen names, and social media locations will all give you valuable information so that you can start your investigation.

Establish the method of the harassment and when it started. Was it a Facebook group? Snapchat? Text messages? Chat rooms? Is a mobile device involved in terms of text messages, missed calls, and more? Has the harassment gone old-school with the use of the post office with physical letters?

Threats of violence may increase the severity of the crime and should not be discounted.

The investigator will need to ensure they get forensically sound copies of the digital evidence to start the investigation. This starts the chain of custody of the digital evidence and is the beginning of the investigation.

We will go into much greater detail about the specific artifacts found in digital evidence, but once you have account usernames and IP addresses that the attacker is using to facilitate their attacks, you have a starting point to identify them.

In the United States, a subpoena is required to obtain subscriber information. This information includes the user's first and last names, physical address, how often they access the account, and the IP address that was used to access the account. It varies between service providers as to how long this information is maintained. Sometimes, it could be as little as weeks and as much as years, depending on the provider. You can also submit legal paperwork asking them to "freeze" the account so that the user cannot disable it or delete any incriminating information.

To gain access to the information contained within the account, such as email content, contents of messages, or anything having to do with content, a search warrant signed by a judge will have to be served on the service provider. If the service provider is within the same jurisdiction of the judicial authority, there are typically no issues. When the service provider is in another jurisdiction within the United States or a jurisdiction outside the borders of the United States, this is when the process becomes much more difficult and sometimes impossible to proceed with.

Some subscriber information you get may or may not be accurate. It is not unusual for a user to complete the registration forms with false information. But what you can do, for example, if you have an email address, is you can do an open source search and see whether the email address was used anywhere else. For example, some online forums will use the email address as a username, and if so, the user may post identifying information in their communications with the other users. That forum now becomes a source of information for which you can issue a subpoena to get the subscriber information.

As you can see, following breadcrumbs of information may lead you to sources you never even considered. It can be quite complicated and time-consuming.

Criminal conspiracy

Criminal conspiracy and digital forensics: how do these aspects intersect in the world of the digital forensic investigator? First, let's define what a conspiracy is: a conspiracy occurs when two or more people agreed to commit an illegal act. However, just deciding to commit the illegal act is not enough; there also have to be actions taken in furtherance of the conspiracy. What does all that mean? For the physical crime of robbery, criminal A contacts criminal B to discuss robbing victim C. The conversation between criminals A and B does not meet the statutory definition of a conspiracy. If criminal A paid criminal B and agreed on the number of funds in exchange for the service of the robbing of victim C, then we have an act in furtherance of the conspiracy to commit robbery. So, what crimes can the digital forensic investigator find within the digital realm? Almost any crime imaginable. Let's take a look at an example of such a crime:

> *"Michelle Theer was convicted of a crime against a person. She conspired with John Diamond to commit the crime against her husband, Marty. Investigators had no direct evidence, no physical evidence, and no eyewitness evidence, but they had digital evidence showing the conspiracy to commit the crime. Investigators recovered over 80,000 emails and instant messages between Diamond and Michelle that showed a personal relationship between the two and the messages showing the conspiracy between them to commit the crime."*

You can read about this case in more detail at `https://caselaw.findlaw.com/nc-court-of-appeals/1201672.html`.

Now more than ever, people are connected to their devices for their everyday activities. It is not a stretch of the imagination that criminals also use their devices to help organize their criminal activities. The digital forensic investigator has to know of all potential sources of digital evidence and recognize that the **Internet of Things** (**IoT**) is an untapped bonanza of digital evidence. What is the Internet of Things?

Home assistance programs such as Siri and Alexa, smartwatches, home security systems, and GPS devices – anything that has an app – might contain evidence and show the intent on the criminals' part to commit the crime. Failure to recognize the digital devices can result in significant damage to your investigation. There have been instances where the subject of an investigation was placed in the interrogation room, and the investigator did not recognize the suspect was wearing a smartwatch. While they left the subject unattended in the interrogation room, the subject was able to communicate with their co-conspirators and direct their efforts in the destruction of evidence and interfere with the investigation. Once the investigators caught on to the subject's actions, they then used the smartwatch to show the criminal conspiracy and used the evidence to generate additional charges for the suspect in custody and their co-conspirators.

Social media is also a source of digital evidence for showing a conspiracy. For example, take the case of Larry Jo Thomas. The government convicted Thomas of committing a crime against Rito Llamas-Juarez. Initially, investigators only knew that Llamas-Juarez was harmed by a specific type of item. As investigators processed the crime scene, a bracelet that was "distinctive" was found and collected as evidence. The investigators examined Thomas's Facebook page and found a photo of Thomas posing with an item similar to what was used at the crime scene. In a different photo, they found the "distinctive" bracelet being worn by Thomas. While the digital evidence did not have a direct impact on the criminality being investigated, it showed how the subject had the means and had been at the crime scene.

Vehicles are also a source of evidence to prove the conspiracy. Newer vehicles are connected to the network and have their own Wi-Fi connection and sync data between mobile devices, GPS data, and the vehicle's black box. Potentially, the investigator can show the subjects performing reconnaissance on their targets, meetings between the conspirators at a shared location, or where they have traveled to and returned using toll passes.

Technology is rapidly changing and advancing as the general population uses technology, and so do the criminals. The general population plans out their day by utilizing technology; criminals also plan out their day of criminal activity using the same technology. I am always amazed when criminals use their mobile devices to plan and execute criminal activity and then take pictures to memorialize their illegal business.

Now that we have learned about criminal investigations, its roles, and the means by which information is being shared, let's move on to the next type of investigation, which is corporate investigations.

Corporate investigations

We will now discuss computer forensics on the civilian side, or non-law enforcement side. Since you are not an agent of the government, the search warrant requirement does not pertain to you. (Your specific jurisdiction may be different.) While you may not have the search warrant requirement, you cannot seize and analyze private property. What do I mean by that? You are the investigator for a large multinational corporation; you have an employee you believe is harassing other employees and may have viewed illicit images on their company laptop. What is the legal requirement for you to examine the contents of the employee's laptop? If you are an agent of the government, the employee has an expectation of privacy. As an employee utilizing the company's equipment, the courts have held that the employee has a limited expectation of privacy on the data in the device.

> **Important note**
>
> This may differ, depending on your local jurisdiction. I was teaching a class in Germany and as I was teaching, the students explained that German law gave an employee a high expectation of privacy. In their jurisdiction, there were specific requirements that had to be met before they could examine an employee's computer.

Other than the search warrant requirement, the corporate investigator's duties are similar to those of law enforcement. They still must acquire the evidence, they must analyze the evidence, and they must present their findings. They could present their findings in an administrative proceeding, or they may forward their findings to law enforcement where they may have to testify in a judicial proceeding. In either case, the digital forensic investigator must ensure that the digital evidence was collected in a forensically sound manner while maintaining the chain of custody of the digital evidence.

If the digital forensic examiner cannot authenticate the evidence, then they cannot testify or present it in the administrative/judicial proceeding. The corporate digital forensic investigator also investigates a wide variety of crimes. Typically, they will not be investigating a crime where a person was hurt or killed, but they can still investigate fraud, forgery, a violation of the company's policies and procedures, corporate espionage, or if they believe an employee has stolen intellectual property or is trying to harm the corporation itself. So, let's now talk about employee misconduct.

Employee misconduct

As a condition of the employee's employment, they must abide by the policies created by their organization. Typically, an employer has an "Employee Handbook" or has a set of policies and procedures that dictate what behaviors are acceptable and which ones are not acceptable. Such policies also include laying out specifications to ensure that the organization treats all employees with dignity and respect in the daily operations of the organization. There may be rules that may specify what is an acceptable use of the organization's desktop and laptop computers, and a violation of those rules could result in an investigation analyzing those devices, as we mentioned earlier.

Now, I use the term "policy and procedures," and I have found there is a large amount of confusion with those two terms, primarily when used together. A policy is a statement from the organization addressing a specific issue, while the procedure is the specific instructions regarding how to accomplish the goals of the policy. For example, the organization could enact a policy to restrict employees from accessing non-organizational emails using the organization's computers. The procedure would have two audiences, all the employees, and the IT staff. The procedure would inform the employees of how to access the organization's email while directing the IT staff regarding how to block non-organizational emails from being accessed.

You need to follow some general guidelines as your organization drafts and implements policies and the accompanying procedures, as follows:

- The policy should be simple to understand. Short and sweet – do not overcomplicate it. If there is a way for an employee to "misunderstand" the policy, then they will dispute whether their actions violated the policy.

- The procedure should specify all the steps needed to implement the task outlined in the policy. Don't assume the reader will understand if you are not specific in what you want them to do.

- The organization must inform the employee of the potential consequences of violating the policy.

- The organization cannot implement policies that violate the law.

- The organization must enforce the policies. There have been many investigations I have conducted where multiple employees have violated the policy, but the organization never enforced the policy. If they do not enforce the policy for 51 weeks and then, during the 52nd week, the organization enforces the policy against some employees and not others, how can the employees be held accountable during week 52?

- There must be documentation that the employee knew and understood that the organization implemented the policy and the penalties for violating the policy.

If an employee violates the organizations' policies or procedures, does law enforcement have to get involved? Of course not. It would depend on the violation and whether it was a criminal act and if the organization had a responsibility to notify law enforcement. Sometimes, the law may mandate the organization to notify law enforcement if they discover the employee has committed a criminal violation. Make sure you are aware of the statutory requirements in your jurisdiction and communicate with in-house counsel during the investigation.

As a digital forensic investigator, it is not typically your decision about whether to notify law enforcement. After you consult with the organizations' legal counsel and C-level executives, they will make that decision. For the digital forensic investigator's purposes, it does not matter whether the investigation relates to a criminal or noncriminal matter.

Remember, we treat *every* investigation as if we may have to go to court and testify because, while the initial investigation may deal with policy violations, during the investigation, you may discover there have been criminal violations that mandate the involvement of law enforcement. The prosecution and defense will scrutinize all of your investigative endeavors before the involvement of law enforcement. If you do not maintain the standards of the investigative process, it could weaken the prosecution.

As a digital forensic investigator for a corporate organization, there are a variety of violations the organization may call on you to investigate. One of the more common incidents is the complaint of harassment or a hostile work environment. This is where one person causes one or more people to be intimidated, harassed, physically threatened, humiliated, or any other activity where it makes the workplace offensive. How would you investigate someone for a hostile work environment? After conducting the interviews with the complaining employees, they may provide statements on how the harassment/hostile work environment was created, if at all.

Your investigation will determine whether the actions were physical, verbal, or carried out on digital media and the frequency of the offending conduct. Was there a single employee whose behavior was offensive or is there a culture within the organization? If a supervisor was notified or if someone asked the offender to stop, what resulted from the efforts to stop the offending behavior? The offending employee could send offensive text messages, emails, or instant messages utilizing the organization's communication network. If the alleged behavior occurred or was facilitated with the organization's devices, you should be conducting your examination to determine whether there is any digital evidence to support or refute the allegations since the property belongs to the organization, which limits the employee's expectation of privacy. (Remember, this may vary by jurisdiction.)

Once you have supervisory approval to conduct the digital forensic examination, the investigation can proceed. With the information at hand, you can filter out a large amount of additional data that may be contained on the storage device. To be efficient while dealing with the extraordinarily large datasets contained within today's high capacity devices, you have to filter out data that is not pertinent to your investigation. For example, if we are dealing with harassing emails, you may restrict your examination to only email traffic.

Now, your investigation may grow based on your findings on the initial exam. For example, while viewing emails, you observe the subject sending out illicit images to other employees. Your investigation has now increased based on the violation and the potential number of violators. Do not limit yourself to only the suspect's computer; you need to examine both the suspect and the complaining witness.

The complaining witness may have evidence of the offending email, while the suspect may have used anti-forensic techniques to remove the source email from their computer. Or you may find the complaining witness had changed the email to contain offensive material. You want to be as thorough as possible and that dictates an examination of the emails from both the sender and the recipient.

You are not typically called upon to determine whether the conduct was offensive – that is a very subjective determination. What one employee considers offensive, another employee may not. Your job will be to recover the artifacts to allow the fact finder to make a well-informed decision as to whether the complaining witness' statement can be substantiated. Human resources or in-house legal counsel will determine whether the employee's conduct was offensive. Your job is to be an impartial third party and to present the findings. This could be through an administrative proceeding such as a hearing, or you could make a presentation to a senior executive. Remember that the organization may be held liable in situations where they have been informed of the employee's offensive behavior and did not take action.

Corporate espionage

In the corporate environment, no matter how large or small, there are specifics about your organization you don't want to share with the entire world. You could provide a proprietary widget to another organization, or you have an exclusive recipe for a consumer food product. In almost every case, your organization is providing a service, and they get paid to provide that service. If a competitor could look inside the internal workings of the organization, that look may mitigate any advantage the organization has over the competition.

We can define corporate espionage as one organization spying on another organization to achieve commercial or financial gain. The same tactics that nation states use against each other are utilized by corporate actors against each other; for example:

- Physical or digital trespassing to gain access to data or information
- Impersonating any employee to gain physical access to an organization's buildings or other facilities
- Intercepting voice or data communications or manipulating a competitor's website
- Manipulating social media against a competitor

Some actions I just listed are not in the digital realm, so how can a digital forensic investigator determine what occurred?

Security

It comes down to physical and digital security. The organization has to be proactive and identify the critical infrastructure that needs protection. Once the critical infrastructure has been identified, the organization can then implement controls for security and documentation. If an attacker is successful, the digital forensic investigator will have to determine how the attacker got past the established protocols. The organization's physical and digital defenses should be multifaceted and not rely on a single aspect. What I mean by this is that there should be a mixture of physical and digital mitigation efforts to protect the organization. Access control is essential; a locked door could be access control, such as controlling access to the server room. Now, the door could be locked and unlocked with a biometric or a physical token. The organization should maintain the access control logs at an off-site facility.

If an employee's access control token was compromised and used by the attacker, a digital forensic investigator can analyze the logs and determine which user identity accessed the server room. Implementing digital surveillance recordings will allow the investigator to observe the compromise and determine whether it was the employee or an unknown third party. With a digital attack, you will have to analyze the logs from the network security devices, for example, antivirus logs, authentication servers, routers, and firewalls, all of which are detective controls. While a detective control allows you to investigate what occurred, it doesn't prevent the incident, nor is it a deterrent. Access control is about protecting an asset; you are controlling users and preventing unauthorized access.

Hackers

You may be the victim of an attack from a "hacker." What is a hacker? Typically, it's a malicious user gaining access to information systems that belong to another. You may see the term "black hat" or "white hat" hacker, where the color of the hat determines the hacker's intent.

A "white hat" hacker is a positive actor. This is a person or persons whose goal is to identify vulnerabilities in the system so that the owner or the vendor of the organization may correct them. A "black hat" hacker is someone who is attacking the system with malicious intent; their goal is to violate and exploit the organization's data system. There is also the "activist hacker," who is looking to exploit vulnerabilities in the system for political reasons. The attack could be the compromising of information maintained in the system or a distributed denial-of-service attack on the organization. The following is a table to help highlight the differences:

White Hat	Black Hat	Activist
They hack into systems to discover the liabilities before the bad actors.	They hack into systems for their own personal gain. (Bad Actor)	They hack into the system to expose activities, harass the owner, or to promote a political agenda. (Bad Actor)

A bad actor will not only rely on accessing the system through technical means; they will also attack an organization through the employees. This is known as using social engineering, which is what we will discuss next.

Social engineering

Social engineering is another attack that is relatively common in the corporate environment. One aspect is a "phishing attack," where the attacker attempts to trick the user into gaining access to confidential information such as a username and passwords. Typically, this attack is made via email, where the sender purports to be a bank, someone in authority, where they're asking the user to provide biographical information, name, date of birth, governmental identification number, username, and passwords.

If the user believes the email and provides that information, the attacker can then impersonate the user and attempt to gain a foothold into the organization's data systems.

There are automated tools designed to use social engineering, such as a phishing attack, against organizations. These tools do not require a significant amount of specialized knowledge to implement. The users of these tools are referred to as a "script kiddies" and could attack your organization using these automated tools. The vendors of the tools state they are to be used by the organization as a method to test their defenses, but there is no method to control what the user does with the software once downloaded.

Gophish

Gophish is one such automated tool. It works on all three of the major operating systems and is freely available for anyone to download. It does not require significant installation skills; you can extract it and run the executable, and the program will be up and running. The following screenshot shows the initial login screen when the software is up and running:

Figure 1.3 – Gophish login

Once you log in, you will be presented with the **Dashboard** of the service.

> **Note**
> This book is not about running Gophish or any other program; it is merely to give you an idea of what is available out there.

Please follow all applicable laws and regulations.

You can create email templates that you can send out to organizations. You can capture members of the organization's emails using **open source intelligence techniques (OSINTs)** and import them into the program:

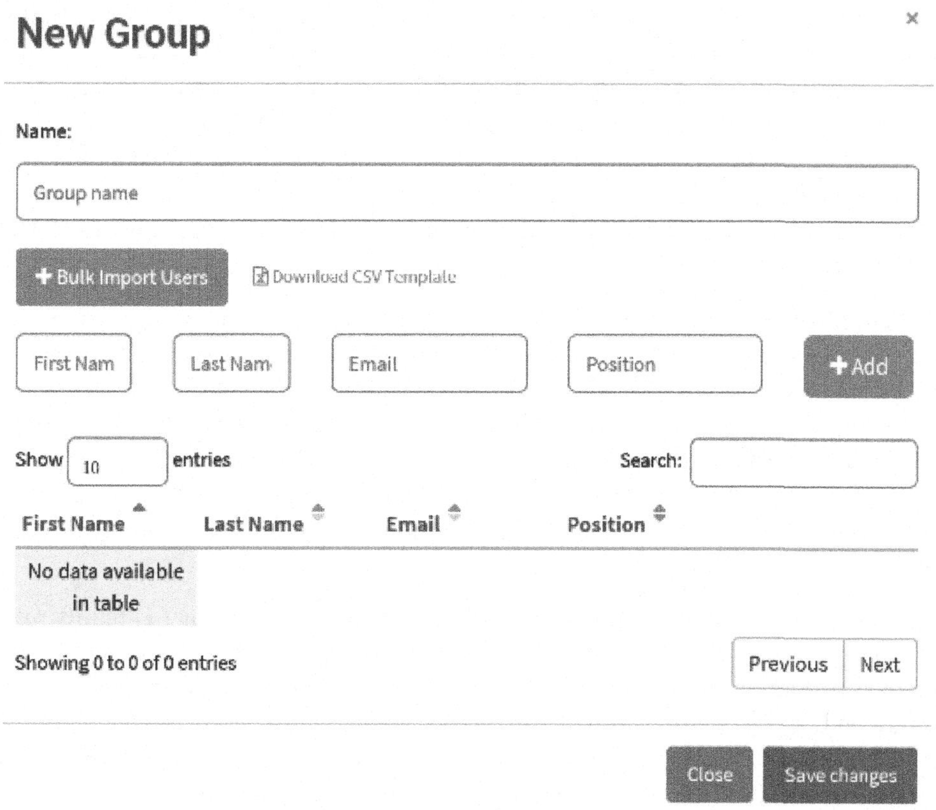

Figure 1.4 – Gophish import emails

A common theme when it comes to phishing the user's credentials is to send them an email asking them to reset their password, and when they do so, it directs them to a clone of the official landing page. After the attackers capture the username and password, the user is redirected to the official page, and they never know what occurred.

Real-world experience

One time, I was hired to conduct a vulnerability analysis of an organization. As part of the scenario, they did not provide me with any information about the internal workings of the data network or the physical security of the building. The building had public access during regular business hours. During regular business hours, I walked around the organization and conducted my reconnaissance to see whether I could identify any vulnerabilities.

To go to the executive levels of the building, I was required to sign in at the security desk and receive a **radiofrequency identification (RFID)** pass. As I signed in, they did not require me to show any identification, nor was I required to state my business or my destination. I signed in and was given a visitor RFID card and was sent on my way. I took the elevator to the top floor and walked around the executive level. I was dressed in the typical business casual clothing, carrying my laptop case. I found an unlocked training room in which I entered and set up my laptop. I plugged into the network and accessed the system. While I was inside the training room, several employees walked in, but none of them questioned why I was there, sitting alone, typing furiously at my computer. I stayed in the room until 4 hours after the building closed. During that time, no one questioned why I was in there. I packed up my laptop and had free rein of the executive level for the rest of the evening.

If I was an actual attacker, how would you be able to investigate what happened? What sources of evidence, maintained by the organization, could you process? The first step would be to identify a potential timeline for what occurred. One control put into place for this vulnerability test was to not damage the network and to access the control file. A control file is a plain document of no value and can be safely manipulated to show unauthorized access. The manipulated file will contain the timestamps to show when the unauthorized access happened. The timestamps will give the investigator a starting point of where to start the investigation.

This will be achieved by examining server logs, firewall logs, and trying to identify my digital footprints within the network. Once they identify the physical device location where the compromise occurred, then they can review the surveillance footage to work backward on how I gained access to the executive level, to the RFID protected elevator, and to the physical security log I completed. Typing out the reaction to the compromise in the system does not address the enormity of the task facing the digital forensic investigator. If the organization identifies the compromise within a timely fashion, that makes the investigation more straightforward, but consider if the compromise isn't recognized for days, weeks, or months. How hard would it be to determine what occurred months later, after the compromise?

Consider the compromise of Sony Pictures in 2014. While the exact duration of the attack is unknown, the attackers spent at least 2 months inside the network copying files, with some reports saying the attackers had access to the internal network for a year. Although it has never been confirmed, the attackers claim to have compromised and transferred over 100 TB of data from Sony Pictures.

The compromise of information was not the only vector of attack; they made employees' computers inoperable, and also compromised some social media accounts for the organization. The employees of the organization were also victimized with the compromising of their personal information by the attackers.

Insider threat

An organization cannot assume the attack will come from an external threat. While the design of most protocols and mitigations is to safeguard the organization from the external threat, the internal threat can be more dangerous than the external threat. No longer can the organization rely upon outward-facing security such as firewalls, building access control systems, intrusion prevention systems, or intrusion detection systems; they must also assess internal vulnerabilities to mitigate the threat from the inside. This is not an easy task; the insider threat has knowledge of the security protocols, the organization's policies, and potential vulnerabilities that the external threat does not.

In 2016, almost 1/3 of all electronic crimes were known/suspected to be caused by the insider threat. The damage caused by the insider was more significant than an external attack. No sector is protected from the internal attacker; in fact, if you are a US federal agency or a defense contractor, the government requires you to create a formal insider threat program, which is not surprising since there have been nearly 100 insider threat incidents within the last 10 years. (We are not talking about espionage incidents.) Almost 3/4 of the insider attackers were actively employed by the federal agency, while 1/3 were not directly employed, such as a contractor or an employee of another agency. A majority of the federal cases dealt with fraud and were committed by the insider for financial gain.

Who typically commits insider attacks? Is it a new employee? A veteran? Remember, for an insider attack to be effective, the insider has to be trusted. If we look at the federal government sector, nearly half of the insiders had been with the organization for over 5 years, with a majority of them abusing their access and creating fraudulent documents. Now, in the information technology sector, the demographics of the insider attack are a bit different. Nearly 75 percent were former employees and were with the organization for less than a year. Almost 20 percent did not have their accounts deactivated when they left the organization. That means they could use their credentials to access the confidential information, despite leaving their employment.

As an investigator, this should be a warning that there is an issue with that organization's policies and procedures that needs to be immediately corrected. Having a procedure at hand to deactivate an employee's account either before termination or shortly after they give their resignation would have stopped 1/5 of the documented attacks.

Investigating an insider threat will be difficult. You are dealing with people/employees who, at some level, have gained the trust of the organization. The investigator has to try and determine what the insider's mindset is underneath the persona that is being shown every day. Are they an opportunist? Are they a disgruntled employee? Are they someone out for revenge against an executive? Those are the potential attackers you may have to deal with. You want to create the groundwork before the attack happens.

Various sections of the organization – Human Resources, Legal, and IT – will be part of planning any potential response as well as being part of the response. The response team will identify who may be involved in an insider threat, such as the following:

- Executive staff
- Directors
- Employees with access to data

If you have to identify any potential "data source(s)" for when we have an investigation, you will need to examine the following:

- Company-issued laptops
- Company-issued tablets
- Cell phones or mobile devices
- Any cloud account access

You will have to correlate the user and the user's devices with access to the critical data, and the team will have to identify the critical data beforehand. When should insider threat investigation be initiated? Typically, this will start with a notification from Legal or Human Resources. The organization could also implement a policy in terms of investigating when an employee leaves the organization. If the employee's position gives them access to sensitive or privileged information, then a review of their activities within the organization should be conducted. This could start in a broad sense; you are looking to gather data from their mobile devices, laptops, desktops, and potentially the cloud. Then, you take that dataset and filter it so that it reflects access to the critical information.

Once the employee has given their resignation or the organization has decided to terminate the employee, the data collection process should start. The data collection process should begin before the employee is told they will be terminated. I recommend that the organization collects between 30 and 90 days' worth of activity for the employee. The more data that's acquired, the better informed the investigator will be of the employee's actions. Some of the artifacts that may help determine whether the employee has exfiltrated data are as follows:

- USB devices
- Cloud accounts
- Sharing of files via social media
- Burning a CD/DVD

You will also analyze the activity around the critical data. This should be a standard activity so that there is an understanding of what is normal. You have to monitor the data to get that normal baseline so that you understand when the unusual traffic occurs. For example, you could monitor the traffic to the critical data and suddenly, access to that data spikes. Does an attack cause this spike or is it normal because it is the end of the pay period and the accountants are accessing the data as part of standard processing?

Another example could be whether the data is being accessed after regular business hours. Is there a legitimate reason for that access? These are the circumstances that need to be identified before the investigation starts. This foreknowledge will allow you to filter out all the baseline information and to only focus on that data outside of the norms.

The investigation may show no malicious intent, or it may indicate there was malicious intent. Either way, you report the findings to the team to determine the next steps. This could lead to a review of policies and procedures and the implementation of new controls to mitigate future attacks.

Summary

In this chapter, you have gained an understanding of the different types of issues you may encounter during a digital forensic examination. You have learned about how the digital world and the physical world interact and how to use the digital world to help prove or disprove allegations. You have gained an understanding of the different procedures and how to collect and manage evidence when investigating allegations of wrongdoing.

In the next chapter, we will discuss the forensic analysis process to maximize the efficiency of your investigation.

Questions

1. Peer-to-Peer filesharing is used to share illegal files only.

   a. True

   b. False

2. What will the first responder identify?

   a. Potential victims

   b. Witnesses

   c. Subjects

   d. All of the above

3. You may find digital evidence in every type of investigation.

   a. True

   b. False

4. Which amendment of the U.S. Constitution protects the rights of citizens from unlawful search and seizure?

   a. First

   b. Second

   c. Third

   d. Fourth

5. What is a "binary"?

   a. A star

   b. An attached file

   c. A USENET post

   d. A web browsing artifact

6. What is required in the United States to obtain subscriber information?

   a. A search warrant

   b. A subpoena

   c. Consent

   d. Hacking

7. Criminals use social media for illegal purposes.

   a. True

   b. False

The answers can be found in the back of this book, under *Assessments*.

Further reading

John Vacca and Michael Erbschloe. *Computer Forensics: Computer Crime Scene Investigation*. Charles River Media, 2002 (available at `https://www.amazon.com/Computer-Forensics-Investigation-CD-ROM-Networking/dp/1584500182`.)

2
The Forensic
Analysis Process

We will now discuss the forensic analysis process. As a forensic investigator, you will need to create a process that will enable you to conduct an efficient investigation. You also need to make sure you are familiar with your tools and the results that they will provide. Without a process, you will waste time examining data that will not have an impact on your investigation and you will not be able to rely on your tools. You want to make sure you are getting valid results from the tools you deploy. To be thorough and efficient, you must use critical thinking to determine the best method of conducting an investigation or exam.

While there are similarities in every investigation, you will find there are differences that will require you to have an exam strategy to be efficient. I am not a fan of keeping an examination checklist because there will be areas that are not applicable, such as different operating systems, physical topography of the network, criminal elements, and suspects. These variables ensure that no two examinations or investigations are the same and will require the investigator to execute a different strategy for each of them.

The forensic analysis process is made up of five subsets:

- Pre-investigation considerations
- Understanding case information and legal issues
- Understanding data acquisition
- Understanding the analysis process
- Reporting your findings

The upcoming sections will discuss each of these in greater detail.

Pre-investigation considerations

The pre-investigation is where you determine your capabilities and equipment specifications to conduct a forensic exam, regardless of whether it is in the field or a lab environment. Now is the time to determine your budget for hardware, personnel, and training. Some of those costs will not be a one-time expenditure but will be part of an ongoing budget expenditure. The equipment has to be updated and personnel training has to be maintained, as well as the purchase of new technology as it becomes available.

Being a digital forensic investigator is not about buying the equipment and going to a training class and never updating either. As technology changes, so do the methods of hiding data or conducting criminal activities, so the investigator must be ready to adjust to these changes.

Before you are ready to begin the investigation, you have to prepare yourself. This will allow greater efficiency and a better work product. This includes preparing your equipment and becoming familiar with the current laws and legal decisions and the organization's policies and procedures.

Some equipment will be reusable and some will not. For the single-use items, make sure someone replaces them as soon as the incident concludes.

> **Note.**
> I cannot tell you how many times I have responded to the scene with my "to go" kit only to find that another detective had already used it and not replaced the consumable equipment. It was my mistake for not checking it before I departed to go to the crime and it was my partner's mistake for not replacing the items.

We will now discuss the equipment you will use as an investigator.

The forensic workstation

Whenever you get forensic investigators together, a common topic of conversation is the forensic workstation. How much RAM? How many SSD drives? Which processor? Which operating system? These are all questions that you might commonly hear. There is always a difference of opinion about the configuration of a forensic workstation. None of the opinions are incorrect because the investigator's workstation configuration depends on their budget and the cases that are being investigated.

Forensic workstations are not cheap. Depending on the skill level of the investigator, they can either build their own or purchase a pre-made forensic workstation. Several vendors will configure a workstation to your specification. For example, consider the vendor Sumuri (`https://sumuri.com`) and their Talino workstations. The base model costs approximately $5,000 and comes with the following:

- An Intel 8700 K processor
- 32 GB of DDR for RAM
- 512 GB SSD

That is a basic forensic workstation and you still have to add storage for the forensic images. The high-end version costs over $18,000 and comes with the following:

- A dual Intel Xeon E5-2690 v4 Broadwell 2.6 GHz 35MB 14-core server processor
- A 1 TB SSD for the operating system
- A 1 TB SSD for temporary files and processing
- 2 TB SSD for databases
- Several 6 to 8 TB hard drives in a RAID configuration
- 640 GB DDR4 RAM
- An 8 GB GDDR5 **graphics processing unit (GPU)**

One bottleneck that a forensic investigator may face with their forensic workstation is the transfer of data. My suggestion is to use SSDs because they have much higher throughput than the typical spinning disk does. A fast CPU and a large amount of RAM enable maximum performance for conducting a forensic analysis. These machines are not portable and you are not always in a position to perform the analysis or to acquire the data from the relative comfort of your workstation. A forensic laptop is also an expensive piece of equipment. At the time of printing, the Talino Omega comes with the following:

- An Intel Core i7 8700K desktop processor

- 64 GB of DDR4 2133 MHz RAM

- An enterprise-class SSD

- Optional: an additional three SSDs

> **Note.**
> You will need to include Gigabit Ethernet on both workstations to communicate on the local area network.

As you can see, you can never have too much CPU, RAM, or storage space on your forensic workstations. The equipment I described is on the higher end; you can conduct digital forensic examinations with less expensive equipment and still achieve the same results. The more high-end equipment will decrease the time involved. If you are a member of a multinational corporation or a large law enforcement agency, you may have the budget for higher-end equipment. A smaller law enforcement agency, a smaller organization, or a single practitioner will have to determine what cost would be more appropriate for their situation.

Sometimes you have to leave the lab, which means you need additional portable equipment. We will now discuss the equipment required in your response kit.

The response kit

The digital evidence is not always delivered to your workspace. Sometimes, you may have to respond to a third-party location to acquire that evidence. The collection of that evidence is the basic building block for any digital forensic examination you may conduct. Just like conducting an examination in your workspace, you need the proper tools and supporting equipment to accomplish this task. You need to create a response kit that includes documentary paperwork, pens, and storage containers to store digital evidence.

A response kit is unique to each digital forensic investigator. No kit is perfect; all kits are always subject to improvement. The goal of your response kit is to have everything you need to collect digital evidence, and we will go over some equipment that, in my experience, I have found useful:

- **Digital camera**: Capable of still and video recording. You need to document the scene as it was when you arrived. If you testify in official proceedings, you will show the fact finder precisely what you saw as you arrived. Some organizations also video record all the actions of the digital forensic investigator's activities as they collect digital evidence.

> **Note.**
> A word of advice: I would disable the microphone so as not to record audio. You may have extended discussions about how to proceed using language that may be regarded as less professional. These discussions and use of language could be used as a distraction by the opposing side in the presentation of evidence.

- **Latex gloves**: These protect several aspects of the evidence collection — you are not leaving your fingerprints and you are also protecting yourself from potential biohazards that may be on the scene. I am talking about blood, urine, feces, and any other biological fluid you can think of.

- **Notepads**: You need to document your actions on the scene. A notepad is a perfect repository to maintain that information. You can take notes about who you talk to, who secured the scene, and the basic facts of the case. When you begin the investigation, a lot of information will be coming at you and it could be easy for you to forget a specific action if you do not record it. Some organizations also make a hand-written sketch of the area where the digital evidence is being collected. Your organization's policies and procedures will determine whether a sketch is required.

- **Organizational paperwork**: This could be a property report for seizing evidence and it lists exactly what was taken, where it was taken from, and any specific identifying marks or serial numbers on the item being taken. You can also include labels or tags to specifically identify items that contain digital evidence.

- **Paper storage bags/antistatic bags**: You have to put the containers of digital evidence somewhere to prevent any unauthorized access. Digital evidence is very fragile and you want to make sure you do not store it in a manner where static electricity can be generated. Static electricity can render the storage media inoperative and you will lose access to any data.

- **Storage media**: Hard drives can be a traditional spinning disk or SSD and USB devices. A corporate digital forensic investigator will not shut down a server to create a forensic image. Instead, they will collect the specific datasets in the form of log files, RAM, or user directories and store them on the appropriately sized storage media.

  A government/law enforcement digital forensic investigator may acquire full forensic images at the scene and they will need larger storage capacity devices. As you become more experienced, you will be able to accurately determine exactly what equipment you need to perform your duties.

- **Write blocking devices**: This could be a hardware device, such as the Tableau TK8u USB 3.0 forensic bridge (`https://www.guidancesoftware.com/tableau/hardware/t8u`), which allows you to access a storage device without changing its contents. We will talk about the acquisition of evidence in much greater detail in *Chapter 3, Acquisition of Evidence*. Alternatively, you can use a forensic boot disk, such as Sumuri's Paladin, which is a Linux distribution based on Ubuntu and allows the collection of digital evidence in a forensically sound manner. Sumuri offers Paladin as a free download at `https://sumuri.com/software/paladin`.

- **Frequency shielding material**: This could include commercial aluminum foil, Faraday bags, or any container that will block radio transmissions. You will use this when you have to seize a mobile device to prevent the user from remotely wiping or resetting the device. Be aware, however, that when you place the device in these containers, the battery will quickly deplete as it will attempt to reconnect to the network. If you have access to the mobile device's menu you can put the device into airplane mode. The device will no longer attempt to connect to the network. Ensure you document any changes you make to the device.

- **A toolkit**: A small precision toolkit with multiple screwdriver bits is used to disassemble laptops, desktops, or mobile devices to access the digital storage container. You want to make sure you have a variety of screw heads to match what the various manufacturers use. Sometimes, the manufacturers will use two or three different screw heads when assembling their devices.

- **Miscellaneous items**: This can include extra power cables, data cables, USB hubs, screws, or anything else that might be difficult to acquire when you are at the subject's location in the middle of the night and no stores are available for you to purchase the missing item. If you are responding to a commercial location, you may want to keep a spare mouse and keyboard if you need to access a server and they are not available. (If you are conducting network-based investigations, you may also want to include a network tap.) This subset is made up of items you did not think you needed until you are onsite and need them.

- **A forensic laptop**: Make sure all of your software is up to date. I recommend creating a folder that contains digital versions of any forms you will use, any processes you need to document, and any applications you find useful to carry out your tasks.

- **Encryption**: If you are traveling out of the country to get to the target site, you might want to encrypt the target drives that contain the acquired data you need to analyze. It is not uncommon for security services or customs to seize devices. This will ensure the data you acquired will not be compromised.

- **Software security keys**: This is also referred to as a dongle. You will find commercial versions of software that require you to insert a USB-based security key to use it. You want to make sure you have them with you because the software cannot be used if you do not have the key inserted.

> Note.
> A program called VirtualHere (`http://virtualhere.com/home`) allows you to use your USB devices remotely. This will require a network connection at your destination and at your home location where the USB keys are plugged in. If you are unsure about the quality of your network connection, I recommend taking the keys with you.

Now, the important question is this: *how do you carry all of this from one location to another?*

My recommendation is a Pelican-type case that is watertight and crushproof to protect the equipment. Also, include a TSA-compliant locking device in case you have to travel via commercial air.

The list of items we have just discussed is only a recommendation. You will add/subtract from this list to meet the needs of the task at hand. There is no right or wrong answer when stocking your response kit. The budget, the organization, and the task at hand are all going to dictate what equipment is needed.

The result is you need to have a response kit when leaving the office to acquire digital data or responding to an incident of any kind. How you stock that kit is entirely up to you as the forensic investigator. This is all about making your job easier and more efficient.

That has covered some of the hardware and physical items needed. We will now move on to discussing software.

Forensic software

This is the software that you will use to analyze data. You have a choice of utilizing commercial software designed for the forensic process or open source tools. You want to make sure that you are using fully licensed software in your work environment. There is nothing more embarrassing than an organization using pirated software to investigate and have that fact come out in the administrative or judicial proceeding. It will be a severe hit to your reputation if you use pirated software to conduct your investigation and it will call into question your integrity, your ethics, the results of your inquiry, and the results provided by the forensic tool. I cannot stress this enough: you have to use fully licensed software in the forensic process. So, what is the difference between open source and commercially available tools?

Vendors make open source software freely available for anyone to use. Typically, there are no restrictions on its use; you can use it for educational, profit, or testing purposes. The positive aspect is that it is available at no cost in most situations. The downside is that you will have little or no technical support if something goes wrong. It will depend entirely on your skillset and level of comfort working with these tools. A lot of open source tools use a **command-line interface** (**CLI**) and not a **graphical user interface** (**GUI**), which can intimidate new users.

A commercial tool will typically have better customer support, documentation, and timely updates. The downside is that you are paying for those services. In reality, for anything that a commercial forensic tool can do, there is an open source tool that can do the same thing. A commercial tool will have the ability to carry out multiple functions while with an open source framework, you may have to use one or more different open source tools to accomplish the same task.

Neither choice is wrong. As a digital forensic investigator, you have to know where the data came from and ensure that the tool is providing an accurate representation of the data. It does not matter if the tool is an open source or commercial version; you have to validate the results provided by any tool. We will talk about validation a little further on in this chapter.

I often get questions about whether a particular piece of software is court-approved. Forensic software is not court-approved, but you need to explain in the administrative/judicial process whether the particular tool you used produces reliable results and is accepted within the forensic community.

In the United States, this is known as the Daubert standard, which comes from the Supreme Court case Daubert v. Merrell Dow Pharmaceuticals Inc., 509 U.S. 579 (1993). This standard is used to determine whether an expert witness's testimony is based on scientifically valid reasoning and can be appropriately applied to the facts of the matter. The factors the court considered are as follows:

- Whether the theory or technique can be or has been tested
- Whether it has been subjected to peer review and publication
- The known or potential error rate
- The existence and maintenance of standards
- Its acceptance within the scientific community

Originally, the standard was only used for scientific testimony but with the Kumho Tire Co. v. Carmichael 526 U.S. 137 (1999) case, the Supreme Court clarified that the factors used in the Daubert decision could also apply to non-scientific testimony, that is, the testimony of engineers and other experts who are not scientists. As you can see, it is not so much the software being used but the expertise of the digital forensic investigator. Commercial forensic tools simplify the process and sometimes have a **find evidence** button. You, as the digital forensic investigator, still have to know where the forensic tool extracted the artifact from within the filesystem.

The **National Institute of Standards and Technology (NIST)** has sponsored the **Computer Forensic Tool Testing Project (CFTT)** (https://www.nist.gov/itl/ssd/software-quality-group/computer-forensics-tool-testing-program-cftt), which has established a methodology for testing computer forensic software tools through the development of general tool specifications, test procedures, test criteria, test sets, and test hardware. This project provides a source for testing the results of forensic tools on its website. They also offer a set of testing media so you can conduct your validation of forensic software. It is part of your best practices to validate the results of your forensic tools at least annually or whenever the tool is updated. It does not matter whether you are a government or private sector digital forensic investigator: you need to have confidence in your tools and be able to testify that you have tested and validated the process.

In 2011, this validation process was called into question during the trial of Casey Anthony. A significant assertion by the prosecution was that someone searched for the term "chloroform" 84 times on Anthony's computer. While the trial was ongoing, it was discovered that the forensic tool used by the digital forensic investigators had misinterpreted the values in the internet history database. The user had only visited the site one time, not 84 as reported. The software designer of the forensic tool realized the mistake while the trial was ongoing and notified the members of the trial team of the error. My recommendation is that you have multiple forensic tools to validate your findings. You could have two commercial forensic tools, one commercial and one open source forensic tool, or two open source forensic tools, but you need to validate your findings.

Some open source forensic tools include the following:

- **Autopsy**: Autopsy is a fully functioning suite of forensic tools that allow you to conduct a full forensic examination. It costs nothing and can be found at `https://www.sleuthkit.org/autopsy/`.

- **SIFT Workstation**: SIFT is a virtual machine that uses the Ubuntu operating system with multiple forensic tools pre-installed. It is free and can be found at `https://digital-forensics.sans.org/community/downloads`.

- **Paladin Forensic Suite**: Paladin is a live Linux distribution based on Ubuntu and has implemented several open source forensic tools in a user interface called the Paladin toolbox. It is free and can be found at `https://sumuri.com/software/paladin/`.

- **CAINE: Computer Aided Investigative Environment (CAINE)** is a digital forensics project that provides a GUI and many open source forensic tools for free. It can be found at `https://www.caine-live.net/`.

These are just a few of the open source forensic suites available. There may be others out there that I haven't mentioned or you may wish to use single-purpose tools. As long as you achieve the goal of finding the artifact to reveal the truth about the matter being investigated, it does not matter which tool you use. The key will be using your training and experience to explain the pertinence of the artifact and how you determined that the tool is providing reliable results.

Here are some commercial forensic tools available for Windows-based users:

- **X-Ways Forensics**: `https://www.x-ways.net/`

- **EnCase**: `https://www.guidancesoftware.com/encase-forensic`

- **Forensic Toolkit (FTK)**: `https://accessdata.com/products-services/forensic-toolkit-ftk`

- **Forensic Explorer (FEX)**: `http://www.forensicexplorer.com/`

- **Belkasoft Evidence Center**: `https://belkasoft.com/ec`

- **Axiom**: `https://www.magnetforensics.com/products/magnet-axiom/`

Here are some Macintosh-based tools:

- **Blacklight**: `https://www.blackbagtech.com/software-products/blacklight.html`

- **Recon Lab**: `https://sumuri.com/software/recon-lab/`

A Linux-based tool is **SMART** (`http://www.asrdata.com/forensic-software/smart-for-linux/`).

This is just a sample of the commercial forensic tools available for use. Each tool will have its strengths and weaknesses, which can be debated endlessly with your fellow practitioners.

Right now, I prefer X-Ways as my primary tool and I supplement it with FEX and Evidence Center.

You can have all of the tools, software, and hardware, but without training, how effective will you be? Next up are some training options for you to consider.

Forensic investigator training

If you travel on the path of a career in digital forensics, you will need to continually upgrade your skills and training and this must be considered an ongoing expense. Just because someone goes through a 40-hour course, this does not automatically make them a digital forensic investigator. They are taking the first steps down that career path but they will need to continue to attend training sessions and associate with other like-minded peers.

Certification is not a guarantee that the user knows what they are doing. A certification shows that the user met the minimum level to achieve that certification. There are a **large** number of certifications available and some are more worthwhile than others. Before joining an organization and taking part in their certification process, you have to do your due diligence and research the costs, availability, and whether that certification is accepted within the forensic community. Most certifying organizations will require annual dues and a yearly training requirement to recertify the certification.

This is a list of some of the organizations that provide forensic investigative training:

- **International Association of Computer Investigative Specialists (IACIS)**: `https://www.iacis.com/`
- **EnCase Certified Examiner (EnCE)**: `https://www.Opentext.com/products-and-solutions/services/training-and-learning-services/encase-training/certifications`

- **Accessdata Certified Examiner (ACE)**: `https://accessdata.com/training/computer-forensics-certification`

- **Computer Hacking Forensic Investigator (CHFI)**: `https://www.eccouncil.org/programs/computer-hacking-forensic-investigator-chfi/`

- **Global Information Assurance Certification (GIAC)**: `https://www.giac.org/certifications`

Now that we have explored the equipment and training options, you still have to prepare by understanding the legal and case information as it pertains to the specifics of an investigation. So, we will discuss legal issues next.

Understanding case information and legal issues

Let's talk about case information and legal issues. This is the information you have to get before you even power up your workstation to look at the digital evidence. You will have to carry out some information gathering from the person requesting your services. You should ask the following questions:

- What is the nature of the investigation? Is it a narcotics case, homicide, or employee misconduct? As you hear this information, you formulate your plan on how you want to proceed.

- What digital evidence do you expect to find at the scene? I've had responses where the investigator was only looking for a single laptop and once we were at the scene, we found multiple laptops, multiple desktops, and many mobile devices. Just remember the information you get may not always be accurate, so you also have to be prepared for that eventuality.

- What is the legal justification? For law enforcement—what is the rationale behind the search? Consent? A search warrant? It doesn't matter whether it is written consent or a written search warrant: you need to read the search warrant and consent to make sure you understand the limits being placed on the search. It may be physical limits within the scene or it may be digital limits on what you can search for on the digital devices.

- As a government and corporate digital forensic investigator, I have had limits on what I can search for or view on digital devices many times. Be aware of those limits; if you find relevant artifacts outside of the scope of the search authority, they cannot be used in the proceedings and you may face sanctions if you do use them.

- Who are the subjects and suspects and what roles do they play in the investigation? Now, depending on your role, you may or may not have any contact with the subjects and suspects involved. If you do have that availability, try talking to them. If you can have a civil conversation with them, you may get additional information about the digital containers and the data.

If you're thinking "We have gathered information from the first respondents and we have gathered information on the other subjects involved; now we can jump right in and collect evidence!"—well, not yet. You want to make sure the crime scene has been adequately documented. For law enforcement, this will include removing extraneous personnel from the scene, restricting access, and allowing someone to record the scene.

The easiest way is to photograph everything. They may call you in to testify in a proceeding 12, 18, 24, or even more months in the future. Lawyers may ask you where a specific item was and, unless you have a photograph (or sketch) of the scene, you may not be able to answer the question.

For a corporate investigation—for example, a hidden camera found in a confidential location—what do you do? The finder's actions may hamper your ability. I had an investigation where a hidden camera was found in a unisex restroom. A user of the restroom found the camera when the tape holding it to the bottom of the shelf released and the camera fell to the ground. The user gave the camera to their supervisor. The supervisor opened the camera and removed the digital storage card. They then placed it into a card reader and plugged it into their computer. At least five other people handled the camera and the SD card, putting it into multiple computers before they contacted me. Every time they plugged the SD card into a computer system, they changed the evidence. When you access the data on an SD card, you change the date and time stamps on the files you access. An organization has to train its members not to look at digital evidence when there is an incident and to call a professional. This will ensure that the evidence is contained in a state that allows it to be presented in a judicial or administrative proceeding.

This case required interviewing all the people involved, processing the digital camera and the SD card, and examining the five workstations. Since this was a corporate environment and initially law enforcement was not going to be involved, I took photographs of the workstations and the connections with the goal of identifying the specific workstations and their users. Remember, we are in a corporate environment and there are multiple versions of the same make and model of computers everywhere.

There will be times when you have been presented the digital evidence after someone else collected it. You still have to ask questions and the source of your answers may only be the investigative reports. You will want to know the following:

- Why was this item seized?

- Does it contain evidence of criminal activity or evidence considered exculpatory?

- Is there a chain of custody for this item?

- How many people have had access to it?

- Where was the item found?

- Was it found in a secured location or a common area of the site?

- Are there any date and time references?

- What should the investigation focus on?

- When does the investigator need the findings of the digital forensic exam?

You need to review the documentation before you start the evidence-collection process. When investigators bring you digital evidence containers such as computers, you need to make sure the search warrant authorized its seizure. There have been several cases where devices containing digital evidence were seized but there was a gray area around the use of digital evidence.

The search warrant will come with limitations on your search. If it is an illicit images investigation, you may be restricted to only viewing images. It is your responsibility to read all the judicial paperwork and to understand what it authorizes and what it does not. Only then can you create a plan for how you stay within the limits.

You also have to anticipate what problems you may encounter as you conduct the digital forensic examination. Is there an aspect of the investigation where your training and experience could be lacking? This is not something to be ashamed of but should be acknowledged so you can reach out for help to increase your training and experience. What resources do you have available to assist you?

Once the legal portion of your preparation is done, we can move on to the next portion of the process. You now have to deal with acquiring the data in a forensically sound manner.

Understanding data acquisition

So, let's recap—you have received training as a digital forensic investigator and you may have received certification. You have built or purchased a digital forensic workstation and a forensic laptop and have created your response kit. You have responded to the scene and ensured that it has been made secure. You have verified that no one has altered the scene and you have documented the scene with photographs. Now, it is time for you to process the scene and collect that digital evidence. We will now discuss the acquisition of data, otherwise known as evidence.

There are multiple scenarios where someone may call on you to acquire data for a digital forensic investigation. As a law enforcement officer, you may respond to the scene, identify potential sources of digital forensic evidence, and then seize those items. As a private sector or corporate investigator, you may be called on to take an employee's workstation or to respond to the server room (either physically or remotely) to collect the data you need to analyze. The procedures we will talk about in the next section can be utilized in every environment.

A source of potential evidence is volatile memory. In the past, the data contained within volatile memory was ignored with a "pull the plug" mentality. This was based on whether officers responded to a scene and the computer was up and running. Best practice required officers to pull the plug to shut the system down. Volatile memory is only available while a system is up and running. When the plug was pulled, they lost all that data, which included any potential evidence. As the field of digital forensics has matured, we have learned that what we once considered best practice was, in reality, not.

To collect volatile evidence, we should start from the most to the least volatile. This is called the **order of volatility**, and it goes like this:

1. Live system
2. Running
3. Network
4. Virtual
5. Physical

We approach the collection of volatile data with the same mindset as the collection of forensic images. You must document the steps you take because you will interact with the machine to collect volatile data and your interaction will change the evidence. In reality, the changes you make typically do not affect what you are investigating. But you should know that changes are being made to the system; you may get asked a question about potential changes to the evidence while testifying at the administrative or judicial proceeding and if you don't know the answer, it could be professionally embarrassing.

The changes you make while collecting the volatile data will impact the processes found in RAM. That is why you need to take notes and document everything you do. Some examples of volatile data we collect are the current state of the system networking information (the ARP table, connections, routing table, and name cache), the logged-on users, running services, running processes, shared drives, remote activity, and open encrypted containers.

We have to balance the changes we will make versus the evidence that may be potentially lost forever. The term "forensically sound manner" means leaving the smallest possible footprint during collection to minimize the amount of data being changed with the collection. The order of collecting volatile data is significant because if you collect volatile data in the wrong order, you may destroy the evidence you are looking for. RAM is considered to be the most volatile of all volatile data, so we would want to collect that first.

Keep the following in mind:

- Collecting the volatile data may not always be possible, depending on the specific set of circumstances you encounter on the scene.

- If you find there is a destructive process running on the machine and the information you want to collect is being altered or overwritten, you may not want to take the time to collect the RAM as evidence is being manipulated.

- If it is a remote connection causing the destructive process to take place, you need to document the connection, sever the connection, and then collect the RAM. It depends on your investigation and the information you are trying to acquire.

- If the attacker is connected remotely and is accessing highly sensitive data, do you want the attacker to maintain access while you collect the RAM or do you want to interrupt the connection? What if it is not critical information?

- Do you want to let the attacker continue to have access while you continue your processing?

Ultimately, the goal of digital forensics is to create a forensic image for analysis and under normal circumstances, it is not appropriate to change digital evidence during the process of collection.

In today's environment, that is not always possible. Due to the easy availability of full disk encryption or full volume encryption, it is no longer acceptable to pull the plug on computer systems.

Let's take a slight detour and talk about what encryption is. At a basic level, encryption is encoding information to protect the confidentiality of the information and allow only the person with the decryption key to access it. All encryption can be broken if the attacker has enough time.

With today's versions of equipment, that time factor is measured in hundreds of years. As technology advances with increases in processing power, the time taken to decrypt top-level encryption decreases. So, what was considered secure encryption in the 1990s is now regarded as weak. That is why it is imperative not to pull the plug on a system where it is possible that encryption is being used. Without gaining access to the decryption key, you cannot get to the data.

Every situation, every crime scene, and every investigation will be different, which means the actions you take will be based on the specific set of circumstances you encounter. Utilize your problem-solving skills and make quick decisions based on the limited information you have available.

Now we have the evidence, how do we keep control of it? Let's talk about the chain of custody.

Chain of custody

Maintaining the **chain of custody** is an integral part of preserving and authenticating evidence, both physical and digital, for an administrative or judicial proceeding. The chain of custody documents all access to the evidence, who accessed it, when it was accessed, and for what purpose it was accessed.

NIST provides a chain of custody document, shown in the following figure. It is a generic chain of custody form for you to use and adjust as needed and can be downloaded at `https://www.nist.gov/document/sample-chain-custody-formdocx`. The form is used to track the chain of custody and will be maintained every time evidence changes hands:

EVIDENCE CHAIN OF CUSTODY TRACKING FORM

Case Number: _____ Offense: _____

Submitting Officer: (Name/ID#) _____

Victim: _____

Suspect: _____

Date/Time Seized: _____Location of Seizure: _____

Description of Evidence		
Item #	Quantity	Description of Item (Model, Serial #, Condition, Marks, Scratches)

Figure 2.1 – An evidence form

As you can see, some fields may not be pertinent to you. For example, as a corporate digital forensic investigator, you may not need the **Victim** field, so you can change it or remove it altogether.

The goal of this form is to track the digital evidence and to maintain control so that you may authenticate the evidence at a later time. In the **Description of Evidence** field, you would describe the container holding the digital evidence. It could be non-reusable media, such as a DVD that has log files burned onto it for later examination.

In the following figure, you can see the **Description of Evidence** section. The **Item** number refers to a sequential numbering system to help track the items. **Quantity** is the physical number of items, and the **Description of Item** field is self-explanatory:

Description of Evidence		
Item #	**Quantity**	**Description of Item** (Model, Serial #, Condition, Marks, Scratches)
CD-001	1	Ultimate DVD contains servers log from AD001
HD-001	1	Samsung SSD 1TB Ser#ABC9876
HD-002	1	Samsung SSD 512 MB Ser# DEF4567
CP-001	1	Pixel XL 128 MB Ser# A5 12 D3 AC FD
TD-001	1	Generic Thumb drive 32MB (green) unknown SN
MD-001	1	Apple iPad 512mb Ser# 09 E3 4D AB Rose Gold

Figure 2.2 – A description of the evidence

As an example, in the previous figure, a DVD is listed as item **CD-001**. You might impound several CDs or DVDs and have the problem of trying to differentiate one disk from another. It's not just CDs or DVDs but also hard drives. It won't be often that you will impound a single item of a specific media type.

I use the following numbering system as a part of my process:

- CD/DVD: CD-XXX
- Hard drive: HD-XXX
- Thumb drive: TD-XXX
- Cellphone: CP-XXX
- Mobile device (not a cellphone): MD-XXX

> **Note.**
> As a side note, you also need to make a permanent mark on the items being seized, you should try to do so in a manner that will not reduce the value of the item.

You can see in the following figure that the hard drive is marked as **HDD001** with the date and the initials of the officer seizing the device:

Figure 2.3 – A hard drive

When the forensic image is created, the device will be referred to as **HDD001** for the rest of the process.

If you cannot write on a device without permanently reducing its value, such as an iPad, do not use a permanent marker to write MD-XXX. Instead, use an adhesive label to mark the information.

> **Note.**
> Use a system that will work for you. When you have developed your system, make sure you use it every time. It will save you from losing evidence or mismarking evidence.

When we are on the scene and seizing evidence and containers containing digital evidence, we want to make sure we do so in a forensically sound manner. We do not analyze the original evidence; we create a copy to do the exam on to ensure we do not make any changes to the original evidence.

We have three choices for making a working copy:

- **A forensic copy**: This is a straight bit-for-bit copy of the source to the destination. This is not common in today's environment. Ensure that your destination device has no old data from previous investigations. You do not want to cause cross-contamination between the current digital forensic investigation and a past investigation. We will recover deleted files, file slack, and partition slack. We will discuss wiping hard drives later on in this book.

- **A forensic image**: We are creating a bit-for-bit copy of the source device but we store that data in a forensic image format. This could be a DD image, an E01 image, or an AFF image. We take that source data and wrap it in a protective wrapper of the forensic image. We will recover deleted files, file slack, and partition slack.

- **A logical forensic image**: Sometimes we are restricted to only accessing specific datasets. They do not allow us to access the entire container. We cannot create a bit-for-bit copy forensic image or a forensic copy. This can be used when we are extracting data from a server and we cannot shut the server down to create a forensic image from the source hard drives. So, we can make logical copies of the files and folders pertinent to the investigation. We will not be able to recover deleted files, the file slack, and partition slack.

Later on in *Chapter 3, Acquisition of Evidence*, we will address creating a forensic image from the devices we have seized or the data seized at the scene.

Now that we have discussed what you need to consider when acquiring a dataset, we will discuss what you need to understand when analyzing data.

Understanding the analysis process

Once you have collected data from the scene, you return to your lab and it is now time to start your forensic analysis. You will find yourself quickly overwhelmed by the sheer amount of data you will find in storage devices. You have to quickly determine whether the information contained within the storage containers is pertinent to your investigation. This is the point where the information gathering that occurred in the case information and legal issues step of the process will play an essential part.

Therefore, you have to capture the five Ws of the investigation (previously mentioned in *Chapter 1, Types of Computer-Based Investigations*). Tie the activity on the computer system with a specific user and identify that user as a real-life person.

If the investigation already has a live suspect identified, you correlate that suspect and the user on the computer system. Some guidelines we are about to discuss can be done with any of the commercial or open source forensic tools. My goal is for you to understand the process without resorting to any specific forensic tool.

Now that we have discussed what you need to consider when acquiring a dataset, we will discuss what you need to understand when analyzing the data.

Dates and time zones

Dates and time zones can cause issues for the digital forensic investigator if they forget to consider them. If you only conduct exams in a specific time zone and all of your seized data comes from the same time zone, then the issues you face are small. But if the data comes from multiple time zones or you travel to various time zones, then they can cause some confusion if you do not take them into account.

Setting the forensic machine and tools to use **universal time** (UTC) as a standard frame of reference helps solve this problem. Also, ensure that you adjust any timeframe where criminal activity may have occurred in UTC. It does not help that operating systems save metadata in a multitude of different time zones. You also have to consider that the suspect may have changed the time zone settings on the computer to hide their illicit activity. Timeline analysis is critical when conducting a forensic exam.

Next, we will need to be able to identify files we know are irrelevant, as well as instantly identify contraband images. We can do that with hash analysis.

Hash analysis

What is a hash value? A hash is a digital fingerprint for a file or piece of digital media. It is generated through the use of a one-way cryptographic algorithm.

The standard cryptographic algorithms used in digital forensics are **Message Digest 5 (MD5)** and the **Secure Hashing Algorithm (SHA-1)**. MD5 creates a 128-bit digital fingerprint while SHA-1 creates a 160-bit digital fingerprint. Using a hashing algorithm allows the use of a variable input to create a fixed-length output. If one bit is changed in the variable input, it will cause a different output. Let's see how this works in the following steps:

1. Create a text file containing the words `This is a test` with a filename of `Hash Test.txt`:

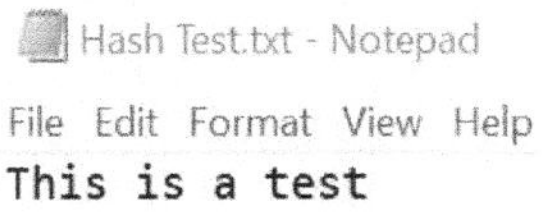

Figure 2.4 – The hash text

2. Use the free Jacksum utility (`https://jacksum.loefflmann.net/en/index.html`) to obtain the hash values:

Figure 2.5 – The Jacksum values

As you can see in the preceding figure, the `ce114e4501d2f4e2dcea3e17b546f339` value is the MD-5 standard length output for the `F:\Hash Test.txt` file. The second value, `a54d88e06612d820bc3be72877c74f257b561b19`, is the SHA-1 output. It doesn't matter which forensic tool I use—these values are the digital fingerprint for this specific file.

3. Change a single part of the contents of the file:

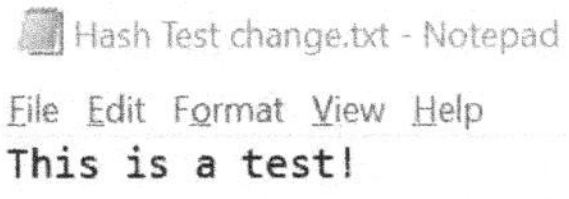

Figure 2.6 – The change in the text

I have added an exclamation point to the end of the sentence—a very small change—but any change will change the hash values.

4. Use Jacksum again and you will get a totally different hash value:

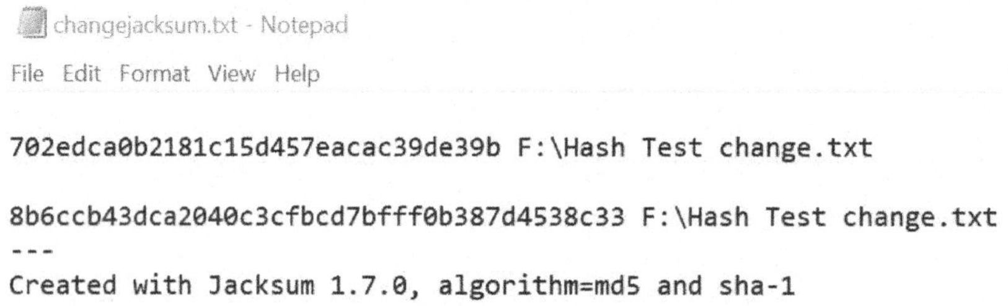

```
changejacksum.txt - Notepad

File  Edit  Format  View  Help


702edca0b2181c15d457eacac39de39b F:\Hash Test change.txt

8b6ccb43dca2040c3cfbcd7bfff0b387d4538c33 F:\Hash Test change.txt
---
Created with Jacksum 1.7.0, algorithm=md5 and sha-1
```

Figure 2.7 – The change in the Jacksum values

The MD5 value is now 702edca0b2181c15d457eacac39de39b, which is different from the original value of ce114e4501d2f4e2dcea3e17b546f339.

The standard output generated by the hashing algorithm is a one-way process. You cannot input the alphanumeric value to reverse the process to get the original dataset that was used in the hashing process. If you have a hash set of known illicit images, the values within that hash set cannot be used to re-create the illicit images.

There are hash sets (which are sets of multiple hash values) that identify known good files. These are files that are of no interest to an investigator. These can be the standard files used in an operating system or application. Using a known good hash set allows you to filter out those files that have no evidentiary value. On the other hand, if you have identified files of interest, such as illicit images or known documents that have been stolen, any data that may interest the investigator can also be highlighted. For the known bad files, someone has to have access to the original file to create the hash value used to identify the file.

Using hash analysis can save you some time and effort during your investigation:

*   You can use it to verify the evidence has not changed.

*   It can be used to exclude files.

*   It can be used to identify files of interest.

NIST has created the **National Software Reference Library** (**NSRL**) (`https://www.nist.gov/software-quality-group/national-software-reference-library-nsrl`), where they have collected software from many sources and created a **Reference Data Set** (**RDS**). The RDS is a large hash set to help identify known good files when conducting your examination. The RDS is freely available to law enforcement, the government, and private industries. Some files identified in the RDS may be considered malicious, such as hacking tools. The investigator still has to put the files in context to see if they were being used for an unlawful purpose. The RDS does not contain hash values of illicit data, such as illegal images.

A collision occurs when two different variable inputs result in the same fixed-length output. This means that two different files have the same hash value, which—based on our previous discussions—you will realize is not good for identifying evidence. There have been efforts by nation states to manipulate variable inputs to create the same fixed-length output and they have been successful.

Does that mean hashing is dead? No, it isn't. There have been no two different files found in the wild that have had the same hash value. All the collisions that have occurred have been files that have been manipulated. When the manipulated files were analyzed, they did not have any user-readable content. While there has been concern that this would negatively affect the admissibility of digital evidence, in 2009 the court case of US versus Schmidt ruled that the odds of a collision of two files were insignificant and were not an issue.

Now that we have determined the digital fingerprint, let's make sure the files are properly identified.

File signature analysis

Your next step is to carry out a file signature analysis, which is to ensure the file extension matches the file type. Many file types you will find in the filesystem have been standardized and possess unique file signatures to identify themselves to the filesystem. This is not the file extension, such as a Microsoft Word document that has a file extension of `.doc` or `.docx`.

A user can change the file extension to hide incriminating evidence. The intention behind carrying out a file signature analysis is to determine whether the file signature and file extension are a match.

The following screenshot shows how X-Ways flags a file when the file extension does not match the file signature:

Name	10534.gif
Type	jpg
Description	existing
Existent	✓
Size	3.0 KB (3,081)
Modified	07/12/2008 21:51:38 +0
Ext.	gif
Type status	mismatch detected, OK
Type descr.	JPEG

Figure 2.8 – A file signature mismatch

The file extension identifies the file as a GIF, but X-Ways has identified the file as a JPEG. The next figure shows the file header for the GIF file in question:

```
Offset   | 0  1  2  3  4  5  6  7   8  9 10 11 12 13 14 15 |        ANSI ASCII
00000000  F D8 FF E0 00 10 4A 46  49 46 00 01 01 00 00 01 ÿØÿà  JFIF
```

Figure 2.9 – A file header

A GIF file should have a hex 47 49 46 38 file signature, not hex FF D8 FF E0. In some cases, the mismatch is through normal usage of the filesystem and not as a result of user interaction. You have to examine the data to make sure the mismatch can be attributed to a specific user.

Gary Kessler has created a website that allows you to search a database based on the file extension or file signature. You can refer to this website at https://filesignatures.net/:

Figure 2.10 – filesignatures.net

You can search by file extension or file signature. Once you input the file extension, in this case JPG, you will be returned the file signatures associated with the JPEG standard:

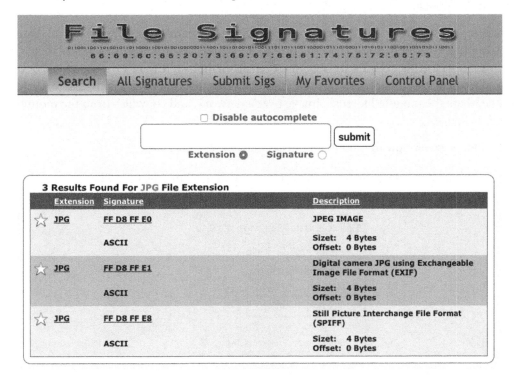

Figure 2.11 – The results for a JPG file signature

After we have ensured that the files have been properly identified, we need to identify any malware that may be on the system. We can do that with antivirus.

Antivirus

A common claim of innocence from a subject accused of wrongdoing that "a virus did it" has occurred in nearly every investigation I have done. Have you determined whether that is a valid claim? Is there malware on the system and did it cause the behavior you are investigating without the user's interaction or knowledge?

This is one reason we collect the volatile data, so we can see what was occurring on the system at the time of collection. If someone else has collected the evidence and all you have is a forensic image, you can still scan that forensic image to help determine whether someone has installed malware. Several forensic tools allow you to "mount" the forensic image as a read-only drive and you can then scan the filesystem to help determine whether there is malware installed.

FTK Imager is a free tool offered by AccessData, available at `https://accessdata.com/product-download/ftk-imager-version-4.2.0`, which allows you to mount the forensic image.

Image mounting allows you to mount a forensic image as a drive or physical device. Your viewing is in read-only mode. You will find many benefits to mounting a forensic image, such as using the file explorer to view the forensic image as if it were a device attached to the computer. You can natively view different file types, use antivirus against the forensic image, share the mounted forensic image over a network, and copy files from the mounted forensic image.

We will now cover how to mount a forensic image with FTK Imager:

1. To mount a forensic image in FTK Imager, you need to select the **File** menu and then select **Image Mounting…** from the menu, as in the following screenshot:

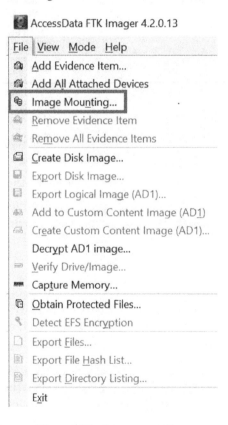

Figure 2.12 – Image mounting

2. It will then present you with the **Mount Image to Drive** menu:

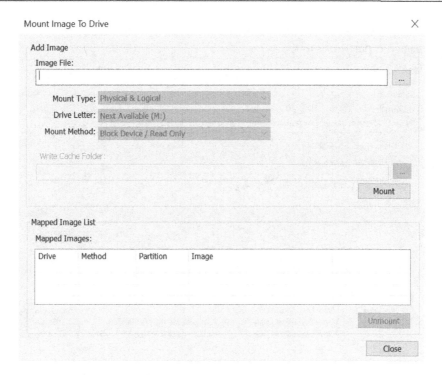

Figure 2.13 – Mount the image

In the dialog box, you will have to select the forensic image you want to mount. If this is a segmented forensic, you only need to point it at the first segment:

- **Mount Type**: You have a choice of **Physical & Logical**, just **Physical**, or just **Logical**. If you select **Physical & Logical**, the software will mount the forensic image as a physical device and mount any logical partitions.

- **Drive Letter**: This is where you want to see the forensic image. In the previous figure, it shows that the next available drive letter is M. You can select any open drive letter you desire.

- **Mount Method**: You have the following choices:

  - **Block Device / Read Only**: This will read the device as a block device, which means a Windows application that performs physical name querying can view the mounted device.

  - **Block Device / Writable**: No changes are made to the original evidence. It will save any changes you attempt to make in a cache file.

  - **File System / Read-Only**: The device as a read-only device that someone can view using Windows Explorer.

In the following screenshot, you can see we have mounted a forensic image and the forensic image has partitions in it:

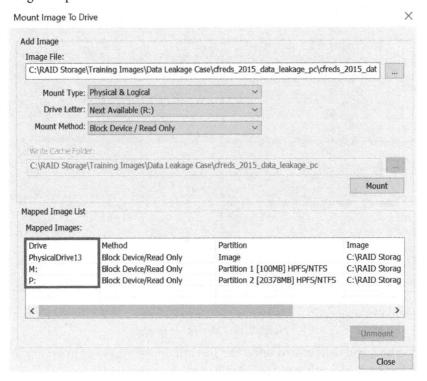

Figure 2.14 – A mounted image

It has mounted the partitions as drive M and drive P. Now, you can run the antivirus of your choice against those volumes to see whether they have installed any malware.

If malware has been installed, that is still not an alibi for the suspect. Determine whether the found malware can do the actions the suspect claims. I have investigated many cases of illicit images where the accused claims the malware downloaded the images. I have yet to find any malware that searches, finds, downloads, and sorts by content the illicit images found on a subject's computer. You still have to analyze the content to determine the context of the digital evidence.

Now, you can begin your analysis of the filesystem and operating system. We will discuss the specific artifacts in the rest of this book. Just to clarify, the **operating system (OS)** is the system in place to communicate between the applications and the hardware. Some typical OSes are Microsoft Windows, Macintosh, and Linux. Almost every action conducted within an OS, whether user- or machine-generated, will leave a footprint somewhere within the OS. You want to analyze these artifacts controlled by the OS to determine whether the user committed any wrongdoing.

A filesystem is the storage mechanism for the data. A filesystem is independent of the OS. The filesystem tracks where the data is stored and what space is available for use. There are many filesystems, such as NTFS, HFS+, FAT 32, and Ext 4. Some are compatible with multiple OSes and some are not. For example, NTFS is utilized by Microsoft Windows as the filesystem of choice.

Once we are sure there is no malware on the system, we can then move on to report the findings of the investigation.

Reporting your findings

We are at the final step of the process: your report. You did all the work of preparing, purchasing the equipment, going to training, and creating your response kit and when the call came, you responded to the scene. When you arrive, you successfully get the case information and navigate any potential legal issues. You collect the volatile data, identify containers of digital evidence, and duly seize the digital evidence while maintaining the chain of custody when transporting it back to your lab. You then conduct your analysis and find artifacts that show that the suspect did or did not do what they were accused of.

Now what? You have to be able to explain your findings to a non-technical person. You have to take a very technical topic and talk about it in a manner that a non-technical person will understand. This is one of the hardest aspects of being a digital forensic investigator to master. You may have to create different versions of the report depending on the audience. Your intended audience will read and interpret your report and you might be questioned on it in a judicial or administrative hearing.

Details to include in your report

You need to include enough details so that you can remember what occurred. Taking notes as you traverse the process will be your friend. There have been many times where I have failed to take that advice and had to go back and redo the process because I did not write something down. Your notes can take many forms, such as handwritten notes, typed notes, screenshots, or notes made with the built-in blogging function of your favorite forensic tool. There is no right or wrong rule on how to take notes, only that you take notes during the process.

So, what do you want to document? The following gives you an idea:

- Communication between the primary investigator and prosecutor
- The condition of the evidence containers
- The specifics of the storage device (the make, model, serial number, and condition)

- Personal identifiers of the suspect, victim, and witness
- The forensic hardware used
- The forensic software used
- What you examined (even if the examination turned up nothing of evidentiary value)
- Your findings

Take all the pieces and put them together so that a non-technical reader will understand the investigations, the steps you have taken, and why you made the conclusions you did. As with everything else in digital forensics, there is not a set standard for the format of your report. You will have input from your employer, the recipients of the report, and your own personal preferences.

I would recommend you include the following in your report. You should break your report into three primary sections:

- Your narrative
- Pertinent exhibits
- Supporting documentation

The narrative is as it sounds. This is where you explain what occurred, what you did, and what it means. You should include an executive summary to hit the key points and conclusions and then move on to a detailed narrative. In your narrative, you should provide screenshots of the artifact you are talking about. Do not add a screenshot without an accompanying narrative. Do not assume the reader will understand what is pertinent about the screenshot. You will have to explain it to the reader. Make sure you focus your screenshot on the artifact you are discussing.

If your report contains screenshots of contraband, such as illicit images, you will need to maintain control of that report so as not to cause an inadvertent release of the contraband images. You will also need to create a second report with the contraband images redacted for readers who cannot legally possess the contraband images.

After the executive summary, you should include basic administrative information. Identify the subjects involved, including the victim, suspect, witness, and other investigators.

Document facts and circumstances

Next, you should describe the facts and circumstances of the investigation. When the investigation was initiated, what investigative endeavors were conducted by other investigators before your involvement? You should include the basis of the search authority.

You have two options regarding listing the evidence that was analyzed. In some larger cases, the listing of digital evidence can take two or more pages. Having a long, drawn-out list does not help the reader understand your report. More likely, the reader will skip the evidence listing and move on. If the investigation does not have a large number of digital devices being examined, then you can list them here, including the devices where you found nothing of evidentiary value. If you have a large number of digital devices, I recommend you only list the devices that had artifacts of evidentiary value, while listing the entire evidence list at the end of the report.

You should also list details about the creation of the forensic images. I typically include a summary of the acquisition details in the narrative portion. I then create a detailed step-by-step process of the forensic image's creation as an exhibit. Once again, having a step-by-step process in the report's narrative does not help the reader understand the process. Giving the reader the high-level details of the forensic image process and then providing the details at a different location improves the readability of the report.

The analysis of the digital evidence will make up the bulk of your report. This is where you will walk the reader through the step-by-step process of the incriminating artifacts you found and why the artifact is important. Many times, I have seen a report where a specific image is highlighted as being important, but then it never explains why the image is important. Is it the location of where the image was found, or is it the image itself? Explain why that specific artifact is important and how you determined it was important.

> **Note.**
> Remember, you are taking a technical subject and explaining it to a non-technical reader. Do not create a list of important files and assume the reader will know what is important.

I find that it's best to present the artifacts in chronological order. For example, if you are examining the illegal downloading of copyright-protected material, you would start by potentially identifying the owner of the computer and any artifacts that can identify a specific user. You can then show any browser searches the user performed when looking for the copyright-protected material and then the steps taken to download that material. If the user had any ongoing communications with other users about the copyright-protected material, you could then use these communications to support your hypothesis about the user's activity of downloading the copyright-protected material.

You can also present the artifacts by subject. If you are investigating the possession and distribution of illicit images, you can present the artifacts showing that the user viewed the images. This will show that the user knew about the images on their system and whether the user actively shared them with other users. Just the image alone is not enough; you also have to find the OS artifacts to support your hypothesis about the image. When you are creating the analysis section, you will need to avoid making any absolute statements. I have seen forensic reports dealing with illicit images where the investigator made the absolute statement that the user knew about the illegal image. They found the image in question in the thumb cache database. The location of an image in a thumb cache database is not absolute proof that the user knew about the image. Images can be included in the thumb cache database without the knowledge of the user. So, you want to be very careful with your language. Do not include opinions—only include factual information.

I have seen reports describing artifacts as "a disturbing image of a child." The term "disturbing image" is not factually based—it is an opinion. You should describe the artifact as it is without projecting your feelings about it. A better description could be "an image depicting a young-looking male, nude, standing in a wooded area." Be careful how you describe the artifacts attributed to a specific user or person. The hardest item to prove is who is behind the keyboard. You can never say with 100 percent certainty that suspect A did the criminal activity unless you have a video showing suspect A was at the keyboard at that specific time. This is not the place for you to offer your opinion; do not assume ownership of an item or the identification of a user.

The report conclusion

The final portion of your narrative is your conclusion. This is the section where you can offer your opinion based on the artifacts you described in the analysis section of the report. You still have to be careful about presenting your opinions. Try to look at the artifacts with no preconceived notions and determine whether the facts again meet your hypothesis. If you cannot decide, include that opinion. Remember, it is not always about trying to prove the subject's guilt. You must also provide evidence if the subject did not do what they are being accused of.

You will probably create an electronic report for distribution; a standard format is PDF. No matter what format you use, make sure you digitally sign the report. The digital signature will show that no one has altered the report since you signed it.

> **Note.**
> Remember, the report is a representation of you and the investigation. If you create a poor report, that will reflect poorly on you, the investigation, and your organization.

Proofreading is essential. Do not proofread the report yourself. You will miss things—typographical errors, poor sentence structures, and unclear findings. What may be clear to you in your mind may not always be accurately transcribed in the written form. If the investigation proceeds to administrative or judicial proceedings, I can guarantee the opposition will dissect your report line by line, looking for inconsistencies and places where you were not objective.

Remember, if the reader does not understand what you are saying about the artifacts you found, then your entire effort in the investigation has been wasted.

Summary

In this chapter, we have discussed the forensic analysis process. You now know how to prepare to conduct a digital forensic examination, from getting the proper equipment to training and getting certification. You now understand the importance of obtaining information before seizing digital evidence and ensuring you talk to other investigators or personnel involved in the situation.

I cannot stress the importance of collecting volatile data enough; if you do not do so, you will lose a large amount of potential evidence. We discussed some strategies to conduct your examination and the differences between an OS artifact and a filesystem artifact. Lastly, we discussed reporting your findings so that they are easily understood by the reader.

In the next chapter, we will go into the specifics of the acquisition of evidence and how to validate your tools to create an error-free forensic image.

Questions

1. Which of the following should be included in your response kit?

    a. A digital camera

    b. Latex gloves

    c. A write-blocking device

    d. All of the above

2. You must use commercial software to perform a valid forensic examination.

    a. True

    b. False

3. What questions need to be asked when you receive digital evidence?

    a. Why was the digital evidence seized?

    b. Where is the chain of custody?

    c. Who has accessed the evidence?

    d. All of the above

4. RAM is the most volatile of evidence.

    a. True

    b. False

5. The chain of custody documents _____.

    a. Who accessed the evidence

    b. Who witnessed the crime

    c. The suspect's fingerprints

    d. None of the above

6. Which of the following is best for a digital forensic exam?

    a. A forensic copy

    b. A forensic image

    c. A logical forensic image

    d. Both B and C

7. Which of the following is a hashing algorithm?

  a. CDC

  b. FBI

  c. MD5

  d. LSD

The answers can be found at the end of the book in the *Assessments* section.

Further reading

Warren Kruse and Jay Heiser, Computer Forensics: Incident Response Essentials (*Addison Wesley, 2001*)

You can purchase the book from `https://www.amazon.com/Computer-Forensics-Incident-Response-Essentials/dp/0201707195`.

3
Acquisition of Evidence

Digital evidence is one of the most volatile pieces of evidence an investigator can handle, and the smallest error or mishandling on the investigator's part can severely impact the investigation. You may lose the data forever, or you might lose pieces of it. Unintentional manipulation of data can call your ability to investigate into question, as well as the integrity of the data in the investigation. This chapter will address how to minimize or eliminate any of these issues by using a tool validation process to create an error-free and validated forensic image.

We will cover the following topics in this chapter:

- Exploring evidence
- Understanding the forensic examination environment
- Tool validation
- Creating sterile media
- Defining forensic imaging

Exploring evidence

What is evidence? The dictionary definition is *the available body of facts or information indicating whether a belief or proposition is true or valid*. Now that seems to be a short, simple, common sense answer to a simple question. In reality, the question becomes far more convoluted when you take into account regulations, the law, and rules of evidence in one jurisdiction, and this grows exponentially when considering multiple jurisdictions. Evidence is a determination made by the trier of fact. The trier of fact will determine if the evidence meets the standards for that proceeding and jurisdiction. Despite the trier of fact, if you accept the evidence, it can still be called into question.

I offer the following example: Let's say you are investigating a murder and you find the victim's and suspect's blood in the suspect's vehicle; the victim's blood on the suspect's socks; and a bloodied glove at the scene, and its matching mate found in the suspect's house.

Based on this evidence, you could believe the government had an airtight case against the suspect. But in this case, the defense was able to successfully argue and challenge the evidence, which resulted in the suspect's acquittal. As you can see, just because something is evidence, if it cannot withstand the challenge of the opposition, then it becomes a liability.

I have worked on both sides of the judicial process regarding digital evidence, and every time, the sheer amount of digital evidence that never sees the light of day amazes me. If the evidence is not presented to the trier of fact and accepted, it does not exist as far as the proceedings are concerned. Neither side will reference it or offer it during the proceedings. It simply will not exist.

How does the opposition attack evidence that has been admitted by the trier of fact? Either by attacking the evidence itself and/or by attacking the process and personnel associated with the collection and analysis of the evidence.

Consider the following example:

An examiner analyzes the thumb cache of the system and sees a URI (The **URI** is a **uniform resource identifier** based on the standard created by the internet engineering task force. In this instance, it is the file path.) pointing to the location of the original image. The original destination folder no longer exists on the system, nor does the source image for the thumbnail in the cache.

As shown in the following screenshot, the source image for the thumbnail in the cache was located in the New folder on the `Picture Drive` of the user account of `bob`. This is the URI that was found in the thumbnail's metadata:

```
URI: file:///media/bob/Picture Drive/New
```

Figure 3.1 – URI image

In the following screenshot, you can see the URI that was found in the metadata of a different thumbnail in the same thumb cache. The path is very similar to the one found in the URI image. There are significant differences here – the user account is bobby, not bob, and the New folder does not exist:

```
URI: file:///media/bobby/Picture Drive/
```

Figure 3.2 – URI image: bobby

On the system that was being analyzed, there was not a bob user account, nor were there any artifacts showing the bob account was ever created or deleted from that system. The digital forensic examiner amended their report and incorrectly stated the Picture Drive was the same in both instances based on the similarities of the URIs. Originally, the digital forensic examiner stated, *The URIs found within the metadata represent file paths that cannot be verified.*

The digital forensic examiner conducted a second exam and found a deleted folder called New on the Picture Drive and amended the report to reflect *The URIs found within the metadata represent evidence item HDD 001.* The New folder was deleted on this date and time. (I am not utilizing exact names or dates for obvious reasons.)

Based on the file path and the current users, there was no way to determine if the New folder referenced in the URI was the same as the deleted New folder. When the digital forensic examiner was confronted about these discrepancies, they admitted that they had made an error. I believe they made the error because of the similarities of the file paths and not paying attention to the specific details. I absolutely believe the error was not malicious or intentional but an honest mistake by the opposition's digital forensic examiner. As you can see, sometimes, an honest mistake can lead to additional questions being asked about the collection of the evidence and the process used to generate the report and the evidence.

In a different case I was brought in on, the suspect was charged with attempting to lure a child. In this specific set of circumstances, the suspect was communicating with an **undercover agent** (**UC**) and sent many illicit images to the UC. When the subject was taken into custody, they were interrogated, confessed, and wrote an apology letter. The confession, over 400 pages of chats, and a dozen illicit images submitted as evidence in the judicial proceedings. Once again, you would expect that there would be a conviction based upon this evidence.

During the trial, it was revealed the government had deleted some text messages and edited the video file of the recording of the confession. The judicial authority informed the jury of the manipulated evidence and that the only conclusion they could consider was that the alteration of the digital evidence was done in a manner to hide facts that would hinder the government's prosecution. The jury then found the subject not guilty of all charges.

If you do not follow the best practices, policies, and procedures of your organization, the evidence will not see the inside of the courtroom and if it is admitted, the opposition's attacks will mitigate its effectiveness. These attacks can create enough reasonable doubt to generate an acquittal.

So, what can we do to mitigate the attack of the opposition? It does not matter which side of the matter you are on; the opposing counsel will attack your findings if it is harmful to their case.

Do not forgo proper evidence handling procedures. Proper evidence handling does not end with the collection of evidence in the field. As it is being transported from the field to the secure location, and whenever someone checks out the evidence, you must ensure the chain of custody and security of the evidence is maintained.

Do not forgo utilizing proper procedures, methodologies, or processes when conducting your digital forensic investigation. Do not take shortcuts.

Validate any procedure, methodology, or process. You have to go through the validation process; you cannot rely on third parties to do the validation for you. Your validation has to repeatedly reproduce the same results when performed by you or anyone else.

If you prepare and conduct your digital forensic examination with the mindset that someone will go through every step you take and question every finding you make, you should be able to mitigate any attack against your digital forensic examination. The key is that you have to prepare. If you are unprepared for the attack, then you may be made to look incompetent while testifying in the judicial/administrative proceedings.

We have discussed the evidence, but what about the environment you will conduct the investigation in? We will now discuss how you should control the examination environment.

Understanding the forensic examination environment

A term that has been pounded into my head since I first went to training with IACIS is the Forensically Sound Examination Environment. While it sounds complicated, it is a relatively simple concept:

- The digital forensic examiner controls the working environment of the digital forensic examination.

- No actions will occur unless the digital forensic examiner intends the action to occur.

- When the action has been completed, the examiner will reasonably know what the expected outcome is.

This concept does not merely apply to a physical location, but anywhere we complete a digital forensic examination or perform actions to support the digital forensic investigation. This could be a lab, office, or in the field where the digital evidence has been collected.

The Forensically Sound Examination Environment is a mindset of the digital forensic examiner. You want to be methodical and thorough as you perform any action to support the digital forensic examination. With this mindset, it will eliminate some mistakes that may occur during the process.

For example, the organization sent two colleagues to a remote location to acquire several workstations. They were able to complete the acquisition of data within 2 to 3 days. No triage or examination was done on the scene, but it was expected to be completed when they returned to the central lab. The remote location was several hundred miles away, and once my colleagues left, they could not return to gain access to the source devices. Upon arrival at the central lab, my colleagues started to conduct their digital forensic examination. Colleague A started to examine one of the forensic images, and as a part of their process, they viewed the folder structure of the filesystem. As they were looking at the installed programs, they were shocked to find a commercial forensic tool installed on the suspects' system. As they drilled down further into the filesystem, they started to find documents with their name on it. They were shocked; how did the suspect gain access to Colleague A's information? The suspect didn't.

Colleague A made an error when creating a forensic image. Instead of imaging the suspects' device, they imaged the system drive of their forensic laptop. They ignored the details as they were creating a forensic image. Luckily, the procedure was for each colleague to make a forensic image of the source device, for a total of two forensic images.

While this story is embarrassing, there were no lasting repercussions because we could use the second copy. Imagine how you would feel if you were Colleague A, and there was not a second backup to use. How do you explain to your supervisor or the client that you could not complete the task as given, and now you do not have access to the source device?

To help stop that from occurring, we will look at tool validation.

Tool validation

Earlier, we discussed potential attacks on you, your exam, and your findings. The opposing counsel will focus on how you did the exam and what tools you used to perform the exam. Your ability to mitigate the opposing counsel attacks is directly related to your preparation and the documentation you created during the exam. Being aware and following best practices is critical in your ability to successfully defend your actions. How do you do this? By continuing your education. The field is always changing, and you have to keep aware of those changes.

The level of detail can easily overwhelm new digital forensic investigators as they need to know how to mitigate the opposing counsel's attack successfully. While you need not know the specific programming or code a particular tool uses, you need to know where the artifact found by the tool is located within the filesystem/operating system so you can adequately explain it as you testify or create your report. Many times, I have seen an examiner rely on a checklist provided by a colleague or one they found on the internet and yet have little to no understanding of why the items are on the checklist or the process used to recover the artifact. It can be as simple as recovering a deleted file. If the digital forensic investigator cannot explain the process of how the specific filesystem processes the user's request to delete a file and how the tool recovered the deleted file, their time testifying will be very uncomfortable. If you cannot explain the basics, all of your findings will be called into question.

You need to determine if your tools produce a valid result. As we saw in our previous discussion in *Chapter 2, The Forensic Analysis Process*, in the matter of Casey Anthony the opposing counsel was successful in mitigating the digital evidence because of an error reported by the forensic tool. If the forensic tool has been found faulty, then the use of the tool may be used as a means to discredit the integrity of the exam and the competence of the examiner.

How do you mitigate the attacks on your process or your tools?

- Understand their functionality
- Document your training
- Take notes during the exam
- Validate the tools

Your testimony about your exam, your findings, and the use of the tools is based on your personal experiences. You cannot testify about someone else's validation. You do not know all the parameters the third party used or did not apply. This is something you have to do personally. Use the tool against a known dataset to see if it performs as expected. If you do not validate your forensic tool, how can you testify that it is providing an accurate result? If you get questioned on the stand, how do you answer the question? It is not uncommon for the opposing counsel to recreate the forensic exam you did. The opposition will attempt to use the same forensic process and the same forensic tools to determine if they can get the same result. What happens if they get a different result using the same method and the same tools? What happens if they get a different result using the same process and different tools? If you do not validate your processes and forensic tools, how can you prepare for that attack against yourself or your examination?

As we mentioned earlier, NIST has created the Computer Forensic Reference Data Set. You can follow this link to assist you in validating your tools: `https://www.cfreds.nist.gov`. These datasets *provide an investigator with documented sets of simulated digital evidence for examination.* NIST has also provided resources for the creation of your test images.

We can use these datasets in a variety of ways:

- Validation testing
- Proficiency testing
- Training

If you use your dataset or a dataset from a third party, you must ensure there is documentation on what is in the dataset and where the testing data is located within the dataset. In the following example, we will use the DCFL control image provided by NIST.

In this example, we will use two forensic tools: the open source tool Autopsy and the commercial tool X-Ways. As shown in the following screenshot, the documentation states there should be two logical files:

```
The following non-system files should be present on the logical level of the disk:

039C8A00   Scientific control.mp3    MD5:    e73a608dfb422a206ce7a62deb90ff9b
029D4A00   Export_me.JPG    MD5:   c0c3892606849fd76a8534ef80956705
```

Figure 3.3 – DCFL control image

The documentation provides us with the logical filename and extension, the hexadecimal offset, and the MD5 hash value for the file. (Remember that the hash value is the digital fingerprint of the file.)

In the following screenshot, we are looking at the interface of Autopsy, which shows that there are two logical files (identified by file extension): one image file and one audio file. So far, that matches the documentation we have been given for the control image:

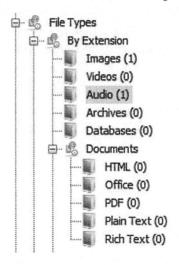

Figure 3.4 – DCFL control image 2

In the following screenshot, we are looking at the interface of X-Ways, and it has also identified two logical files, whose filenames match the control:

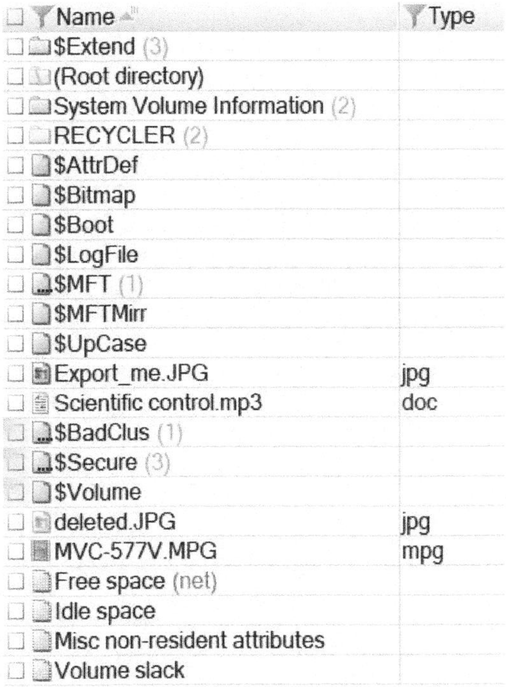
Name
Type
$Extend (3)
(Root directory)
System Volume Information (2)
RECYCLER (2)
$AttrDef
$Bitmap
$Boot
$LogFile
$MFT (1)
$MFTMirr
$UpCase
Export_me.JPG jpg
Scientific control.mp3 doc
$BadClus (1)
$Secure (3)
$Volume
deleted.JPG jpg
MVC-577V.MPG mpg
Free space (net)
Idle space
Misc non-resident attributes
Volume slack

Figure 3.5 – DCFL control image 3

In the following screenshot, we are looking at the metadata of the image file as provided by Autopsy, and we can see that the filename, extension, and hash values match the information provided in the control documents:

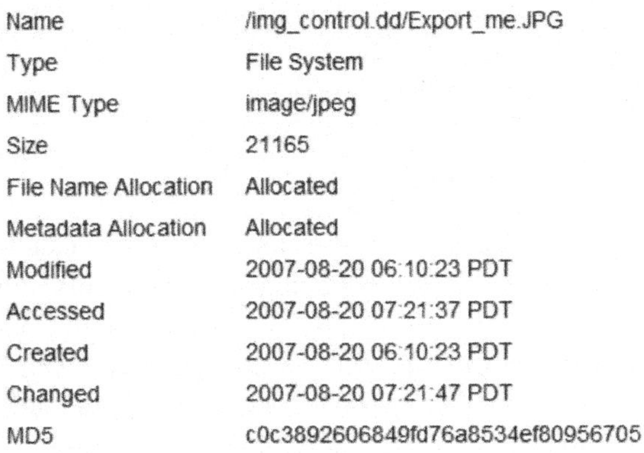
Name /img_control.dd/Export_me.JPG
Type File System
MIME Type image/jpeg
Size 21165
File Name Allocation Allocated
Metadata Allocation Allocated
Modified 2007-08-20 06:10:23 PDT
Accessed 2007-08-20 07:21:37 PDT
Created 2007-08-20 06:10:23 PDT
Changed 2007-08-20 07:21:47 PDT
MD5 c0c3892606849fd76a8534ef80956705

Figure 3.6 – DCFL control image 4

In the following screenshot, we are looking at the metadata for the same file in the X-Ways interface, and find it also matches the information provided in the control documents:

Evidence object	control
Name	Export_me.JPG
Type	jpg
Description	existing
Existent	✓
Size	20.7 KB (21,165)
Created	08/20/2007 13:10:23 +0
Modified	08/20/2007 13:10:23 +0
Accessed	08/20/2007 14:21:37 +0
Record changed	08/20/2007 14:21:47 +0
Record changed²	08/20/2007 13:10:23 +0
Ext.	JPG
Type status	confirmed, OK
Type descr.	JPEG
Category	Pictures
Path	\
Full path	\Export_me.JPG
Parent name	\
Attr.	A
1st sector	85,669
FS offset	43897856
ID	29
Int. ID	22
Int. parent	6
Unique ID	0-22
Unique ID as GUID	00000016-0000-4000-B0E330CC71024E5F
Owner	S-1-5-21-3958095517-222395546-2225589205-500
Link count	°1
Pixels	0.4 MP
Analysis	0% skin tones
Hash¹ (MD5)	C0C3892606849FD76A8534EF80956705
Hash² (SHA-1)	4F90640F999271C41A1E77804FD7AAA4F0340D9D
Generator signature	60F38468 (U:Standard 75 Edited)
Device type	unknown
Relevance	3.59

Figure 3.7 – DCFL control image 5

You will work your way through the rest of the control image to ensure the forensic tool of choice is functioning correctly and is producing accurate results. There are multiple control datasets you can use to validate your tools. You cannot be sure your tool works properly until you conduct the validation test. Your organization should have a policy dictating when the validation should occur and how to document and record the results of the validation test. If you do not log the validation tests, the opposing counsel can call it into question when they request those records.

That covers the validation of your tools, but what about the storage containers? Let's discuss sterile media and define what it is.

Creating sterile media

Sterile media is also a concept that was emphasized when I first trained. Now, there is a discussion regarding whether sterile media is still needed in today's forensic environment. The decision to use sterile media to store the forensic data will be based on the acquisition and the type of examination you will use. Sterile media can be used before the start of the forensic process and at the end of the forensic process. There are multiple reasons to use sterile media, which we will now discuss. When digital forensics was first starting, we did not have the capability to create a forensic image; we were forced to create a forensic copy to perform our examination on. Remember, we talked about a forensic copy in *Chapter 2*, *The Forensic Analysis Process*, and defined a forensic copy as follows:

"A straight bit-for-bit copy of the source to the destination. This is not common in today's environment; ensure that your destination device has no old data from previous investigations. You do not want to cause cross-contamination between the current digital forensic investigation and a past investigation. We will recover deleted files, file slack, and partition slack."

If your source and destination were the same make, model, and capacity, then you would potentially not have an issue. In real life, this rarely happens, so you would use a larger capacity device and you would copy the data from the source device to the destination device. As a result, you would have unallocated space not used on the destination device. If you did not wipe or use sterilized media as your destination device, it is possible that there would be pre-existing data on your destination device, and this creates the possibility for the co-mingling of data. So, when using the forensic copy process and you look for data in unallocated space or slack space, you must use sterilized media.

There have been cases where the examiner has used a newly purchased storage device or had the storage device provided to them; they still must wipe the drive and sterilize it of all pre-existing data. If you do not and the destination device is provided to the opposing counsel and they find data not relevant to the matter at hand, it can call into question the integrity of the exam and the competence of the examiner.

What do you do with old storage devices that contained digital evidence? Do you destroy them? Do you recycle them? Do you turn them over to your organization and not worry about it? Before the storage device leaves your control, you must wipe that device to ensure no confidential information or contraband is released to an unauthorized entity. That way, you can be positive that there is no way data relating to any digital forensic exam can be released without your approval.

So, what exactly is sterile media? It is simply where every byte on the device is overwritten with a hexadecimal 00. Technically, you can use any character you like, but it is much easier to verify whether the sterilization of media was successful if you use the hexadecimal 00. We use the 64-bit checksum to validate the sterilization process. If you run the 64-bit checksum against the sterile media, you will get zeros as the generated checksum value. I do not recommend using the MD5 or SHA–1 hashing algorithms to verify the sterilization process. They will not give you a value you can use to immediately identify the successful sterilization process.

Let's look at the sterilization process. We will use Paladin from Sumuri Forensics. Paladin is a live bootable version of Ubuntu. This means you have to have Paladin installed on a USB or a DVD/CD. Using a USB or CD/DVD will allow the computer to boot to the operating system contained on the USB/CD/DVD. Paladin allows you to access the host computer while modifying none of the digital evidence. The Paladin toolbox allows us to create forensic images, convert forensic images, and create sterile media.

In the following screenshot, I have opened the Paladin toolbox and selected **Disk Manager**:

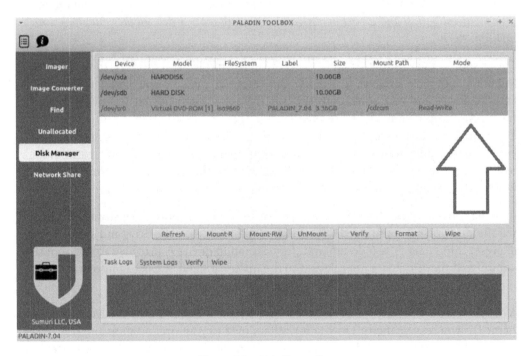

Figure 3.8 – Paladin toolbox

As we look at the preceding screenshot, we see that there are three devices on the system: two 10-GB hard drives and a CD-ROM drive. The CD-ROM is the Paladin operating system, while the two hard drives are the storage drives on the computer. We will wipe one of these storage drives, in this case, /dev/sdb. As you look at the interface, below the device listing, you will see a variety of options. At the far right, we have a button titled **Wipe**. This is the button we will select after we left-click on the device we want to wipe. You do not want to mount the device before wiping it.

Once Paladin has completed the wiping/sterilization process, it will show you a log of the processes being used. In the following screenshot, we can see that it input the pattern 00 and the number of sectors that were overwritten. The last line tells us when the operation was completed. You need to save this log and store it with the storage device you have just wiped:

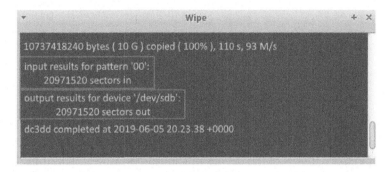

Figure 3.9 – Paladin toolbox 2

But how do we verify the results to ensure the tool works as expected? Here, we will use the commercial tool X-Ways Forensics. X-Ways Forensics is a commercial tool offered by X-Ways Software Technology AG and is my go-to tool when conducting a digital forensic exam. Its ease of installation, price, and the ability to use it on many platforms are what I find attractive about this tool. It's not that other tools are not worthwhile; this is just my personal preference.

We have added the device into X-Ways, and now we want to verify the sterilization process we used with Paladin. Follow these steps to do so:

1. Right-click on the device and select **Properties**:

Figure 3.10 – X-Ways 1

2. The **Properties** window of the device will appear. Toward the bottom right, you will find the **Compute hash** button. When we left-click it, we will see the hashing options available to us:

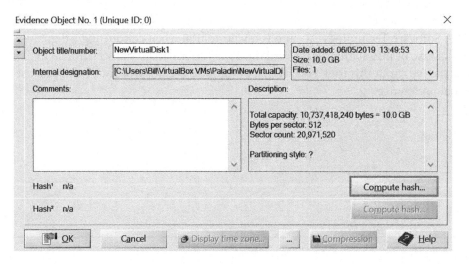

Figure 3.11 – X-Ways 2

3. You will want to select **Checksum (64 bit)**, which will return zeros if the sterilization process worked correctly:

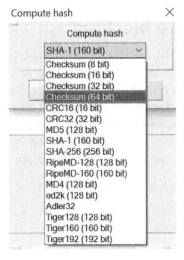

Figure 3.12 – X-Ways 3

If you choose MD5, SHA–1, or any other hashing algorithm, you will get a value for the device, but that value will not let you determine if there is any residual data left on the device.

4. As shown in the following screenshot, the checksum result is a string of zeros. This informs us that the media sterilization process has worked correctly. We have also just validated another aspect of our forensic tools:

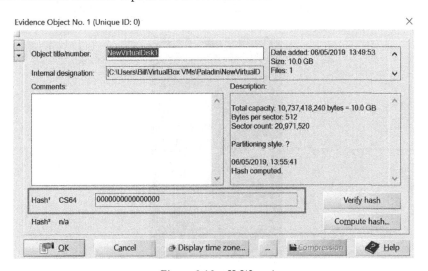

Figure 3.13 – X-Ways 4

We now have sterile media, but how do we protect the original evidence? The answer is to perform write blocking, which we will discuss next.

Understanding write blocking

Write blocking is at the core of the forensic examination environment. With the fragility of digital evidence, we want to ensure we do not change a single bit of data on the source device. Evidence handling is an essential function of the examination process, and we must ensure that we meet all the requirements to avoid altering or damaging the evidence. If I plug the device into a Windows-based computer system, to enhance the user's experience, the operating system scans and makes writes on that device that change the evidence. To prevent the alteration of the source device, we must use a write blocker.

You have a choice of utilizing a "hardware write blocker" or a "software write blocker."

Hardware write blocker

As the operating system issues commands, it will read/write from the source device. A hardware write blocker is a device that intercepts and prevents any modification to the source device. It is physically connected between the computer and the source device to accomplish this. There are also standalone hardware write blockers that are self-contained that allow you to attach the source and destination device and then create the forensic image.

In the following image, we can see the Tableau Forensic SATA/IDE Forensic bridge T35u that the Department of Homeland Security tested in October 2018. This device allows you to forensically acquire SATA and IDE devices by using the computer's USB 3.0 connection:

Figure 3.14 – Tableau

NIST has created the Computer Forensics Tool Testing Program, which lists the testing results for hardware write blockers (https://www.nist.gov/itl/ssd/software-quality-group/computer-forensics-tool-testing-program-cftt/cftt-technical/hardware). Here, you can find the report on the T35u and other devices.

Software write blocker

Software write blocking is where a change is made to the operating system to stop it from making writes to the device. For a Windows-based system, there is a registry change you can make to prevent rights to attached USB devices. This will require you to have a hard drive dock to connect to the system.

Another option is to utilize a bootable operating system, such as Paladin or Win FE.

In the following screenshot, we can see the Paladin toolbox, and it is listing the drives in the system. By default, Paladin mounts none of the attached storage devices. This means it makes no modifications and doesn't look at the devices until you tell the software to mount:

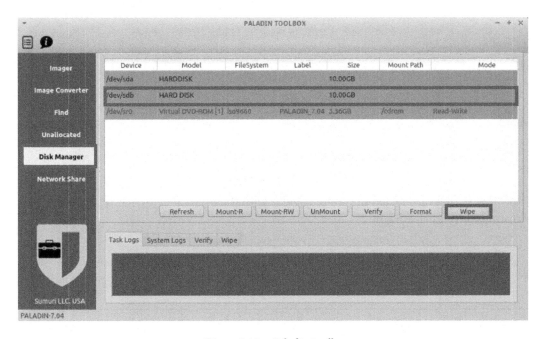

Figure 3.15 – Paladin toolbox

There are two options when you mount a device:

- Read-only
- Read/write

You should not mount a device read/write unless you want to change the device. If you create a forensic image of the device, then you should mount read-only.

As shown in the following screenshot, there is a column listed as **Mode**, and we can see that the CD-ROM is mounted as read/write and is highlighted in red, while the hard disk is green and shows read-only:

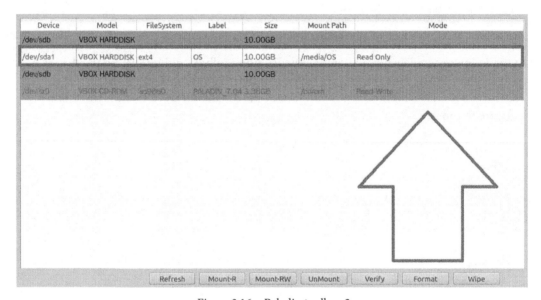

Device	Model	FileSystem	Label	Size	Mount Path	Mode
/dev/sdb	VBOX HARDDISK			10.00GB		
/dev/sda1	VBOX HARDDISK	ext4	OS	10.00GB	/media/OS	Read Only
/dev/sdb	VBOX HARDDISK			10.00GB		
/dev/sr0	VBOX CD-ROM	iso9660	PALADIN_7.04	3.38GB	/cdrom	Read-Write

Refresh   Mount-R   Mount-RW   UnMount   Verify   Format   Wipe

Figure 3.16 – Paladin toolbox 2

Now that we have protected the source device with the original evidence, let's move on to creating the forensic image.

Defining forensic imaging

I continue to stress that we never want to change the source device/digital evidence. That is why we never conduct a digital forensic examination on the original device. You should only conduct your digital forensic analysis on a copy and not the original. You must remember the forensic copy you make will also be considered the evidence and will have the same evidentiary weight as the original source device in terms of evidence. What are we transferring from the source device into our forensic copy? Everything! I want to look at allocated files, deleted files, slack space, unallocated space, and unpartitioned space. I want to collect every bit on the source device. Earlier in this book, in *Chapter 2, The Forensic Analysis Process*, I gave you the following definitions:

- **Forensic copy**: This is a straight bit-for-bit copy of the source to the destination. This is not common in today's environment, so ensure that your destination device has no old data from previous investigations. You do not want to cause cross-contamination between the current digital forensic investigation and a past investigation. We will recover deleted files, file slack, and partition slack. We will discuss wiping hard drives later on in this book.

- **Forensic image**: We are creating a bit-for-bit copy of the source device, but we store that data in a forensic image format. This could be a DD image, an E01 image, or an AFF image. We take that source data and wrap it in a protective wrapper of the forensic image. We will recover deleted files, file slack, and partition slack.

- **Logical forensic image**: Sometimes, we are restricted to only accessing specific datasets. They do not allow us to access the entire container. We cannot create a bit-for-bit copy of a forensic image or a forensic copy. This could be when we are extracting data from a server, and we cannot shut the server down to create a forensic image from the source hard drives. Due to this, we can make logical copies of the files and folders pertinent to the investigation. We will NOT be able to recover deleted files, file slack, and partition slack.

For the forensic copy and the forensic image, we will acquire every bit on the source device; if there are restrictions, then we will only be able to copy the logical files. We will then put the logical files into a forensic container, which will then encapsulate them in a protective format to prevent any alteration to the data after we've collected it. These are not backups, as you might see in the corporate environment. In the corporate environment, they have not created those backups in a forensically sound manner and they will not contain any information about file slack, unallocated space, deleted files, or any piece of data that is not maintained by the filesystem. I do not recommend doing digital forensic examinations in which commercial/open source backup software was used to collect the evidence. Only use a trusted and verified forensic tool that will collect all the information, and do so in a forensically sound manner.

There are two common formats for a forensic image. (There are others, but DD and E01 are the two formats I consistently see used by government and corporate digital forensic investigators.) Let's take a look at them now.

DD image

DD is a UNIX command, and some call it the oldest imaging tool available that has migrated to other platforms. You can find versions of DD that work on Linux, Windows, or Mac and they all work in relatively the same manner. They designed it to copy data from a source device to a destination device. Relatively simple, is it not?

With a DD image, you can do a forensic copy, which is every byte from the source device to the destination device. You also have the option of creating a flat-file/RAW image of the source device. The image file can be a single file, or we can segment it into multiple pieces. It does not compress the forensic image, so you must ensure that your destination device is of the same capacity or greater than the source device.

In the following screenshot, you can see an example of a DD image that has not been segmented and is 21 GB in size. Depending on the format of your storage device, you may have to segment the forensic image to meet the filesystem's constraints. You may also see different file extensions for the DD image; .001, .dd, and .img are common file extensions:

| cfreds_2015_data_leakage_pc.dd | 4/21/2015 11:17 AM | DD File | 20,971,520 KB |

Figure 3.17 – DD image

dcfldd (http://dcfldd.sourceforge.net/) is a version of the dd command that has incorporated additional features, such as the following:

- Hashing on the fly

- Status output

- Disk wiping

- Verifying an image or wipe

- Multiple outputs

- Splitting outputs

- Piped output and logs

dcfldd was written by Nick Harbor (former employee of DCFL).

> **Note**
>
> dcfldd has an issue with imaging faulty drives. NIST reported that dcfldd will misalign the data in the image after a faulty sector is encountered on the source device. You can visit this link to find out more: `https://www.dhs.gov/sites/default/files/publications/DCFLDD%201%203%20 4-1%20Test%20Report_updated.pdf`.

dc3dd (`https://sourceforge.net/projects/dc3dd/`) is another version of the dd command. Where dcfldd is a fork of the dd command, dc3dd is a patch of the dd command. While these options are similar, they have a slightly different code base and feature sets. When the dd command is updated, dc3dd is also automatically updated.

Some features available on dc3dd include the following:

- Ability to have on-the-fly hashing
- Ability to write errors directly to the file
- Ability to create error log pattern wiping
- Ability to verify mode
- Ability to create progress reports
- Ability to split outputs

Jesse Kornblum developed dc3dd at the DoD Cybercrime Center. The next format we will discuss is the EnCase evidence file.

EnCase evidence file

The other forensic image format we will talk about is the EnCase evidence file, commonly referred to as e01 or the expert witness file format. Where the dd command is a direct bit-for-bit copy, the e01 format is also a bit-for-bit copy, but includes additional data within the forensic image.

EnCase Forensics is a commercial forensic tool created by Guidance Software (now Open Text) and was one of the first commercial digital forensic tools available for use. They created the forensic image file known as the e01 format, **Expert Witness Format** (**EWF**), or the EnCase image file format.

The e01 file format is a forensic image that encapsulates the raw data from the source device to prevent changes from occurring after acquisition without informing the user about the changes. While the dd image only contains the data from the source device, the e01 forensic image contains header information such as evidence name/number, acquisition dates and times, investigator notes, and information about the forensic tool used to create the forensic image. The e01 forensic image also has additional security features to ensure the validity of the forensic image. There is a CRC calculation every 64 sectors as the forensic image file is created. It stores the CRC value within the forensic image so that every time the forensic image is utilized, your forensic tool can verify it.

As seen in the following screenshot, you can see the layout of the e01 file format. The **Case Information** is at the head of the file, a **CRC** is created from the header information, and then a 64-sector block is added to the image file and a **CRC** value is created for that 64-sector block and added to the forensic image. The **data** block and the corresponding **CRC** block process continues until it acquires the entire source device. Once the process has reached the end of the source device, an **MD5** hash value is generated of all the data blocks (and only the data blocks) and attached to the end of the forensic image. With the e01 forensic image, you also can enable compression; you do not have that ability with a dd image:

Figure 3.18 – e01

Next, we need to discuss SSD drives, because SSD devices have some special considerations when it comes to imaging.

SSD device

Solid State Storage (SSD) is a new type of storage device that is becoming more prevalent in the business and consumer market. As the price of storage devices comes down, their use will increase. SSDs create a unique issue regarding digital forensics. There are automated processes that are run through the firmware of the device. The digital forensic examiner has no way to stop or to intercept the commands of the firmware on the storage device. Wear leveling is a feature that ensures the storage blocks on the device are used at a similar rate. If some blocks on the storage device are overused or if the blocks are not equal, it can lead to premature failure of some storage blocks. The firmware will decide on where to move the data on the storage device. Plugging in the solid state device can cause the firmware to move data around.

Garbage collection is the other firmware function that causes concern in the digital forensic world. When a user deletes a file, formats a partition, or deletes partitions, the firmware starts the garbage collection process with the `trim` command. This causes the now unallocated space to be wiped, and the deleted data will no longer be accessible.

It is possible that after you create the forensic image of the source device and you have your pre- and post- hash values of the source device, if you go back days, weeks, or months later and hash the source device, it may come back with a different hash value. It also may also be possible with large drives with long imaging times that the pre- and post-imaging hash values do not match, depending on how much "idle time" the drive has during the imaging process.

As long as you are able to explain the issues with SSD drives, you should have no issues, so we will move on to imaging tools.

Imaging tools

Remember that you do not want to conduct your investigation on the original media, especially SSD devices. As I mentioned in the prior section, the wear leveling and `trim` commands will result in a change in the original evidence. There are many forensic tools for you to use for your imaging needs; we will now discuss two freely available tools and how to create a forensic image.

FTK Imager

FTK Imager is a free tool offered by AccessData. You can visit `https://accessdata.com/product-download/ftk-imager-version-4.2.0`, which will help you create a hash value for the source device, image it, and then create the post hash value to verify that no changes were made to the source device during the imaging process:

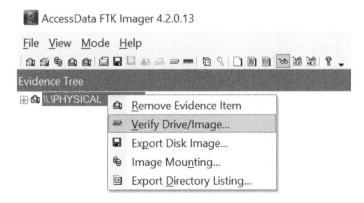

Figure 3.19 – FTK Imager

After using the appropriate write blocker, we attached a 2-GB USB thumb drive to the system. We will now obtain the pre-hash of the device. This hash value gives us the starting value of the device. This value will be used to determine if any alterations have occurred on the source device. In the preceding screenshot, you can see we have loaded the physical device into FTK Imager and then right-clicked to bring up the **Verify Drive/Image** menu. Simply click on **Verify Drive/Image** and let FTK Imager do its work. The results will be displayed after, as shown in the following screenshot:

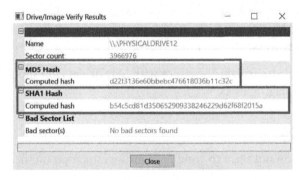

Figure 3.20 – FTK Imager 2

Now that we know what the starting hash value is, we can proceed with the creation of the forensic image:

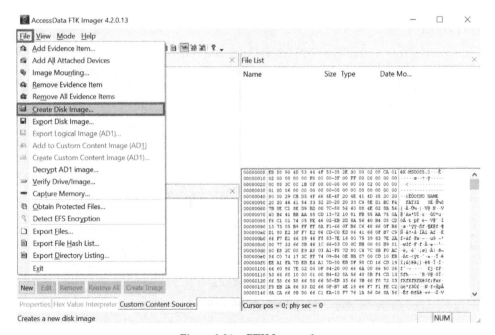

Figure 3.21 – FTK Imager 3

As shown in the preceding screenshot, click on the **File** menu and select **Create Disk Image**.

From here, you will select your source. With FTK Imager, we have some choices to make:

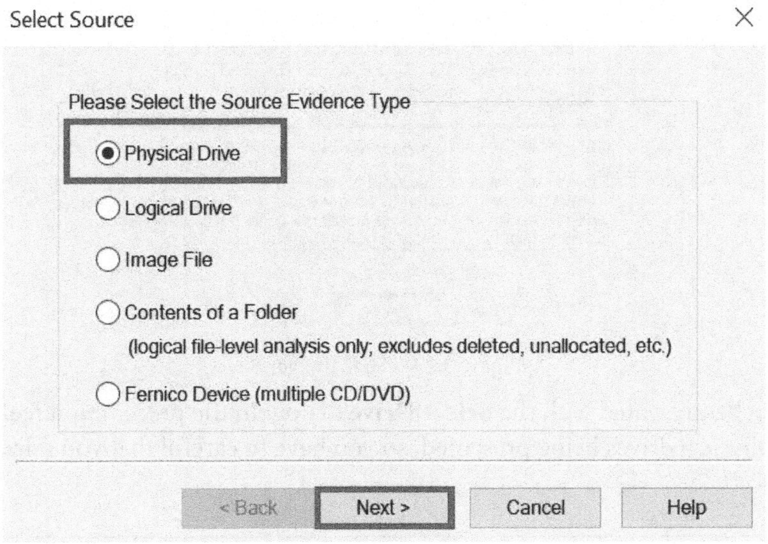

Figure 3.22 – FTK Imager 4

Let's discuss each option in detail:

- **Physical Drive**: The physical device will give us every bit of data on the source.

- **Logical Drive**: You will only get the data within the partition boundaries. If there are deleted partitions or data outside of the boundaries on the source device, you will not be able to recover that data.

- **Image File**: If you want to change the format of the forensic image; for example, change it from an e01 to a dd image.

- **Contents of a Folder**: You will only get the logical data. You will not get deleted data or unallocated space. Sometimes, you may not be able to shut the system down to create a physical image, such as a server, so you have to grab the logical files for analysis.

- **Fernico Device**: Use this option if you have a Fernico FAR system.

Since we want to get all of the data on the device, we will select **Physical Drive**:

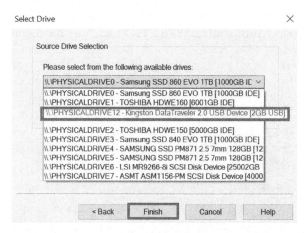

Figure 3.23 – FTK Imager 5

You will then be presented with the **Select Drive** dialog. In the preceding screenshot, there are a lot of physical drives being presented, so you have to careful that you select the correct device!

> **Note**
>
> You can use Windows (or your OS of choice) disk manager to get the physical device number.

We want to select physical device 12, which is the Kingston Data Traveler:

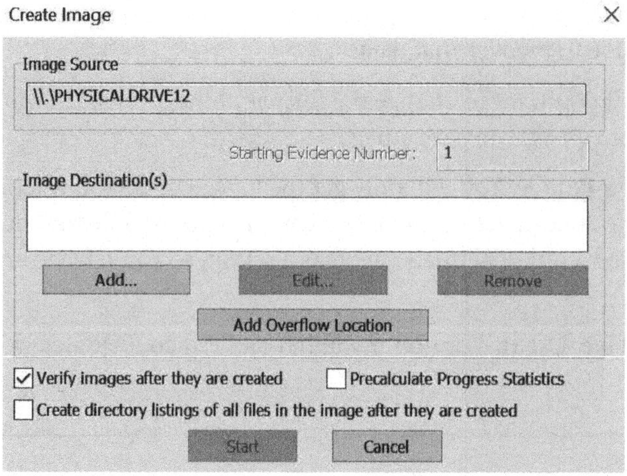

Figure 3.24 – FTK Imager 6

Now, left-click on the **Add** button to select where you want to save the forensic image and what kind of forensic image you wish to create:

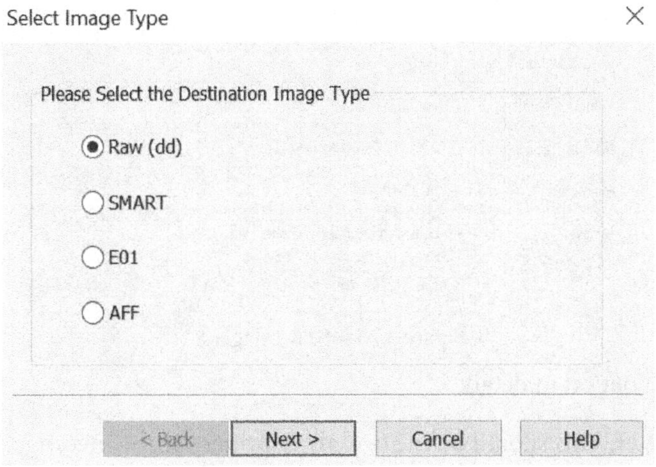

Select Image Type   ×

Please Select the Destination Image Type

◉ Raw (dd)

◯ SMART

◯ E01

◯ AFF

    < Back   Next >   Cancel   Help

Figure 3.25 – FTK Imager 7

What kind of forensic image do you want to create? You have the choice of four options:

- **Raw (dd)**
- **SMART**
- **E01**
- **AFF**

We have already discussed the two most common formats: dd and e01. You can also create two other types of forensic images:

- **SMART**: SMART forensics is a commercial forensic tool on the Linux platform offered by ASR that can be found at http://www.asrdata.com. It can create compressed or uncompressed forensic images and has the ability to segment forensic images.

- **AFF: Advanced Forensics Format (AFF)** is an open source format for the creation of forensic images. The goal of the designers was to create a nonproprietary forensic imaging format. Simson Garfinkel and Basis Technology originally developed AFF.

I do not recall creating a forensic image that was not in the EnCase format or a dd image. My preference is to create a dd image because it is faster than creating an e01 forensic image. Once the examination is complete, I convert the dd image into the e01 format with high compression to help reduce the file size.

Once you've selected the forensic image format, you will be asked to enter the evidence item information (as shown in the following screenshot), which comprises the following:

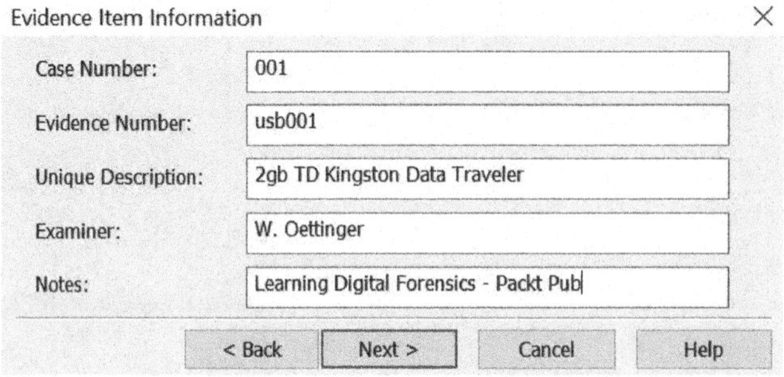

Figure 3.26 – FTK Imager 8

Let's discuss each option in detail:

- **Case number**: This should be the overall identifier for the investigation.

- **Evidence number**: This should be an identifier to help you track the digital evidence. If you have an extensive investigation with multiple source devices, this will help you accurately identify what forensic image you are working on.

- **Unique description**: This is where I would add the make, model, capacity, and serial number of the source device.

- **Notes**: This is where I would add some specific details about where the source device came from, such as a laptop, desktop, and so on.

Your next option is to select the destination (as shown in the following screenshot) for the forensic image in the image destination folder. This could be a storage device attached to the local computer, a connected RAID device, or a form of **network-attached storage** (**NAS**):

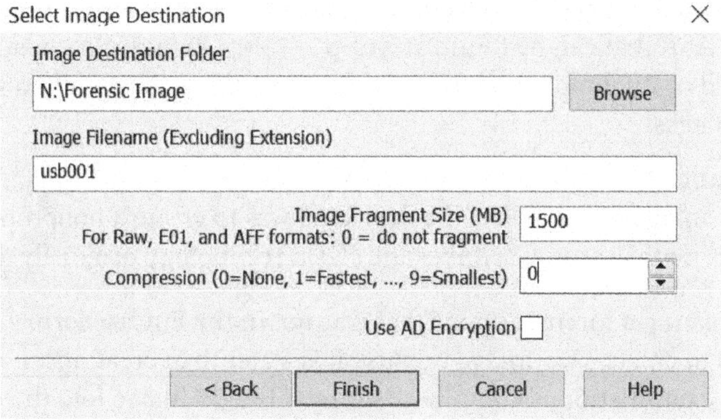

Figure 3.27 – FTK Imager 9

Next, you need to make a selection regarding filing. I recommend using a similar identifier as the evidence number to help avoid confusion.

Image Fragmentation Size will come into play, depending on the filesystem on the storage device and how you will archive the data. In the past, I used a 2 GB fragment size to ensure the forensic image could be used with multiple filesystems. If I do not expect the forensic image to leave my environment, then I will not use a fragmented image. Just know which filesystems have a file size limitation.

I rarely use compression because of the increase in time used to create the forensic image.

Your last option is to encrypt the forensic image. If you encrypt the forensic image, make sure you use a password you will not forget. If you forget the password, you cannot use the forensic image.

Once you have completed answering the requested information, as depicted in the preceding screenshot, you will see the **Create Image** window, showing the options you have selected. You also have the option to add a second destination to create two forensic images at a time:

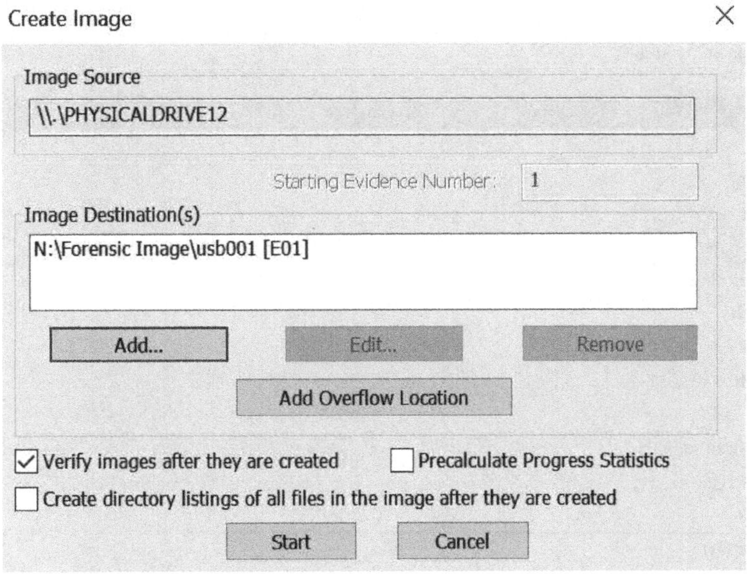

Figure 3.28 – FTK Imager 10

Once FTK Imager has completed creating the forensic image, it will provide you with a status update showing the elapsed time:

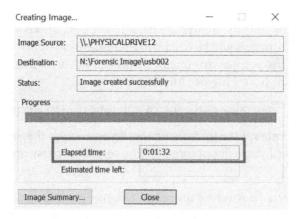

Figure 3.29 – FTK Imager 11

This will also show you the results window, as shown in the following screenshot (a text file is also automatically created and stored in the same location as the forensic image):

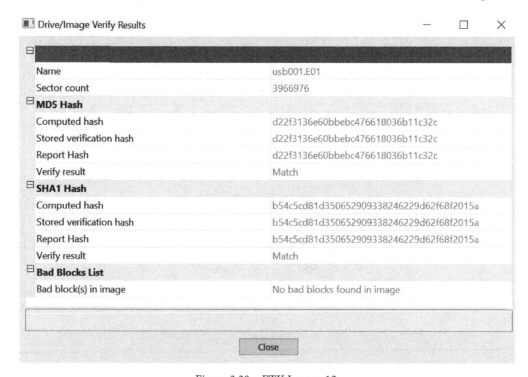

Figure 3.30 – FTK Imager 12

FTK Imager is not the only tool you can use to create a forensic image. An open source forensic tool you can use is Paladin. Paladin has many features, but we will only discuss how it creates a forensic image here.

Paladin

Sumuri's Paladin is a Linux distribution based on Ubuntu that allows the collection of digital evidence in a forensically sound manner. The following screenshot shows the desktop you will see when you boot up Paladin:

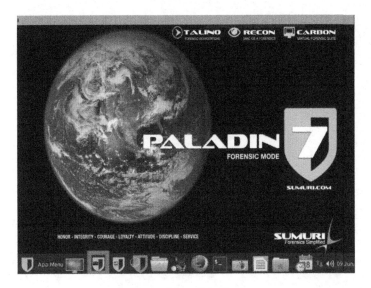

Figure 3.31 – Paladin 1

To create a forensic image with Paladin, we will follow the same general steps that we did for FTK imager, with the exception that we do not have to use a hardware write blocker. Paladin is a live distribution of Ubuntu, so you will have to boot your computer to either a USB device or a CD/DVD. Once you see the desktop shown in the preceding screenshot, you are ready to start imaging:

1. Left-click on the Paladin toolbox icon to get started.
2. Once the Paladin toolbox opens, left-click on **Disk Manager** (as shown in the following screenshot) to see what devices are attached to the system. You will see there are three SATA devices on the system:

    SDA–20-GB hard drive.

    SDB–256-GB thumb drive with one partition (sdb1).

    SDC–2-GB thumb drive. All three devices are represented in black text.

3. Once you've mounted the device, the text will change to green for read-only access and to red for read/write access:

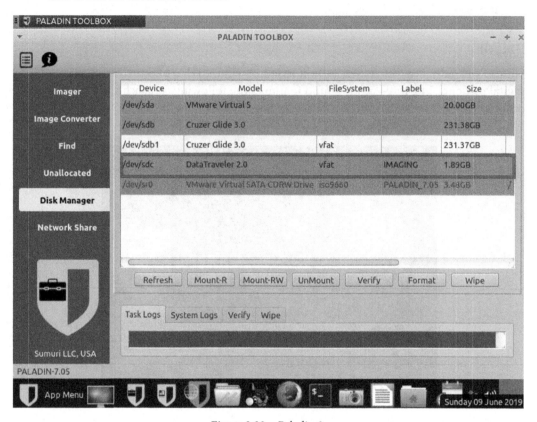

Figure 3.32 – Paladin 2

4. Before starting the forensic imaging process, we must pre-hash the source device. Just select the source device and then click the **Verify** button while in **Disk Manager**. You will see the output shown in the following screenshot:

dc3dd 7.2.641 started at 2019-06-09 16:43:43 +0000
compiled options:
command line: dc3dd of=/dev/null hash=md5 hash=sha1 if=/dev/sdc hlog=/tmp/
000AEBFFB4C45B8903020517_06-09-2019-16-43-43_verify.log

input results for device `/dev/sdc':
  d22f3136e60bbebc476618036b11c32c (md5)
  b54c5cd81d350652909338246229d62f68f2015a (sha1)

output results for File `/dev/null':

Figure 3.33 – Paladin 3

5. In the following screenshot, you now have the option to choose the source device, the forensic image you want to create, and the destination location:

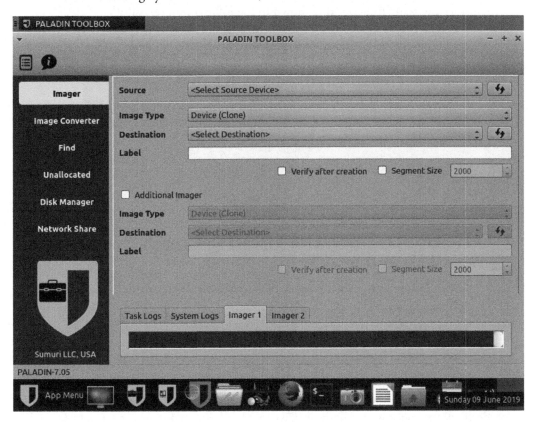

Figure 3.34 – Paladin 4

6. When you select the dropdown for the source device, you will see a list of devices recognized by the system. This is the same list of devices we saw in the Device Manager. It is essential to choose the correct device when creating your forensic image. Here, we will select the sdc device:

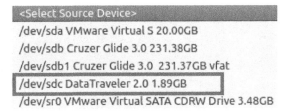

Figure 3.35 – Paladin 5

7. When you select the image format drop-down menu, you will be presented with more choices. We have discussed dd, e01, and SMART forensic images, so let's consider the remaining options shown in the following screenshot:

Figure 3.36 – Paladin 6

Let's discuss them in detail:

ex01: This is an updated format of the e01 forensic image. It was introduced with the release of EnCase 7.

Dmg: This is a proprietary Apple disk image file. It is considered to be a RAW forensic image.

vmdk: VMware Virtual Disk Format. This is a virtualization disk image.

vhd: Virtual Hard Disk. This is a virtual hard disk format typically used by Microsoft Virtual PC, Virtual Server, and Hyper V Server.

8. Your next option is to select the destination. With Paladin, you must ensure the destination device is mounted read/write. I have ensured that sdb1 has been mounted read/write and has sufficient capacity to store the forensic image:

Figure 3.37 – Paladin 7

9. All that remains is to add a label, that is, a filename. I recommend using the same
    naming convention to identify the different pieces of evidence. Since it is a USB
    device and it is the first device I have imaged, I will label it `usb001`:

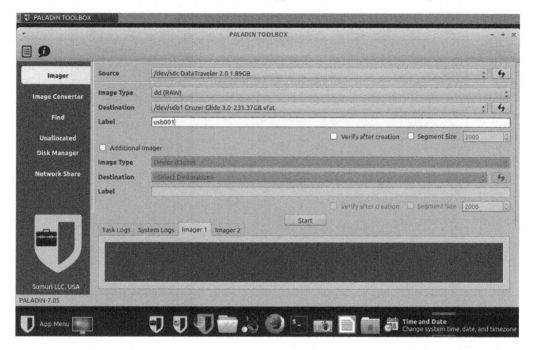

Figure 3.38 – Paladin 8

You also have the option to **Verify after creation** and whether you want to create a
forensic image with segments.

You also have the option to create a second forensic image at the same time.

Once the forensic image creation process has completed, Paladin will present you with the log of the process. As shown in the following screenshot, Paladin is using dc3dd to create the forensic image:

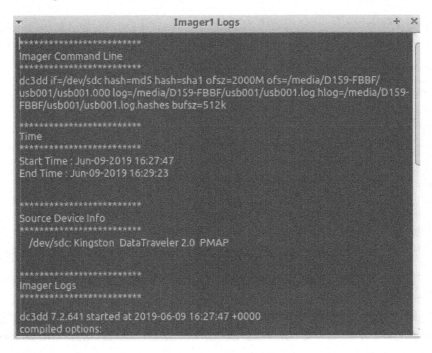

Figure 3.39 – Paladin 9

With that, you have just created a forensic image with Paladin.

Summary

In this chapter, we have discussed evidence and how you need to ensure you validate your processes and your forensic tools to make sure you are getting accurate results. You learned about the Forensically Sound Examination Environment and how you have to maintain control of the environment. The environment is not just in the lab but encompasses when you start the Forensic Analysis Process. We have gone over how to validate your forensic tools, create sterile media, and explored the different write blocking options that are available. We have gone through creating a forensic image utilizing forensic tools such as FTK Imager and Paladin and gone into detail about the different formats available for the creation of a forensic image. Now, we can move on and explore how the computer operates and explore different filesystems.

In the next chapter, we will go into the workings of the computer system and the storage devices you may encounter.

Questions

1. Digital evidence is _____.

   a. Volatile
   b. Non-volatile
   c. Good to have
   d. Not needed when you have a confession

2. Why would it be a good idea to wipe a drive before reusing it to store evidence?

   a. Chain of custody.
   b. To make sure it is formatted correctly.
   c. To ensure no prior data exists on the device.
   d. It's the examiner's choice (the examiner can decide the course of action).

3. You must use a write blocker on the source device when creating a forensic image.

   a. True
   b. False

4. Who controls the Forensically Sound Examination Environment?

   a. Suspect
   b. First responder
   c. Examiner
   d. Depends on the situation

5. The examiner must validate all tools before use.

   a. True
   b. False

6. When creating a forensic image, which is the best option?

   a. Forensic copy
   b. Forensic image
   c. Logical forensic image
   d. Backup copy

7. A dd image can be compressed.

   a. True
   b. False

The answers can be found at the back of this book, under *Assessments*.

Further reading

Zatyko, K., 2011. Commentary: Defining Digital Forensics.

Retrieved from `http://www.forensicmag.com`.

4
Computer Systems

As we discussed in previous chapters, a digital forensic investigator must be able to control the environment in which they operate. The diversity of computer hardware, operating systems, and filesystems requires the digital forensic investigator to have a firm understanding of all the different and potential configurations they may encounter. This requires the digital forensic investigator to have procedures or controls in place to protect the integrity of the digital evidence and the processes used to examine it. If you do not understand the boot process and how the system reacts when it starts or which filesystem is in use on the storage devices, you could make a fatal mistake. You have to understand how they work together. Failure to understand these basic components could lead you to alter the digital evidence. You will also find that you will be less effective when you testify in judicial or administrative proceedings.

In this chapter, we will cover the following topics:

- Understanding the boot process
- Understanding filesystems
- Understanding the NTFS filesystem

Understanding the boot process

In order to control the environment as we start our investigation, we must understand the environment. Here, digital evidence is being stored, created, and accessed. In most cases, this will be a computer system. I use the term "computer system," and what that comprises is the operating system, the filesystem, and the hardware bundled together to create a computer. To be effective, you must understand the physical media the data is stored on, the filesystem used on the storage device, and how that data is tracked and accessed while on the storage device. Once you understand the process, you can then implement controls to protect the integrity of the digital evidence.

So, what is the boot process? Well, when you push the power button and electricity energizes the system, a series of commands is issued. As it executes the commands, the system is taking steps (just like on a ladder) to achieve the goal of a running operating system. If something breaks any of those steps, then the system will not load.

The first step is the **Power-On Self-Test** (**POST**); the CPU will access the **Read-Only Memory** (**ROM**) and the **Basic Input/Output System** (**BIOS**) and test essential motherboard functions. This is where you hear the beep sound when you turn the power on to the computer system. If there is an error, then the system will notify you of the error through the use of beep codes. If you do not have the motherboard manual, do a search to determine the meaning of the specific beep code.

Once the **POST** test has successfully completed, the BIOS is activated and executed. Note that the system has not accessed the storage media. All the program executions are taking place at the motherboard level and not in the storage devices. The user can access the BIOS by using the correct key combination as it is displayed on the screen.

> **Note**
> The time allowed for you to hit the correct key can sometimes be quite short. If you are unsuccessful, the system will continue booting and will access the storage device. If you are trying to access the suspect's computer system, disengage the storage devices if they are accessible before starting the process. This will ensure that you are not booting to the suspect's storage device and destroying evidence.

The BIOS will have the basic information of the system: the amount of RAM, the type of CPU, information about the attached drives, and the system date and time. The easiest way to document this information is to take a photograph of it as it is displayed on the screen. This is also where you can change the boot sequence. Typically, the system checks the CD/DVD first and then the designated hard drive. This is where you would be able to change the setting of the boot device when we create the boot media later on in the chapter. Changing the boot device tells the BIOS to access the device we are providing, and not the suspect's.

In 2010, the BIOS function was replaced by the **Unified Extensible Firmware Interface (UEFI)**. It provides the same service as the BIOS, but has been enhanced, as follows:

- By providing better security at the pre-boot process
- Faster startup
- Will support drives larger than 2 TB
- Support for 64-bit device drivers
- Support for the **GUID partition table (GPT)**

The Secure Boot feature allows us to use authenticated operating systems when booting the computer system. This can be an issue if you are attempting to use an alternative booting device.

As you can see in the following diagram, once the power is turned on and it has completed the POST test, depending on the system, it may boot with the BIOS, or it may boot with the UEFI scheme:

Figure 4.1 – Boot process

The BIOS will look for the **Master Boot Record (MBR)** of the boot device. The MBR is located at sector zero and holds information about the partitions, filesystems, and the boot loader code for the installed operating system. Once the MBR is found in the boot loader and has been activated, control is then passed over to the operating system to complete the booting process.

The UEFI will look for the GPT; the GPT will have a protective MBR to ensure legacy systems will not mistakenly read this as being unpartitioned and overwrite the data. It will also contain the partition entries and backup partition table header. A GPT disk can contain up to 128 partitions for a Windows operating system. Just like in the BIOS scheme, once the active partition and boot loader have been found, the operating system will take over the booting process.

Since you now understand the boot process, we still want to control the boot environment with the creation of forensic boot media, which we will discuss next.

Forensic boot media

It is a widespread practice to remove the hard drive from the system to create a forensic image. However, sometimes, the storage device cannot be removed from the system, and you have to create a forensic image. To accomplish this task, you need to use a bootable CD/DVD or USB device to create a forensic environment in order to create a forensic image.

Using boot media, you will want to ensure that it will create that sound forensic environment and not cause any changes to the source device. As we discussed during the boot process, we want to intercept any potential changes to that source device, and we want to have the system boot inside an environment we control. While it is still possible to boot using a CD/DVD, it is becoming more common to find systems without an optical drive. Without an optical drive, we must use a boot USB device to create a sound forensic environment to access the storage device.

Linux is a standard operating system that has been used to create a USB-based (live) operating system to create the forensic environment needed to examine these devices. As discussed in *Chapter 3*, *Acquisition of Evidence*, Paladin is one such tool. It is freely available to download and to purchase if you wish to have it preinstalled on a USB device. Sumuri also provides some limited technical support in the operation of Paladin.

There is also a Windows-based bootable environment known as **WinFE** (**Windows Forensic Environment**). WinFE was developed by Troy Larson in 2008 and has spawned other tools such as Mini-WinFE, which was developed by Brett Shavers and Misty (`http://reboot.pro/files/file/375-mini-winfe/`). The benefit of using the Windows bootable environment is that you now have access to Windows-based forensic tools. It is possible to run X-Ways or FTK Imager from this secure environment. I would not recommend using a tool that is resource-heavy. What I mean by this is that some forensic suites such as EnCase Forensic or FTK require significant resources to run effectively. X-Ways can be run from a USB device, as can some artifact-specific tools such as RegRipper.

As with any tool or procedure, you must validate it to ensure you are getting the expected results. This means that before you go out into the field and boot a suspect's computer utilizing a forensic USB device, you must test it in the laboratory environment to ensure no changes are made. Some of the challenges that you, as the examiner, need to be concerned with when using a bootable USB device include the following:

- Ensuring the system will boot to the device and not the internal hard drive by changing the boot order in the BIOS.

- In some systems, it's difficult to access the BIOS in the time provided during the boot process.

- Ensure the system can boot to a USB device – some older systems cannot.

- Knowing which filesystems the bootable device can write-protect and which ones it cannot.

- Dealing with the secure boot feature of the UEFI boot process.

As mentioned earlier, secure boot is a security feature of the UEFI process that allows trusted software to boot the system. If we want to use a bootable forensic operating system, the secure boot feature must be disabled.

You must enter the UEFI environment by pressing the catch key such as *F2* or *F12* (this will vary depending on the computer manufacturer). Once you have entered the setup utility, navigate to the **Security** menu (this might also vary depending on the computer manufacturer) and disable the secure boot option. Some Linux distributions and WinFE have received signed status and will boot a system that has secure boot enabled.

You must document your steps as you go through this process. If you miss hitting the catch key and start the boot process in the host operating system, then you must document that it occurred. Even starting a partial boot will change the timestamps and make entries in various logs in the operating system.

Now that you understand what a bootable forensic device is, let's go ahead and create one in the next section.

Creating a bootable forensic device

To create a bootable forensic device, you will need a USB (I recommend using an 8-GB, or larger, device) and an ISO file for the operating system you wish to install. I will demonstrate using an ISO for Paladin and free software called Rufus (`https:/rufus.ie/`). Rufus is a utility used to create bootable USB devices.

Once you download Rufus, execute the executable and the program will run:

Figure 4.2 – Rufus

Something similar to the preceding screenshot (Rufus) will appear, and you will have to select the appropriate choice from the drop-down menus:

- **Device**: This is the destination. It is the USB device you want to host the bootable operating system.

- **Boot selection**: This will be the "live" operating system. Here, I am using an ISO file for Paladin 7.04.

- **Partition scheme**: You have a choice of using MBR or GPT. Using MBR will give you greater flexibility in the devices you can boot.

- **Target system**: With the MBR selection for the partition scheme, you can use the device on either a BIOS or UEFI system. If you select GPT for the partition scheme, you can only target UEFI systems.

Under **Format Options**, accept the default values and then click on the **START** button. Once the program completes, you will have a fully functioning, bootable forensic environment.

We have created a forensic boot environment; let's discuss the storage media you will encounter. We will now discuss hard drives.

Hard drives

The term "physical drive storage device" refers to the hard disk drive itself. That is, a physical device that contains platters or solid state storage that holds data. The term "logical device/volume/partition" refers to the formatting of the physical device. A physical device can contain one or more logical devices/volumes/partitions. It is a common misconception that the term "C drive" refers to the physical device, when, in actuality, it refers to a logical partition on the physical device.

Several components make up the interior of the hard drive (as shown in the following figure). If you were to open the case, you would find the hard drive comprised one or more platters. There could be one or more platters stacked together with a spindle in the center. The platters, which are made of a metal alloy or glass, are coated with a magnetic substance in which the heads magnetically encode information on the platters. The heads can write data on both sides of the platter. The spindles of the hard disk cause the disks to rotate at thousands of revolutions per minute; the faster the spindle causes the platters to spin, the higher the efficiency of accessing the data encoded on the platters. To read or write data to the platters, the heads are positioned less than .1 microns from the surface of the platter. Additionally, the actuator controls the heads; it swings across the platter, placing the head in the correct position to read/write the data. The storage devices are manufactured with tight tolerances and can be damaged by sudden sharp movement or a mechanical shock:

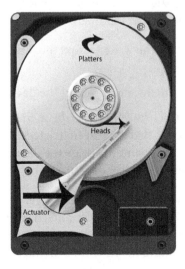

Figure 4.3 – Hard drive

A hard drive can have different interfaces, for example, you may run into some of the following:

- **Small Computer System Interface (SCSI)**: An older standard that is typically seen in the corporate environment. Limited to 16 chained devices and will have a terminator at the end of the chain.

- **Integrated Drive Electronics (IDE/EIDE)**: An older standard, but may still be found in older consumer computer systems.

- **Serial Advanced Technology Attachment (SATA)**: A current standard found in many consumer and commercial environments.

- **Serial Attached SCSI (SAS)**: A current standard that is typically found in commercial environments.

Solid state drives (SSDs) are storage devices that contained no moving parts. Instead, they are made up of memory chips. As we discussed earlier, a traditional hard drive has several moving parts in which to read/write data to the spinning platters. With an SSD storage device, all of the data is stored in memory chips, allowing for the following:

- Less weight

- Increased reliability

- Improved data access speed

- Reduced power consumption

For an SSD to function reliably, there are several operations controlled by the firmware of the device. We know these functions as follows:

- **Wear leveling**: This spreads the writes across the different chips so that it uses the chips at the same rate.

- **Trim**: This will wipe the unallocated space of the device.

- **Garbage collection**: As the firmware scans the memory modules, it may identify pages within the data blocks that have been deleted. The firmware will move the allocated pages to a new block and will wipe the data block so that it can reuse the blocks. The firmware can only delete data in blocks.

The real-world effect on forensics is that we can no longer recover data that is, or was, in unallocated space. Since these operations are conducted at the firmware layer, as soon as we give power to the device, these operations start automatically. Currently, there is no way to stop the firmware from doing the functions mentioned previously.

The drive geometry of a platter drive details how data is stored on the device; the drive geometry defines the number of heads, the number of tracks, the cylinders, and the sectors per track. The manufacturer performs what it refers to as a low-level format, which creates the basic structure of the disk by defining the sectors and tracks. A track is a circular path on the surface of the platter, as indicated in the following diagram. The red circle (**A**) is a single track and each side of the platter will have its own set of tracks. They then subdivide the track into sectors. A sector (**B**) is the smallest storage unit on the device. Originally, a sector used to be 512 bytes in size; however, newer disks are being formatted with a sector size of 4,096 bytes:

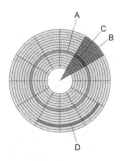

Figure 4.4 – Drive diagram

The platters have an addressing scheme so that they can locate the data; originally, **Cylinder, Head, Sector (CHS)** was used. Here, **Cylinder** refers to the vertical axis of the same sectors on all the platters. **Head** refers to the read/write heads; each platter has two heads. And, in this case, **Sector** refers to the number of sectors per track. This addressing scheme worked for large capacity hard drives; however, as the storage capacity increased, the CHS scheme could not scale because of file size limitations, so **Logical Block Addressing (LBA)** was created. With the LBA scheme, you can address the sectors with a sector number starting from zero.

So, we have discussed the physical components of the device. We will now dive deeper and examine some of the internal aspects.

MBR (Master Boot Record) partitions

Three steps are required before the computer system can use the storage device. We have discussed the low-level format conducted by the manufacturer, but now we will discuss partitioning.

Partitioning occurs when we divide the physical device into logical segments called "volumes." With the MBR partitioning scheme, we are restricted to four primary partitions. With one physical device, you can have a primary partition used to host the Windows operating system, and you can have a second primary partition that hosts a Linux operating system. Note that you must have a primary partition to boot into an operating system. When a user selects the booted operating system, this is known as the **active partition**.

To get around the partition limit, developers created the extended partition. One of the four partition records is designated as an extended partition, which can then be divided into logical volumes.

As we discussed previously, we can find the MBR at sector zero. The MBR contains the information needed by the system to boot. The MBR will be contained in sector zero, so it will be no longer than 512 bytes. The partition table will show us which partition is the active partition. Once the starting sector or the active partition is located, the boot process will continue:

```
Offset      0  1  2  3   4  5  6  7   8  9  A  B   C  D  E  F     ANSI ASCII
00000000   33 C0 8E D0  BC 00 7C FB  50 07 50 1F  FC BE 1B 7C   3ÀŽÐ¼ |ûP P ü¼ |
00000010   BF 1B 06 50  57 B9 E5 01  F3 A4 CB BD  BE 07 B1 04   ¿  PW¹å ó¤Ë½¾ ±
00000020   38 6E 00 7C  09 75 13 83  C5 10 E2 F4  CD 18 8B F5   8n | u fÅ âôÍ ‹õ
00000030   83 C6 10 49  74 19 38 2C  74 F6 A0 B5  07 B4 07 8B   fÆ It 8,tö µ ´ ‹
00000040   F0 AC 3C 00  74 FC BB 07  00 B4 0E CD  10 EB F2 88   ð¬< tü» ´ Í ëò^
00000050   4E 10 E8 46  00 73 2A FE  46 10 80 7E  04 0B 74 0B   N èF s*þF €~ t
00000060   80 7E 04 0C  74 05 A0 B6  07 75 D2 80  46 02 06 83   €~ t ¶ uÒ€F f
00000070   46 08 06 83  56 0A 00 E8  21 00 73 05  A0 B6 07 EB   F fV è! s ¶ ë
00000080   BC 81 3E FE  7D 55 AA 74  0B 80 7E 10  00 74 C8 A0   ¼ >þ}Uªt €~ tÈ
00000090   B7 07 EB A9  8B FC 1E 57  8B F5 CB BF  05 00 8A 56   · ë©‹ü W‹õË¿ ŠV
000000A0   00 B4 08 CD  13 72 23 8A  C1 24 3F 98  8A DE 8A FC   ´ Í r#ŠÁ$?˜ŠÞŠü
000000B0   43 F7 E3 8B  D1 86 D6 B1  06 D2 EE 42  F7 E2 39 56   C÷ã‹Ñ†Ö± Òî B÷â9V
000000C0   0A 77 23 72  05 39 46 08  73 1C B8 01  02 BB 00 7C   w#r 9F s » |
000000D0   8B 4E 02 8B  56 00 CD 13  73 51 4F 74  4E 32 E4 8A   ‹N ‹V Í sQOtN2äŠ
000000E0   56 00 CD 13  EB E4 8A 56  00 60 BB AA  55 B4 41 CD   V Í ëäŠV `»ªU´AÍ
000000F0   13 72 36 81  FB 55 AA 75  30 F6 C1 01  74 2B 61 60   r6 ûUªu0öÁ t+a`
00000100   6A 00 6A 00  FF 76 0A FF  76 08 6A 00  68 00 7C 6A   j j ÿv ÿv j h |j
00000110   01 6A 10 B4  42 8B F4 CD  13 61 61 73  0E 4F 74 0B   j ´B‹ôÍ aas Ot
00000120   32 E4 8A 56  00 CD 13 EB  D6 61 F9 C3  49 6E 76 61   2äŠV Í ëÖaùÃInva
00000130   6C 69 64 20  70 61 72 74  69 74 69 6F  6E 20 74 61   lid partition ta
00000140   62 6C 65 00  45 72 72 6F  72 20 6C 6F  61 64 69 6E   ble Error loadin
00000150   67 20 6F 70  65 72 61 74  69 6E 67 20  73 79 73 74   g operating syst
00000160   65 6D 00 4D  69 73 73 69  6E 67 20 6F  70 65 72 61   em Missing opera
00000170   74 69 6E 67  20 73 79 73  74 65 6D 00  00 00 00 00   ting system
00000180   00 00 00 00  00 00 00 00  00 00 00 00  00 00 00 00
00000190   00 00 00 00  00 00 00 00  00 00 00 00  00 00 00 00
000001A0   00 00 00 00  00 00 00 00  00 00 00 00  00 00 00 00
000001B0   00 00 00 00  00 2C 44 63  C8 7E C8 7E  00 00 00 01   ,DcÈ~È~
000001C0   01 00 DE FE  3F 0A 3F 00  00 00 0C B2  02 00 80 00   þ? ? ² €
000001D0   01 0B 07 FE  FF FF 4B B2  02 00 74 38  51 02 00 00   þÿÿK² t8Q
000001E0   00 00 00 00  00 00 00 00  00 00 00 00  00 00 00 00
000001F0   00 00 00 00  00 00 00 00  00 00 00 00  00 00 55 AA   Uª
```

Figure 4.5 – MBR map

The preceding MBR map depicts sector zero of a hard disk. This is the MBR for the physical disk. The first 440 bytes are highlighted; this is the boot code. The next 4 bytes are the disk signature and identify the disk to the operating system. The following 64 bytes comprise the partition table. Each 16-byte entry refers to a specific partition. Remember, it restricts us to 4 primary partitions utilizing the MBR partitioning scheme. The final 2 bytes is the signature for the MBR. It identifies the ending of the MBR and will be the last 2 bytes of the sector.

In the following table, I have extracted the four partition tables and reformatted the hex values for easier reading. The first byte will designate which partition is the active partition. A value of x/80 identifies the active bootable partition. A value of x/00 shows the non-active (bootable) partition:

```
00 01 01 00 DE FE 3F 0A 3F 00 00 00 0C B2 02 00
80 00 01 0B 07 FE FF FF 4B B2 02 00 74 38 51 02
00 00 00 00 00 00 00 00 00 00 00 00 00 00 00 00
00 00 00 00 00 00 00 00 00 00 00 00 00 00 00 00
```

Figure 4.6 – Partition tables

Typically, you would see the first partition marked as the active partition; in this case, it is the second partition, which is bootable. The next three bytes represent a starting sector for the CHS calculation. So, when we examine the partition table, we can see that the physical device has as a partition of 0 and a partition of 1 with the entries for partition 2 and 3 being zeroed out. This tells us that there are only two partitions on this physical device.

The fifth byte represents the filesystem on the partition. For partition 0, we can see the hex value of **DE,** which tells us that it is part of the Dell Power Edge Server utilities. Partition 1 has a hex value of **07**, which shows the NTFS filesystem.

If I found the hexadecimal values of 05 or fh, then that would show an extended partition. We would then have to look into the extended boot records of the extended partitions.

> **Note**
> You can find a full list of partition identifiers at https://www.win.tue.nl/~aeb/partitions/partition_types-1.html.

The next three bytes are the values for the ending sector of the CHS calculation. The next four bytes show the starting sector of the partition, and the last four bytes show the size of the partition.

The sector values used in the CHS calculation are legacy values for older storage devices. The values showing the start sector and the total number of sectors (partition size) are being used for the current drives using LBA.

Each partition will have a **Volume Boot Record** (**VBR**) at sector zero of the partition. The system uses the VBR to boot the operating system in that volume. It is an operating system-specific artifact and is created when the partition is formatted. It will also appear on unpartitioned devices, such as removable media, for example, a USB or floppy disk.

Primary partitions are not the only partitions that you may encounter; you can also encounter an extended partition, which is the subject of the next section.

Extended partitions

The limitation of the MBR of only allowing four primary partitions resulted in the creation of the extended primary partition. Here, it takes the place of one (and only one) primary partition and enables the user to create additional logical partitions over the four primary partitions.

The following partition map illustrates the replacement of a primary partition with an extended partition:

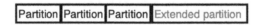

Figure 4.7 – Partition map

The following diagram shows the extended partition. Here, the user has created multiple logical partitions within the extended partition boundary:

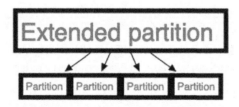

Figure 4.8 – Extended partition map

The extended partition will not have a VBR. It will have an **extended boot record (EBR)**, which will point to the first extended logical partition. The first extended logical partition will contain information about itself and a pointer to the next extended logical partition. In effect, this will create a daisy chain of pointers from one extended logical partition to the next.

We have now covered the aspects relating to the MBR; let's now go over the GPT formatted aspects.

GPT partitions

A GUID is a **globally unique identifier** and uses a 128-bit hexadecimal value to identify different aspects of the computer system uniquely. A GUID comprises five groups and is formatted as `00112233-4455-6677-8899-aabbccddeeff`, and, while there is no central authority to ensure uniqueness, it is doubtful that you would get a repeating GUID.

RFC 4122 defines the five different GUIDs as follows:

- **Version 1**: Date-time and MAC address: The system generates this version using both the current time and client MAC address. This means that if you have a version 1 GUID, you can figure out when it was created by inspecting the timestamp value.

- **Version 2**: DCE Security: This version isn't explicitly defined in RFC 4122, so it doesn't have to be generated by compliant generators. It is like a version 1 GUID except that the first four bytes of the timestamp are replaced by the user's POSIX UID or GID, and the upper byte of the clock sequence is replaced by either the POSIX UID or GID domain. (**UID** stands for **User Identifier**. **POSIX** stands for **Portable Operating System Interface**, which is a set of standards to ensure compatibility between operating systems.)

- **Version 3**: MD5 hash and namespace: This GUID is generated by taking a namespace (for example, a fully qualified domain name) and a name, converts it into bytes, concatenates it, and hashes it. Once it has specified the special bits such as version and variant, it then converts the resulting bytes into hexadecimal form. The special property regarding this version is that the GUIDs generated from the same name in the same namespace will be identical even if they were generated at different times.

- **Version 4**: Random: The system creates this GUID using random numbers. Of the 128 bits in a GUID, it reserves 6 for special use (version + variant bits) giving us 122 bits that can be filled at random.

- **Version 5**: SHA-1 hash and namespace: This version is identical to version 3 except that SHA-1 is used in the hashing step in place of MD5.

The GPT is a partitioning scheme that is used for newer storage devices and is part of the new UEFI standard. The UEFI standard replaces the BIOS, while the GPT replaces the MBR partitioning scheme.

The GPT petitioning scheme uses LBA and a protective MBR that can be found in the physical sector zero. The protective MBR allows for some backward compatibility and helps to remove any issues when dealing with legacy utilities that do not recognize the GPT partitioning scheme. There is no boot code available in the protective MBR. As you can see in the following diagram, this is the first partition entry of the partition table of the protective MBR. The partition is identified by hex value **EE**, which shows it is a GPT partition disk, as shown in the following GPT hex:

```
00000001B0 65 6D 00 00 00 63 7B 9A   00 00 00 00 00 00 00 00
00000001C0 02 00 EE FE FF 33 01 00   00 00 FF FF FF FF 00 00
00000001D0 00 00 00 00 00 00 00 00   00 00 00 00 00 00 00 00
00000001E0 00 00 00 00 00 00 00 00   00 00 00 00 00 00 00 00
00000001F0 00 00 00 00 00 00 00 00   00 00 00 00 00 00 55 AA
```

Figure 4.9 – GPT hex

While the MBR contains the partition table within physical sector 0, GPT houses the partition table header at physical sector 1. The GPT header can be identified by the **EFI** signature of hexadecimal values 45 46 49 20 50 41 52 54, as shown in the following diagram:

```
0000000200 45 46 49 20 50 41 52 54   00 00 01 00 5C 00 00 00   EFI PART      \
0000000210 6C D3 30 12 00 00 00 00   01 00 00 00 00 00 00 00   lÓ0
0000000220 AF 12 9E 3B 00 00 00 00   22 00 00 00 00 00 00 00   ¯ ž;        "
0000000230 8E 12 9E 3B 00 00 00 00   A2 60 8A D3 0D 63 00 43   Ž ž;    ¢`ŠÓ c C
0000000240 9F 9D 39 BD FB 81 B3 9E   02 00 00 00 00 00 00 00   Ÿ 9½û ³ž
0000000250 80 00 00 00 80 00 00 00   64 96 AF 89 00 00 00 00   €   €    d–¯‰
0000000260 00 00 00 00 00 00 00 00   00 00 00 00 00 00 00 00
```

Figure 4.10 – EFI PART

The following table shows the layout of the GPT header, which you can use to identify the layout of the desk:

GPT header format

Offset	Length	Contents
0 (0x00)	8 bytes	Signature ("EFI PART", 45h 46h 49h 20h 50h 41h 52h 54h)
8 (0x08)	4 bytes	Revision (for GPT version 1.0 (through at least UEFI version 2.7 (May 2017)), the value is 00h 00h 01h 00h)
12 (0x0C)	4 bytes	Header size
16 (0x10)	4 bytes	CRC32 checksum of the GPT header
20 (0x14)	4 bytes	Reserved; must be zero
24 (0x18)	8 bytes	Current LBA (location of this header copy)
32 (0x20)	8 bytes	Backup LBA (location of the other header copy)
40 (0x28)	8 bytes	First usable LBA for partitions (primary partition table last LBA + 1)
48 (0x30)	8 bytes	Last usable LBA (secondary partition table first LBA – 1)
56 (0x38)	16 bytes	Disk GUID in mixed endian
72 (0x48)	8 bytes	Starting LBA of array of partition entries (always 2 in primary copy)
80 (0x50)	4 bytes	Number of partition entries in array
84 (0x54)	4 bytes	Size of a single partition entry (usually 80h or 128)
88 (0x58)	4 bytes	CRC32 checksum of the of the partition table
92 (0x5C)	*	Reserved; must be zeroes for the rest of the block (420 bytes for a sector size of 512 bytes; but can be more with larger sector sizes)

Figure 4.11 – GPT header format

The GPT partition entries are typically found in physical sector 2. The following diagram shows the GPT partition table entries:

```
Offset      0  1  2  3  4  5  6  7   8  9  A  B  C  D  E  F      ANSI ASCII
0000000400 A4 BB 94 DE D1 06 40 4D  A1 6A BF D5 01 79 D6 AC   ¤»"ÞÑ @M¡j¿Õ yÖ¬
0000000410 C4 04 7F C0 41 4E 2D 46  9C B1 AA A1 9A A8 07 FC   Ä  ÀAN-Fœ±ª¡š¨ ü
0000000420 00 08 00 00 00 00 00 00  FF 9F 0F 00 00 00 00 00        ÿŸ
0000000430 01 00 00 00 00 00 00 80  42 00 61 00 73 00 69 00     €B a s i
0000000440 63 00 20 00 64 00 61 00  74 00 61 00 20 00 70 00   c   d a t a   p
0000000450 61 00 72 00 74 00 69 00  74 00 69 00 6F 00 6E 00   a r t i t i o n
0000000460 00 00 00 00 00 00 00 00  00 00 00 00 00 00 00 00
0000000470 00 00 00 00 00 00 00 00  00 00 00 00 00 00 00 00
0000000480 28 73 2A C1 1F F8 D2 11  BA 4B 00 A0 C9 3E C9 3B   (s*Á øÒ ºK  É>É;
0000000490 4A 0C 5D 1C 1C 51 E1 4F  94 D5 FC 6D 48 0F 27 86   J ] QáO"ÕümH '†
00000004A0 00 A0 0F 00 00 00 00 00  FF B7 12 00 00 00 00 00      ÿ·
00000004B0 00 00 00 00 00 00 00 80  45 00 46 00 49 00 20 00     €E F I
00000004C0 73 00 79 00 73 00 74 00  65 00 6D 00 20 00 70 00   s y s t e m   p
00000004D0 61 00 72 00 74 00 69 00  74 00 69 00 6F 00 6E 00   a r t i t i o n
00000004E0 00 00 00 00 00 00 00 00  00 00 00 00 00 00 00 00
00000004F0 00 00 00 00 00 00 00 00  00 00 00 00 00 00 00 00
0000000500 16 E3 C9 E3 5C 0B B8 4D  81 7D F9 2D F0 02 15 AE   ãÉã\ ¸M }ù-ð  ®
0000000510 C2 6D C0 11 34 28 79 4E  87 FA CD 56 0B 1D F1 C3   ÂmÀ 4(yN‡úÍV ñÃ
0000000520 00 B8 12 00 00 00 00 00  FF 37 13 00 00 00 00 00   ¸   ÿ7
0000000530 00 00 00 00 00 00 00 80  4D 00 69 00 63 00 72 00     €M i c r
0000000540 6F 00 73 00 6F 00 66 00  74 00 20 00 72 00 65 00   o s o f t   r e
0000000550 73 00 65 00 72 00 76 00  65 00 64 00 20 00 70 00   s e r v e d   p
0000000560 61 00 72 00 74 00 69 00  74 00 69 00 6F 00 6E 00   a r t i t i o n
0000000570 00 00 00 00 00 00 00 00  00 00 00 00 00 00 00 00
0000000580 A2 A0 D0 EB E5 B9 33 44  87 C0 68 B6 B7 26 99 C7   ¢ Ðëå¹3D‡Àh¶·&™Ç
0000000590 21 1F 93 09 AF 7F A9 44  81 D8 1E 73 C1 4B 9E AF   ! " ¯ ©D Ø sÁKž¯
00000005A0 00 38 13 00 00 00 00 00  FF 0F 9E 3B 00 00 00 00   8    ÿ ž;
00000005B0 00 00 00 00 00 00 00 00  42 00 61 00 73 00 69 00           B a s i
00000005C0 63 00 20 00 64 00 61 00  74 00 61 00 20 00 70 00   c   d a t a   p
00000005D0 61 00 72 00 74 00 69 00  74 00 69 00 6F 00 6E 00   a r t i t i o n
00000005E0 00 00 00 00 00 00 00 00  00 00 00 00 00 00 00 00
00000005F0 00 00 00 00 00 00 00 00  00 00 00 00 00 00 00 00
```

Figure 4.12 – GPT sector 2

Each partition entry is 128 bytes and provides information about the partitions. The following table shows the contents of the partition entries, which include the partition type GUID, the GUID that is unique to that specific partition, the starting and ending sectors, and the partition name in Unicode:

GUID partition entry format		
Offset	Length	Contents
0 (0x00)	16 bytes	Partition type GUID
16 (0x10)	16 bytes	Unique partition GUID
32 (0x20)	8 bytes	Starting LBA
40 (0x28)	8 bytes	Ending LBA
48 (0x30)	8 bytes	Attribute flags
56 (0x38)	72 bytes	Partition name

Figure 4.13 – GUID

A partition should hold all of the data on the disk within the partition's boundaries; however, there are spaces on the disk outside of the normal partition boundaries where a technical user may hide data. We will discuss those areas next.

Host Protected Area (HPA) and Device Configuration Overlays (DCO)

HPA and DCO are hidden areas on the hard drive created by the manufacturers. The HPA is used by the manufacturer to store recovery and diagnostics tools and cannot be changed or accessed by the user. The DCO is an overlay that allows the manufacturer to use standard parts to build different products. It allows the creation of a standard set of sectors on a component to achieve uniformity. For example, the manufacturer might use one set of parts to create a 500-GB hard drive, and while using the same components, can also create a 600-GB hard drive. Once again, usually, the user would not have access to this location. Some utilities to do so are freely available, however, and could be used by a user to access these locations and store data.

The following screenshot shows you how an HPA may appear in X-Ways:

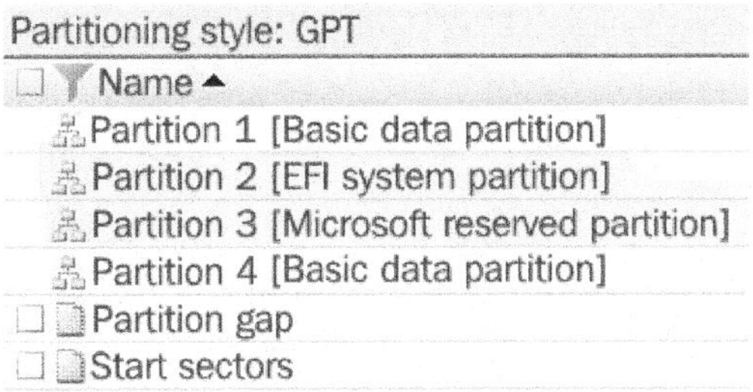

Partitioning style: GPT

☐ ▼ Name ▲
  Partition 1 [Basic data partition]
  Partition 2 [EFI system partition]
  Partition 3 [Microsoft reserved partition]
  Partition 4 [Basic data partition]
☐ Partition gap
☐ Start sectors

Figure 4.14 – HPA 1

The following screenshot shows you how an HPA may appear in FTK Imager:

Figure 4.15 – HPA 2

Let's move on and discuss some potential filesystems that you may encounter.

Understanding filesystems

A hard drive can have multiple partitions on it, and, in each partition, there will be (in most cases) a filesystem. There might be hundreds of thousands to millions of files contained within a partition. The filesystem tracks where every file is and how much space is available within the partition boundaries.

We discussed sectors earlier in the *Hard drives* section, and they are the smallest units that are available to store data. The filesystem stores data based on clusters. Clusters are one or more sectors. A cluster is the smallest allocation unit the filesystem can write to. Now, there are many filesystems available, and some are restricted to specific operating systems unless the user enables drivers that will allow the operating system to read the filesystem.

We will now look at some of the common filesystems you may encounter.

The FAT filesystem

The **File Allocation Table** (**FAT**) filesystem has been around since the early days of home computing, and it is one of the few filesystems that nearly all operating systems can read. It is the de facto standard filesystem for removable devices.

As time has gone by, the FAT filesystem has gone through numerous changes:

- FAT 12: The first version was created in 1977 and used 12 bits (hence, the FAT 12 designation) to address available clusters. This limited its use to only storage devices that could contain 4,096 clusters. It is rarely seen nowadays, but you might find it on a floppy diskette.

- FAT 16: This was created in 1984 and used 16 bits (I see a pattern) to address the available clusters. It had the same issues as the FAT 12, as it could not be scaled to be used with larger capacity devices.

- VFAT: This was introduced with Windows 95 and added the Virtual File Allocation Table. It added the use of the **long filename** (**LFN**) and additional timestamps.

- FAT32: This uses 28 bits to address available clusters, theoretically allowing for a maximum volume size of 2.2 TB. Microsoft implemented restrictions that limited the volume size to 32 GB with a maximum file size of 4 GB. It is still in use today and can be found on most removable devices.

We will discuss the FAT32 filesystem for the remainder of this section on the FAT filesystem.

The FAT filesystem is laid out in two areas (as shown in the following diagram, *Figure 4.16 – FAT areas*):

- **System Area**: This stores the volume boot record and FAT tables.

- **Data Area**: This stores the root directory and files:

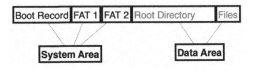

Figure 4.16 – FAT areas

Next, we will discuss what falls under **System Area**.

Boot record

In the system area, we have the **Volume Boot Record (VBR)**. We can find it in logical sector 0 (LS 0), which is the first sector within the partition boundaries. The boot process creates the VBR when the partition is formatted and contains information about the volume and boot code to continue the boot process for the operating system. If it is a primary partition, the VBR will consist of several sectors, typically, sectors 0, 1, and 2 with a backup in sectors 6, 7, and 8. The VBR and backups are stored in a "reserve area," which is typically 32 sectors before the first file allocation table begins:

```
EB 58 90 4D 53 44 4F 53   35 2E 30 00 02 08 2A 20
02 00 00 00 00 F8 00 00   3F 00 FF 00 80 00 00 00
00 E8 3F 00 EB 0F 00 00   00 00 00 00 02 00 00 00
01 00 06 00 00 00 00 00   00 00 00 00 00 00 00 00
80 00 29 D9 7C BE FC 4E   4F 20 4E 41 4D 45 20 20
20 20 46 41 54 33 32 20   20 20 33 C9 8E D1 BC F4
7B 8E C1 8E D9 BD 00 7C   88 56 40 88 4E 02 8A 56
40 B4 41 BB AA 55 CD 13   72 10 81 FB 55 AA 75 0A
F6 C1 01 74 05 FE 46 02   EB 2D 8A 56 40 B4 08 CD
13 73 05 B9 FF FF 8A F1   66 0F B6 C6 40 66 0F B6
D1 80 E2 3F F7 E2 86 CD   C0 ED 06 41 66 0F B7 C9
66 F7 E1 66 89 46 F8 83   7E 16 00 75 39 83 7E 2A
00 77 33 66 8B 46 1C 66   83 C0 0C BB 00 80 B9 01
00 E8 2C 00 E9 A8 03 A1   F8 7D 80 C4 7C 8B F0 AC
84 C0 74 17 3C FF 74 09   B4 0E BB 07 00 CD 10 EB
EE A1 FA 7D EB E4 A1 7D   80 EB DF 98 CD 16 CD 19
66 60 80 7E 02 00 0F 84   20 00 66 6A 00 66 50 06
53 66 68 10 00 01 00 B4   42 8A 56 40 8B F4 CD 13
66 58 66 58 66 58 66 58   EB 33 66 3B 46 F8 72 03
F9 EB 2A 66 33 D2 66 0F   B7 4E 18 66 F7 F1 FE C2
8A CA 66 8B D0 66 C1 EA   10 F7 76 1A 86 D6 8A 56
40 8A E8 C0 E4 06 0A CC   B8 01 02 CD 13 66 61 0F
82 74 FF 81 C3 00 02 66   40 49 75 94 C3 42 4F 4F
54 4D 47 52 20 20 20 20   00 00 00 00 00 00 00 00
00 00 00 00 00 00 00 00   00 00 00 00 00 00 00 00
00 00 00 00 00 00 00 00   00 00 00 00 00 00 00 00
00 00 00 00 00 00 00 00   00 00 00 00 0D 0A 44 69
73 6B 20 65 72 72 6F 72   FF 0D 0A 50 72 65 73 73
20 61 6E 79 20 6B 65 79   20 74 6F 20 72 65 73 74
61 72 74 0D 0A 00 00 00   00 00 00 00 00 00 00 00
00 00 00 00 00 00 00 00   00 00 00 00 00 00 00 00
00 00 00 00 00 00 00 00   AC 01 B9 01 00 00 55 AA
```

Figure 4.17 – VBR

In the preceding diagram, we can see a volume boot sector, which helps to decipher the following information:

- x00: We will find the jump instructions for the system to continue booting.

- x03: The OEM ID shows which operating system was used to format the device.

- x0B: Bytes per sector.

- x0E: Number of reserve sectors.

- x10: Number of FATs (this should be 2).

- x11: Unused root entries (for FAT32, this should be 0 because the root directory is in the data area).

- x13: Number of sectors (this will be 0 if the number of sectors exceeds 65,536).

- x15: Media descriptor (xF8 will show a hard disk, while xF0 will show a removable device).

- x16: Number of sectors per FAT (for FAT32, this should be 0).

- x18: Number of sectors per track (this should be 63 for hard disks).

- x1A: Number of heads (this should be 255 for hard disks).

- x1C: Number of hidden sectors (the number of hidden sectors before the start of the FAT volume).

- x20: Number of total sectors (that is, the total sectors for the volume).

- x24: Logical sectors per FAT.

- x28: Extended flags.

- x2A: FAT version.

- x2C: The starting root directory cluster (usually, cluster 2).

- x30: Location of the FS information sector (typically, this is set to 1).

- x32: Location of the backup sector(s) (usually, this is set to 6).

- x34: Reserved (set to 0).

- x40: Physical drive number (x80 for hard drives).

- x41: Reserved

- x42: Extended boot signature (this should be x29).

- x43: Volume serial number (a 32-bit value is usually generated from the date and time; this can track removable devices).

- x47: Volume label (this might not be accurate; different OSes may not use this field).

- x52: Filesystem type.

Next, we will take a look at the file allocation table.

File allocation table

The next component of the FAT filesystem is the file allocation table, which immediately follows the VBR. By default, there are two file allocation tables (FAT1 and FAT2). FAT2 is a duplicate of FAT1.

The purpose of the file allocation table is to track the clusters and to track which files occupy which clusters. Each cluster is represented within the file allocation table starting with cluster 0. The file allocation table uses 4 bytes (32 bits) per cluster entry. The file allocation table will use the following entries to represent the cluster's current status:

- Unallocated: x0000 0000

- Allocated: The next cluster that is used by the file (for example, it represents cluster 7 as x0700 0000)

- Allocated: The last cluster that is used by the file (xFFFF FFF8)

- Bad cluster: Not available for use (xFFFF FFF7)

A cluster is the smallest allocation unit the filesystem can address. A sector is the smallest allocation unit on the disk. A cluster is made up of one or more sectors. It is very easy to get confused if you comingle those terms. Consider the following cluster example:

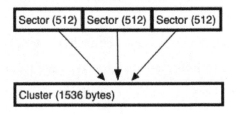

Figure 4.18 – Cluster example

As users add files to the data area, the system will update the file allocation table. A file may occupy one or more clusters. Additionally, the clusters may not be sequential, so you could have the data of a file spread in different physical locations on the disk; we typically refer to this as fragmentation.

In the following diagram, we can see a representation of the file allocation table; in this scenario, we have a single file occupying three clusters: **Cluster 4**, **Cluster 5**, and **Cluster 6**. You can see that **Cluster 4** is pointing to **Cluster 5** and **Cluster 5** is pointing to **Cluster 6**. **Cluster 6** has the hexadecimal value for **end of file (EOF)**:

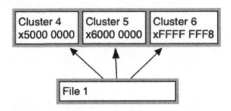

Figure 4.19 – Non-fragmented file entry

In the following diagram, we can see a similar representation of the file allocation table with some changes. We now have two files, with file number 1 occupying clusters **4** and **6**. We can see that **Cluster 4** is pointing to the next cluster containing the file data, which is **Cluster 6**. This is an example of file fragmentation. File number 2 is wholly contained within the cluster boundaries of **Cluster 5**. **Cluster 5** will not point to a subsequent cluster; instead, it has the EOF hexadecimal value:

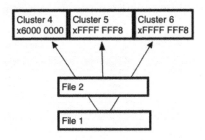

Figure 4.20 – Fragmented file entry

We have covered the system area of the FAT; we will now discuss the data area of the FAT filesystem.

Data area

The root directory is housed in the data area because, when it was stored in the system area, it was unable to grow enough to work with larger capacity devices. The critical component of the root directory is the directory entry. If there is a file, directory, or subdirectory, then there will be a corresponding directory entry.

Each directory entry is 32 bytes in length and helps to track the name of the file, starting cluster, and file size in bytes.

In the following diagram, we can see a FAT32 directory with multiple file entries. The filesystem will stop looking for file entries when it runs into a hexadecimal 00, and all values following the hexadecimal 00 will be ignored:

```
E5 6C 00 6F 00 6E 00 67    00 66 00 0F 00 D4 69 00    ål.o.n.g.f...Õi.
6C 00 65 00 6E 00 61 00    6D 00 00 00 65 00 2E 00    l.e.n.a.m...e...
E5 4F 4E 47 46 49 7E 31    54 58 54 20 00 6B B0 6D    åONGFI~1TXT .k°m
D3 4E D3 4E 00 00 B1 6D    D3 4E 00 00 00 00 00 00    ÓNÓN..±mÓN......
E5 48 4F 52 54 20 20 20    54 58 54 20 18 6B B0 6D    åHORT   TXT .k°m
D3 4E D3 4E 00 00 B1 6D    D3 4E 00 00 00 00 00 00    ÓNÓN..±mÓN......
42 74 00 78 00 74 00 00    00 FF FF 0F 00 D4 FF FF    Bt.x.t...ÿÿ..Ôÿÿ
FF FF FF FF FF FF FF FF    FF FF 00 00 FF FF FF FF    ÿÿÿÿÿÿÿÿÿÿ..ÿÿÿÿ
01 6C 00 6F 00 6E 00 67    00 66 00 0F 00 D4 69 00    .l.o.n.g.f...Õi.
6C 00 65 00 6E 00 61 00    6D 00 00 00 65 00 2E 00    l.e.n.a.m...e...
4C 4F 4E 47 46 49 7E 31    54 58 54 20 00 6B B0 6D    LONGFI~1TXT .k°m
D3 4E D3 4E 00 00 A8 6D    D3 4E 00 00 00 00 00 00    ÓNÓN.."mÓN......
53 48 4F 52 54 20 20 20    54 58 54 20 18 6B B0 6D    SHORT   TXT .k°m
D3 4E D3 4E 00 00 93 6D    D3 4E 00 00 00 00 00 00    ÓNÓN...mÓN......
24 52 45 43 59 43 4C 45    42 49 4E 16 00 30 B5 6D    $RECYCLEBIN..0µm
D3 4E D3 4E 00 00 B6 6D    D3 4E 06 00 00 00 00 00    ÓNÓN..¶mÓN......
00 00 00 00 00 00 00 00    00 00 00 00 00 00 00 00    ................
00 00 00 00 00 00 00 00    00 00 00 00 00 00 00 00    ................
```

Figure 4.21 – FAT directory entry

In the following FAT directory map, we can see the layout of the directory entry and a **short filename** (**SFN**) directory entry with the specific offsets highlighted:

Offset (hex)	Size (Bytes)	Description
x00	1	The first character of the file name or status byte
x01	7	Filename (padded with spaces if required)
x08	3	Three characters of the file extension
x0B	1	Attributes
x0C	1	Reserved
x0D	1	Created time and date of the file
x0E	2	File creation time
x10	2	File creation date
x12	2	Last accessed date
x14	2	Two high bytes of FAT32 starting cluster
x16	2	Time of the Last Write to File (last modified or when created)
x18	2	Date of the Last Write to File (last modified or when created)
0x1A	2	Two low bytes of the starting cluster for FAT32
0X1C	4	File size (zero for a directory)

```
53 48 4F 52 54 20 20 20  54 58 54 20 18 6B B0 6D   SHORT   TXT .k°m
D3 4E D4 4E 00 00 E9 5E  D4 4E 08 00 27 00 00 00   ÓNÔN..é^ÔN..'...
```

Figure 4.22 – FAT directory map

If the first byte is xE5, then the filesystem will consider that entry as deleted. The remaining bytes of the file or directory name will remain, as will the other metadata.

The short filename must conform to the specifications as follows:

- Eight characters are allowed; if there are less than eight characters, then the name will be padded with x20.

- Three characters are allocated for the file extension (if there are less than three characters, then the name will be padded with x20).

- Spaces and the following characters are not permitted: "+ * , . / : ; < = > ? [\] |

The directory entry will always be stored in uppercase. The attribute byte (offset x0B) is considered a packed byte, which means the different values have different meanings.

The following diagram shows that bit values in the Attribute flag can be combined, and the resulting hex value will reflect the combinations. If a file had the **READ ONLY** flag and the **HIDDEN** flag, then that would give us a value of 0000 0011, and, when converted to hexadecimal, we get the value of x03:

0000 0001	READ ONLY
0000 0010	HIDDEN FILE
0000 0100	SYSTEM FILE
0000 1000	VOLUME LABEL
0000 1111	LONG FILENAME
0001 0000	DIRECTORY
0010 0000	ARCHIVE

Figure 4.23 – Packed byte

When we look at the example at the bottom of the preceding FAT directory map, we find the hexadecimal value of 20 at the offset x0B; when we convert the hexadecimal into binary, we get 0010 0000. This tells us that the file is an archive.

We can also encounter a **Long Filename (LFN)**; the technique for handling the LFN is a little bit more complicated. We will discuss the LFN in the next section.

Long filenames

When a user creates an LFN, the system will generate an alias that conforms to the SFN standard. It will format the alias so that the first three characters after the file extension dot will become the extension. The first six characters will be converted to uppercase and will be used for the alias. The alias will then add a ~ character with a following number. It will start with the number 1 and increase incrementally if there are additional files with the same alias name.

The following diagram shows a directory entry for a file with an LFN; the filename is long filename.txt:

```
42 74 00 78 00 74 00 00    00 FF FF 0F 00 D4 FF FF    Bt.x.t...ÿÿ..Ôÿÿ
FF FF FF FF FF FF FF FF    FF FF 00 00 FF FF FF FF    ÿÿÿÿÿÿÿÿÿÿ..ÿÿÿÿ
01 6C 00 6F 00 6E 00 67    00 66 00 0F 00 D4 69 00    .l.o.n.g.f...Ôi.
6C 00 65 00 6E 00 61 00    6D 00 00 00 65 00 2E 00    l.e.n.a.m...e...
4C 4F 4E 47 46 49 7E 31    54 58 54 20 00 6B B0 6D    LONGFI~1TXT .k°m
D3 4E D3 4E 00 00 A8 6D    D3 4E 00 00 00 00 00 00    ÓNÓN..¨mÓN......
```

Figure 4.24 – LFN

Since this is an LFN, the filesystem will create additional directory entries. In this specific case, there will be two additional directory entries to facilitate the use of the LFN. The first byte of each additional directory entry is the sequence byte. The right nibble is the sequence number. As we look at the directory entry depicted in preceding diagram, the directory entry above the SFN entry has a hexadecimal value of x01. Here, the value of 1 tells us that this is the first value in the sequence. When we move up to the second directory entry, we can see that it has a hexadecimal value of x42, the right nibble informs us this is the second directory entry for this LFN file. The left nibble of the value, 4, tells us this is the last directory entry for the file. In each of the LFN directory entries, you will find that the attribute byte is x0F.

But what happens when a file is deleted? Well, you may be able to recover the file and its associated metadata. In the next section, we will discuss recovering deleted files.

Recovering deleted files

When a file is deleted in the FAT filesystem, the data itself does not get changed. The first character of the directory entry will change to xE5 and the file allocation table entries are reset to x00. When the filesystem reads the directory entries and encounters xE5, it will skip that entry and start reading from the subsequent entries.

To recover deleted files, we need to reverse the process that the filesystem used to delete the files. Remember, it has not changed the file contents, and they still physically reside in their assigned clusters. We now need to reverse engineer the deletion and recreate the file entry and the entries in the file allocation table. To do this, we need to find the first cluster of the file, the size of the file, and the size of the clusters in the volume.

In the following diagram, we have a directory entry showing us that a file has been deleted. We can see xE5 at the start of the directory entry. (Note that this will require the use of a hex editor to make the changes.)

Then, we have to determine the starting cluster, which is x00 x08 (but is shown as x08 x00 in the diagram). This value is referring to cluster number 8. To determine the file size, take a look at the last four bytes, x27 x00 x00 x00 (remember that the FAT filesystem stores data in little endian, which means the least significant byte is on the left, so we would read that value as x00 x00 x00 x27, and when we convert it into a decimal, we have a value of 39 bytes for the file size):

| E5 48 4F 52 54 20 20 20 | 54 58 54 20 18 6B B0 6D | åHORT TXT .k°m |
| D3 4E D4 4E 00 00 E9 5E | D4 4E 08 00 27 00 00 00 | ÓNÔN..é^ÔN..'... |

Figure 4.25 – Deleted entry

Now we have to determine how many sectors make up a cluster and what the sector size is. You will need to go to the boot record to get that information. The boot record shows us that there are 512 bytes per sector, and there are 8 sectors per cluster, which gives us a cluster size of 4,096 bytes (as shown in the following diagram):

| Bytes per sector | 011 | 512 | 15 |
| Sectors per cluster | 013 | 8 | 114 |

Figure 4.26 – Boot record

This means that our file will only occupy a single cluster. We then go to the file allocation table and look at the entry for cluster 8 and see that it is zeroed out:

```
00 00 00 00 FF FF FF 0F   0B 00 00 00 0C 00 00 00
0D 00 00 00 0E 00 00 00   0F 00 00 00 10 00 00 00
```

Figure 4.27 – Deleted FAT

To recover the deleted file, perform the following steps:

1. You need to change the entry in the file allocation table from x0000 0000 to xFFFF FFF8 or xFFFF FF0F. If this were a larger file, you would need to change the file allocation table entry to point to the next cluster until you reach the last cluster and the end of the file size. As you are rechaining the entries, if you come to an entry marked as allocated, when you were expecting to find the entry unallocated, then you may be dealing with a fragmented file. Another alternative is when the clusters were made available for use to the filesystem, a new file was placed in the now-available sectors, which would cause the data to be overwritten. There are not a lot of options available if you run into either one of these situations. If the data is overwritten, then you are stuck. If it is fragmented then you have to try and guess where the next cluster will be, which is not very likely with a large capacity device.

2. The next step is to go back to the directory entry and replace xE5 with another character. When replacing the xE5 character of the filename in the directory entry, be careful to not to guess what the character is. If you select the incorrect character, you could change the meaning or create a bias with the new filename, and that would be improper. I recommend that when recovering a deleted file, you replace that first character with an underscore or a dash so there is no misunderstanding about the filename.

When recovering a file with an LFN, it is important to relink the LFN to the SFN. This is because when the additional directories are created to accommodate the LFN, the system creates a checksum based on the data of the SFN. When you change the xE5 value on the SFN entry, you also want to use the same replacement character for the subsequent xE5 entries for the LFN directory entries. The reason you link the LFN to the SFN is that the SFN directory entry contains information such as the date and time, the starting cluster, and the file size.

It is still possible to recover scraps of data that previously existed on the disk but no longer have any artifacts in the filesystem. This information will be stored in slack space, which is discussed in the next section.

Slack space

Now is the time to bring up slack space. Remember that the smallest unit the filesystem can write to is a cluster and that clusters are made up of one or more sectors. The reason I keep repeating this is that I have seen people who are new to the field get confused about the difference between the two. The reason this is important is that files come in a variety of sizes; almost no files will conveniently fit within the cluster boundaries. So, you will have files that spill over into the next cluster. The space between the end of the logical file and the cluster boundary is called "file slack." This slack space can contain data from the previous file. Until it is overwritten, that data will remain for you to examine.

You might find evidence of document files, digital images, chat history, or emails; that is, for any data that has been stored on the device, you may find remnants in slack space after the user has deleted the file.

This concludes the *FAT filesystems* section; next up is NTFS.

Understanding the NTFS filesystem

The **New Technology File System** (**NTFS**) is the default filesystem for Microsoft Windows operating systems. FAT32 had some significant shortcomings, which required a filesystem that was more reliable and efficient, along with additional administrative improvements to help Microsoft remain viable in the corporate environment. They initially designed NTFS for the server environment; however, as the hard drive capacity has increased, it is now the default filesystem in the commercial and consumer market for the Windows operating system.

NTFS is far more complicated than the FAT filesystem; however, the overall purpose remains the same:

- To record the metadata of a file, that is, the filename, the date timestamps, and the file size
- To mark the clusters the file occupies
- To record which clusters are allocated and which clusters are unallocated

The NTFS filesystem comprises the following system files:

$MFT	**Describes all files on the volume, including file names, timestamps, stream names, and lists of cluster numbers where data streams reside, indexes, security identifiers, and file attributes**
$MFTMirr	**Duplicate of the first vital entries of $MFT, usually 4 entries (4 kb)**
$LogFile	**Contains transaction log of file system metadata changes**
$Volume	**Contains information about the volume, namely the volume object identifier, volume label, file system version, and volume flags**
$AttrDef	**A table of MFT attribute that associates numeric identifiers with names**
$ (Root file name index)	**The root folder**
$Bitmap	**Tracks the allocation status of all clusters in the partition**
$Boot	**Volume boot record**
$BadClus	**A file that contains all the clusters marked as having bad sectors**
$Secure	**Access control list database**
$UpCase	**Converts lowercase characters in Unicode by storing an uppercase version of all Unicode characters in this file**
$Extend	**A file system directory containing various optional extensions, such as $Quota, $ObjId, $Reparse or $UsnJrnl**

Figure 4.28 – NTFS table

To identify a partition with NTFS, we need to look at the MBR or the GPT, depending on which formatting scheme was used. In the following diagram, we can see the MBR for the hard drive and the partition table highlighted after the boot code:

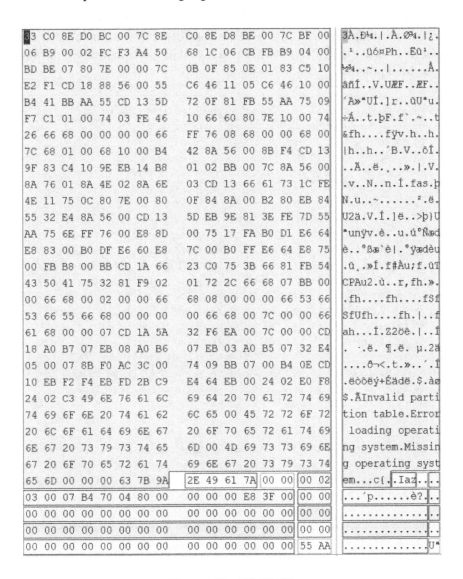

Figure 4.29 – NTFS MBR

Looking at the partition table, we can see that there is a single partition, and, at offset decimal `11` from the start of the partition table, we can see the hexadecimal value of `07`. As we discussed earlier in this chapter, this is the filesystem identification for NTFS.

With an NTFS-formatted partition, there is no system or data area like we saw with a FAT-formatted partition. Everything in NTFS is considered a file to include the system data. When we look at the VBR, we can see that it contains information for the system to continue the boot process:

```
EB 52 90 4E 54 46 53 20    20 20 20 00 02 08 00 00    ëR.NTFS    .....
00 00 00 00 00 F8 00 00    3F 00 FF 00 80 00 00 00    .....ø..?.ÿ.....
00 00 00 00 80 00 80 00    FF E7 3F 00 00 00 00 00    ........ÿç?.....
AA A9 02 00 00 00 00 00    02 00 00 00 00 00 00 00    ª©.............
F6 00 00 00 01 00 00 00    66 20 92 02 61 92 02 7C    ö.......f ..a..|
00 00 00 00 FA 33 C0 8E    D0 BC 00 7C FB 68 C0 07    ....ú3À.Ð¼.|ûhÀ.
1F 1E 68 66 00 CB 88 16    0E 00 66 81 3E 03 00 4E    ..hf.Ë....f.>..N
54 46 53 75 15 B4 41 BB    AA 55 CD 13 72 0C 81 FB    TFSu.´A»ªUÍ.r..û
55 AA 75 06 F7 C1 01 00    75 03 E9 DD 00 1E 83 EC    Uªu.÷Á..u.éÝ...ì
18 68 1A 00 B4 48 8A 16    0E 00 8B F4 16 1F CD 13    .h..´H....ô..Í.
9F 83 C4 18 9E 58 1F 72    E1 3B 06 0B 00 75 DB A3    ..Ä..X.rá;...uÛ£
0F 00 C1 2E 0F 00 04 1E    5A 33 DB B9 00 20 2B C8    ..Á.....Z3Û¹. +È
66 FF 06 11 00 03 16 0F    00 8E C2 FF 06 16 00 E8    fÿ........Âÿ...è
4B 00 2B C8 77 EF B8 00    BB CD 1A 66 23 C0 75 2D    K.+Èwï¸.»Í.f#Àu-
66 81 FB 54 43 50 41 75    24 81 F9 02 01 72 1E 16    f.ûTCPAu$.ù..r..
68 07 BB 16 68 52 11 16    68 09 00 66 53 66 53 66    h.».hR..h..fSfSf
55 16 16 16 68 B8 01 66    61 0E 07 CD 1A 33 C0 BF    U...h¸.fa..Í.3À¿
0A 13 B9 F6 0C FC F3 AA    E9 FE 01 90 90 66 60 1E    ..¹ö.üóªéþ...f`.
06 66 A1 11 00 66 03 06    1C 00 1E 66 68 00 00 00    .f¡..f.....fh...
00 66 50 06 53 68 01 00    68 10 00 B4 42 8A 16 0E    .fP.Sh..h..´B..
00 16 1F 8B F4 CD 13 66    59 5B 5A 66 59 66 59 1F    ....ôÍ.fY[ZfYfY.
0F 82 16 00 66 FF 06 11    00 03 16 0F 00 8E C2 FF    ....fÿ........Âÿ
0E 16 00 75 BC 07 1F 66    61 C3 A1 F6 01 E8 09 00    ...u¼..faÃ¡ö.è.
A1 FA 01 E8 03 00 F4 EB    FD 8B F0 AC 3C 00 74 09    ¡ú.è..ôëý.ð¬<.t.
B4 0E BB 07 00 CD 10 EB    F2 C3 0D 0A 41 20 64 69    ´.»..Í.ëòÃ..A di
73 6B 20 72 65 61 64 20    65 72 72 6F 72 20 6F 63    sk read error oc
63 75 72 72 65 64 00 0D    0A 42 4F 4F 54 4D 47 52    curred...BOOTMGR
20 69 73 20 63 6F 6D 70    72 65 73 73 65 64 00 0D    is compressed..
0A 50 72 65 73 73 20 43    74 72 6C 2B 41 6C 74 2B    .Press Ctrl+Alt+
44 65 6C 20 74 6F 20 72    65 73 74 61 72 74 0D 0A    Del to restart..
00 00 00 00 00 00 00 00    00 00 00 00 00 00 00 00    ................
00 00 00 00 00 00 8A 01    A7 01 BF 01 00 00 55 AA    ........§.¿...Uª
```

Figure 4.30 – NTFS VBR

The information in the VBR is a file; the $Boot record contains all of the information that we would expect to find in the VBR. The following $Boot diagram shows the data structure for the $Boot file:

JMP instruction	000	EB 52 90	EB 52 90
OEM ID	003	NTFS	NTFS
BIOS Parameter Block	**00B**		
Bytes per sector	00B	512	512
Sectors per cluster	00D	8	8
Reserved sectors	00E	0	0
(always zero)	010	00 00 00	00 00 00
(unused)	013	00 00	00 00
Media descriptor	015	248	248
(unused)	016	00 00	00 00
Sectors per track	018	63	63
Number of heads	01A	255	255
Hidden sectors	01C	128	128
(unused)	020	00 00 00 00	00 00 00 00
Signature	024	80 00 80 00	80 00 80 00
Total sectors	028	4,188,159	4,188,159
$MFT cluster number	030	174,506	174,506
$MFTMirr cluster number	038	2	2
Clusters per File Record Se...	040	246	246
Clusters per Index Block	044	1	1
Volume serial number	048	66 20 92 02...	66 20 92 02 61 92 02 7C
Checksum	050	0	0
Bootstrap code	054	FA 33 C0 8E...	FA 33 C0 8E D0 BC 00 7C
Signature (55 AA)	1FE	55 AA	55 AA

Figure 4.31 – $boot

Arguably, the most essential system file in the NTFS filesystem is the $MFT (master file table). The MFT tracks all of the files in the volume to include itself. It tracks each file within the MFT through the use of file entries called a file record. Each file record is uniquely numbered and is 1,024 bytes. Each file record starts with a header, with the ASCII text "FILE", and has an EOF marker of hexadecimal FF FF FF FF. As it adds files to the volume, a new file record is created. If a file has been deleted, the file record will zero out and make it available for reuse. The MFT will look for an empty file record and use it prior to creating a new record. It is possible for the file record to be reused rather quickly, which would overwrite the previous data in the file record.

As shown in the following NTFS file record example, we can see a file record and file header starting with the ASCII values of FILE. If the record were corrupted or had an error, you would see the ASCII value of BAAD. The file header is 56 bytes:

46	49	4C	45	30	00	03	00	39	6B	20	00	00	00	00	00	FILE0...9k ....
01	00	01	00	38	00	01	00	D8	01	00	00	00	04	00	00	...8...Ø......
00	00	00	00	00	00	00	00	04	00	00	00	28	00	00	00	........(...
03	00	00	00	00	00	00	00	10	00	00	00	60	00	00	00	........` ...
00	00	00	00	00	00	00	00	48	00	00	00	18	00	00	00	........H......
BB	0E	D4	A1	6C	27	D5	01	E9	FC	2A	E5	DF	26	D5	01	».Ô¡l'Õ.éü*åß&Õ.
58	0B	C7	E9	DF	26	D5	01	BB	0E	D4	A1	6C	27	D5	01	X.Çéß&Õ.».Ô¡l'Õ.
20	00	00	00	00	00	00	00	00	00	00	00	00	00	00	00	....
00	00	00	00	08	01	00	00	00	00	00	00	00	00	00	00	....
00	00	00	00	00	00	00	00	30	00	00	00	80	00	00	00	........0......
00	00	00	00	00	00	02	00	62	00	00	00	18	00	01	00	........b......
05	00	00	00	00	00	05	00	BB	0E	D4	A1	6C	27	D5	01	........».Ô¡l'Õ.
BB	0E	D4	A1	6C	27	D5	01	BB	0E	D4	A1	6C	27	D5	01	».Ô¡l'Õ.».Ô¡l'Õ.
BB	0E	D4	A1	6C	27	D5	01	00	00	00	00	00	00	00	00	».Ô¡l'Õ........
00	00	00	00	00	00	00	00	20	00	00	00	00	00	00	00	....
10	00	6C	00	6F	00	6E	00	67	00	66	00	69	00	6C	00	..l.o.n.g.f.i.l.
65	00	6E	00	61	00	6D	00	65	00	2E	00	74	00	78	00	e.n.a.m.e...t.x.
74	00	00	00	00	00	00	00	80	00	00	00	18	00	00	00	t.......
00	00	18	00	00	00	01	00	00	00	00	00	18	00	00	00	....
80	00	00	00	A0	00	00	00	00	16	18	00	00	00	03	00	....
53	00	00	00	48	00	00	00	63	00	6F	00	6D	00	2E	00	S...H...c.o.m...
64	00	72	00	6F	00	70	00	62	00	6F	00	78	00	2E	00	d.r.o.p.b.o.x...
61	00	74	00	74	00	72	00	69	00	62	00	75	00	74	00	a.t.t.r.i.b.u.t.
65	00	73	00	00	00	00	00	78	9C	AB	56	4A	29	CA	2F	e.s.....x.«VJ)Ê/
48	CA	AF	88	4F	CB	CC	49	CD	4C	89	CF	C9	4F	4E	CC	HÊ¯.OËÌIÍ.ÏÉONÌ
51	B2	52	A8	56	CA	4D	4C	CE	C8	CC	03	89	25	96	94	Q²R¨VÊMLÎÈÌ..%..
14	81	85	52	12	4B	12	81	0C	25	4F	83	82	82	AC	0A	...R.K...%O...¬.
F3	D0	1C	A7	50	97	F4	8A	E2	74	67	93	FC	80	74	47	óÐ.§P.ô.âtg.ü.tG
5B	5B	A5	DA	DA	5A	00	CB	B7	1C	B0	00	00	00	00	00	[[¥ÚÚZ.Ë·.°.....
FF	FF	FF	FF	82	79	47	11	00	00	00	00	00	00	00	00	ÿÿÿÿ.yG........

Figure 4.32 – NTFS file record

In the following NTFS file record map, we can see the data structure of a file record header:

Signature (must be 'FILE')	000	FILE
Offset to the update sequence	004	0x30
Update sequence size in words	006	3
$LogFile Sequence Number (LSN)	008	2,124,601
Sequence number	010	1
Hard link count	012	1
Offset to the first attribute	014	0x38
Flags	016	01 00
Real size of the FILE record	018	472
Allocated size of the FILE record	01C	1,024
Base FILE record	020	0
Next attribute ID	028	4
ID of this record	02C	40
Update sequence number	030	03 00
Update sequence array	032	00 00 00 00
Attribute $10	**038**	
Attribute $30	**098**	
Attribute $80	**118**	
Attribute $80	**130**	
End marker	1D0	0xFFFFFFFF

Figure 4.33 – NTFS file record map

The file record also contains defined data blocks called file attributes. These store specific types of information about the file. The following file attributes table shows several common file attributes that you are likely to see in almost every record:

$Standard Information -0x10	Includes information such as timestamp and link count.
$Attribute List - 0x20	Lists the location of all attribute records that do not fit in the MFT record.
$File Name - 0x30	A repeatable attribute for both long and short file names. The long name of the file can be up to 255 Unicode characters. The short name is the 8.3 case-insensitive name for the file. Additional names, or hard links, required by POSIX can be included as additional filename attributes.
$Security Descriptor - 0x50	Describes who owns the file and who can access it.
$Data - 0x80	Contains file data. NTFS allows multiple data attributes per file. Each file type has one unnamed data attribute. A file can also have one or more named data attributes.

Figure 4.34 – File attributes table

Let's take a look at each of these attributes in detail.

$Standard_Information Attribute (0x10): The file attributes follow the file header and contain information about the file and, sometimes, the actual file itself. The following diagram depicts a file attribute. The first four bytes show the attribute type; in this case, it is the $10 Standard Information Attribute, which contains general information, flags, accessed, written, and created times, the owner, and security ID. It is identified by the hexadecimal header: x/10 00 00 00. The file attribute map contains the decoded values:

```
03 00 00 00 00 00 00 00    10 00 00 00 60 00 00 00
00 00 00 00 00 00 00 00    48 00 00 00 18 00 00 00
BB 0E D4 A1 6C 27 D5 01    E9 FC 2A E5 DF 26 D5 01
58 0B C7 E9 DF 26 D5 01    BB 0E D4 A1 6C 27 D5 01
20 00 00 00 00 00 00 00    00 00 00 00 00 00 00 00
00 00 00 00 08 01 00 00    00 00 00 00 00 00 00 00
00 00 00 00 00 00 00 00    30 00 00 00 80 00 00 00
```

Figure 4.35 – File attribute

Here is a map of the values you will find in the attribute:

Attribute $10	038	
Attribute type	038	0x10
Length (including header)	03C	96
Non-resident flag	040	0
Name length	041	0
Name offset	042	0x00
> Flags	044	00 00
Attribute ID	046	0
Length of the attribute	048	72
Offset to the attribute data	04C	0x18
Indexed flag	04E	0
Padding	04F	0
∨ $STANDARD_INFORMATION	050	
File created (UTC)	050	6/20/2019 1:32 PM
File modified (UTC)	058	6/19/2019 8:45 PM
Record changed (UTC)	060	6/19/2019 8:45 PM
Last access time (UTC)	068	6/20/2019 1:32 PM
> File Permissions	070	20 00 00 00
Maximum number of versions	074	0
Version number	078	0
Class Id	07C	0
Owner Id	080	0
Security Id	084	264
Quota Charged	088	0
Update Sequence Number	090	0

Figure 4.36 – File attribute map

$File_Name Attribute (0x30): The next attribute is the $30 File Name Attribute. This attribute stores the name of the file attribute and is always resident. The maximum filename length is 255 Unicode characters. It is identified by the hexadecimal header of x/ 30 00 00 00:

```
00 00 00 00 00 00 00 00   30 00 00 00 80 00 00 00
00 00 00 00 00 00 02 00   62 00 00 00 18 00 01 00
05 00 00 00 00 00 05 00   BB 0E D4 A1 6C 27 D5 01
BB 0E D4 A1 6C 27 D5 01   BB 0E D4 A1 6C 27 D5 01
BB 0E D4 A1 6C 27 D5 01   00 00 00 00 00 00 00 00
00 00 00 00 00 00 00 00   20 00 00 00 00 00 00 00
10 00 6C 00 6F 00 6E 00   67 00 66 00 69 00 6C 00
65 00 6E 00 61 00 6D 00   65 00 2E 00 74 00 78 00
74 00 00 00 00 00 00 00   80 00 00 00 18 00 00 00
00 00 18 00 00 00 01 00   00 00 00 00 18 00 00 00
```

Figure 4.37 – Filename attribute

The following is a map of the values you will find in the attribute:

Attribute $30	098	
Attribute type	098	0x30
Length (including header)	09C	128
Non-resident flag	0A0	0
Name length	0A1	0
Name offset	0A2	0x00
> Flags	0A4	00 00
Attribute ID	0A6	2
Length of the attribute	0A8	98
Offset to the attribute data	0AC	0x18
Indexed flag	0AE	1
Padding	0AF	0
∨ $FILE_NAME	0B0	
Parent directory file record number	0B0	5
Parent directory sequence number	0B6	5
File created (UTC)	0B8	6/20/2019 1:32 PM
File modified (UTC)	0C0	6/20/2019 1:32 PM
Record changed (UTC)	0C8	6/20/2019 1:32 PM
Last access time (UTC)	0D0	6/20/2019 1:32 PM
Allocated size	0D8	0
Real size	0E0	0
> File attributes	0E8	20 00 00 00
(used by EAs and reparse)	0EC	0
File name length	0F0	16
File name namespace	0F1	0
File name	0F2	longfilename.txt

Figure 4.38 – Filename attribute map

$Data Attribute (0x80): The next attribute for this entry is the $80 Data Attribute. The data attribute contains the contents of the file or points to where the contents are located in the volume. This attribute is the file data itself.

If the data attribute content is resident, we only use the attribute header and the resident content header. The resident content of the attribute is the file's data. Only tiny files have a resident data attribute. We will discuss resident versus non-resident data later on in this chapter.

You may find multiple data attributes per file. In this record, the second $80 Data attribute, Dropbox, has added some information to the file:

```
74 00 00 00 00 00 00 00   80 00 00 00 18 00 00 00
00 00 18 00 00 00 01 00   00 00 00 00 18 00 00 00
80 00 00 00 A0 00 00 00   00 16 18 00 00 00 03 00
53 00 00 00 48 00 00 00   63 00 6F 00 6D 00 2E 00
64 00 72 00 6F 00 70 00   62 00 6F 00 78 00 2E 00
61 00 74 00 74 00 72 00   69 00 62 00 75 00 74 00
65 00 73 00 00 00 00 00   78 9C AB 56 4A 29 CA 2F
48 CA AF 88 4F CB CC 49   CD 4C 89 CF C9 4F 4E CC
51 B2 52 A8 56 CA 4D 4C   CE C8 CC 03 89 25 96 94
14 81 85 52 12 4B 12 81   0C 25 4F 83 82 82 AC 0A
F3 D0 1C A7 50 97 F4 8A   E2 74 67 93 FC 80 74 47
5B 5B A5 DA DA 5A 00 CB   B7 1C B0 00 00 00 00 00
FF FF FF FF 82 79 47 11   00 00 00 00 00 00 00 00
```

Figure 4.39 – Data attribute

The following is a map of the values you will find in the attribute:

Attribute $80	130	
Attribute type	130	0x80
Length (including header)	134	160
Non-resident flag	138	0
Name length	139	22
Name offset	13A	0x18
> Flags	13C	00 00
Attribute ID	13E	3
Length of the attribute	140	83
Offset to the attribute data	144	0x48
Indexed flag	146	0
Padding	147	0
Attribute name	148	com.dropbox.attributes
✓ $DATA	178	
Data	178	78 9C AB 56 4A 29 CA 2F 48
End marker	1D0	0xFFFFFFFF

Figure 4.40 – Data attribute map

When examining the $Data Attribute 0x80, the contents of the file may be stored within the MFT file record itself. Since the file record is 1,024 bytes long, it would have to be a tiny file. When the data content of the file fits within the file record, it is called "resident data":

Figure 4.41 – Resident data

In the current example, we have a file named resident.txt that is 23 bytes in size. This is smaller than the 1,024 bytes of the file record. To look at the data of the file, we need to look at the $Data Attribute 0x80 of the file record, as follows:

```
96 6A E0 D5 5E A7 04 37   80 00 00 00 30 00 00 00   .jàÕ^§.7....0...
00 00 18 00 00 00 01 00   17 00 00 00 18 00 00 00   ................
54 68 69 73 20 69 73 20   72 65 73 69 64 65 6E 74   This is resident
20 64 61 74 61 2E 20 00   80 00 00 00 A0 00 00 00   data. ..... ...
```

Figure 4.42 – Resident data example

On examining the attribute, we can see the ASCII and hex representation of the file content we observed in the preceding resident data example. When dealing with a non-resident file, such as the one depicted in the following diagram, we can see that the nonresident.txt file, which is 145 KB in size, is larger than the 1,024-byte file record:

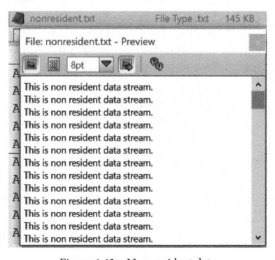

Figure 4.43 – Non-resident data

When you look at the $Data Attribute 0x80 of the file, as shown in the preceding diagram, we do not see the contents of the file, but we have pointers to the location of the file within the volume boundaries. We consider this to be non-resident content. Once the content of the attribute becomes non-resident, it can never become resident again. We commonly refer to the pointers in the file record of the attribute as a "run list" for the data runs of the non-resident data:

96 6A E0 D5 5E A7 04 37	80 00 00 00	48 00 00 00	.jàÕ^§.7....H...
01 00 00 00 00 00 06 00	00 00 00 00 00 00 00 00	.|..|..|........
24 00 00 00 00 00 00 00	40 00 00 00 00 00 00 00	$......@.|..|....
00 50 02 00 00 00 00 00	30 43 02 00 00 00 00 00	.P......0C......
30 43 02 00 00 00 00 00	11 25 26 00 00 00 00 00	0C......%&......

Figure 4.44 – Non-resident data example

You can have a single data run, or multiple data runs, within the $Data Attribute 0x80. Deciphering the run list for the data runs can be tricky. In the following run list, we have the $Data Attribute 0x80 with two run lists:

80 00 00 00 50 00 00 00	01 00 00 00 00 00 04 00	....P...........
00 00 00 00 00 00 00 00	1A 00 00 00 00 00 00 00	....
40 00 00 00 00 00 00 00	00 B0 01 00 00 00 00 00	@......°
00 B0 01 00 00 00 00 00	00 B0 01 00 00 00 00 00	.°......°
31 07 E8 E3 48 31 14 44	47 17 00 00 00 00 00 00	1.èãH1.DG.......
FF FF FF FF 82 79 47 11	00 00 00 00 00 00 00 00	ÿÿÿÿ.yG.........

Figure 4.45 – Run list

If the file is not fragmented, then you will have one run list pointing to the data run in the volume. If the file is fragmented (which is very common), then you will have multiple run lists providing information about the starting cluster for each fragment. I have taken the two run lists highlighted in the preceding list and created the following chart:

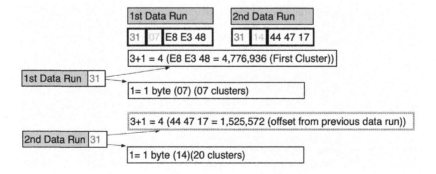

Figure 4.46 – Run list map

The first run list comprises the hexadecimal values of 31 07 E8 E3 48. Take the first byte of the header (x/31) and add the left and right nibble (3+1=4). 4 is the number of bytes in the run list entry (this is x/07 E8 E3 48). The right nibble (x/1) tells us that 1 byte represents the number of clusters being used for this fragment. We find a value of x/07 in the length field, which represents 7 clusters for this fragment. The left nibble (x/3) informs us that 3 bytes (x/E8 E3 48) will represent the logical starter cluster of the fragment. At the end of the first run, we have a second run list of x/31 14 44 47 17. Like the prior run list, we take the first byte of the header (x/31) and add the left and right nibble (3+1=4). 4 is the number of bytes in the run list entry (which is x/14 44 47 17). The right nibble (x/1) tells us that 1 byte represents the number of clusters being used for this fragment. We find a value of x/14 in the length field, which represents 20 clusters for this fragment. The left nibble (x/3) informs us that 3 bytes (x/44 47 17) will represent the offset from the previous run list cluster. This process will keep going until the system hits x/ 00 00 00 00, which shows the end of the run lists.

That concludes our adventure into the world of NTFS. If you find yourself with a headache, you are not alone! This is just the basics of the filesystem. You can find entire books that have been written about NTFS, if you want to go into much greater detail.

Summary

In this chapter, we looked at how physical disks are constructed and prepared in order to store data. We discussed different partition schemes and how they address the creation of logical partitions. We also learned how filesystems differ and how data is organized.

In the next chapter, we will learn about the computer investigative process and how to analyze timelines, analyze media, and perform string searching for data.

Questions

1.   Newer computer systems utilize the BIOS booting method.

     a. True

     b. False

2.   A UEFI-based computer system will utilize _____ to boot from.

     a. MBR

     b. VBR

     c. GPT

     d. LSD

3. A cluster is the smallest storage unit on a hard drive.

    a. True

    b. False

4. An MBR-formatted disk can have more than four primary partitions.

    a. True

    b. False

5. A FAT32-formatted partition is laid out in two areas: a system area and a
    _____ area.

    a. Disk

    b. Doughnut

    c. Data

    d. Designer

6. In a FAT32-formatted partition, the root directory is in the system area.

    a. True

    b. False

7. In a NTFS formatted partition, the filename is stored in the _____
    attribute.

    a. Standard information

    b. Filename

    c. Data

    d. Security descriptor

The answers can be found in the rear of the book under *Assessment*.

Further reading

Carrier, B. File System Forensic Analysis. Addison-Wesley, Reading, PA., Mar. 2005
(available at `https://www.kobo.com/us/en/ebook/file-system-forensic-analysis-1`).

Section 2: Investigation

In this section, you will learn how to identify the evidence you have collected, analyze it, and draw conclusions to determine whether the facts and circumstances found in the digital evidence support the hypothesis that a crime/incident did or did not occur.

The following chapters are in the section:

5
Computer Investigation Process

Being a digital forensic examiner requires you to have a plan to conduct the investigation. For instance, there is the kitchen sink approach – where the person requesting the examination states, *I want it all*. However, this is not practical when the smallest drive from a system might contain hundreds of thousands of pages or events. While the kitchen sink approach is a plan, it may not be the most efficient.

In reality, your search method will depend on the crime you are investigating, and whether there are limitations to the scope of the search. In some investigations, the judicial authority may restrict an investigator's access to digital evidence to only email messages, or you may be limited to a specific date and time within the forensic image.

In this chapter, we will first go through timeline analysis, where a user's activity is analyzed *temporally*. Then, we will examine the storage containers that are used by the user. You will also learn about string search, in which you search a dataset using matching strings of characters. Finally, in the last section, we will analyze data that has been deleted from the filesystem.

In this chapter, we will learn about the following topics:

- Timeline analysis
- Media analysis

- String search
- Recovering deleted data

Timeline analysis

During the investigation, you may find artifacts that appear to show the guilt (or innocence) of the accused. We cannot construe the mere presence of the artifact as a sign of the suspect's guilt (or innocence). The artifact needs to be placed within the context of the user and system activity.

For example, I was brought in as a consultant on a case that was being brought to trial; they accused the suspect of physically abusing another person. One piece of evidence that was considered against the suspect was the high number of Google searches about how to treat an injury. They attributed the searches to the accused, who was the father. The hardest piece of evidence to prove is the identity of the user behind the keyboard when the contested actions occurred. Since the items were present in the internet history (we will go into much greater detail in *Chapter 9*, *Internet Artifacts*), I wanted to check the context of when the searches were made. The wife was the primary owner of the laptop, but the husband was also a frequent user of the laptop. So, how do you attribute the searches to a specific user especially when you have multiple people using the same laptop with the same user account?

A person's internet viewing habits can almost be as distinctive as a fingerprint. As I reviewed the one million-plus lines of internet history, I could differentiate the two different users on the laptop. I could correlate social media use with each user and could attribute the Google searches to the mother of the child. When she was confronted with the findings, the mother admitted that she made searches on how to treat her child's injuries. After being presented with the evidence and testimony of the mother, the jury found the client not guilty of child abuse.

If they had done a timeline analysis prior to making their decision, I believe the father would not have been charged, as the only evidence against him was the digital evidence found on the wife's laptop.

Your ability to create a timeline to analyze the system and actions of the user create a much deeper and thorough understanding of digital evidence. When I first started in the field, the use of timelines was rudimentary and was typically based on the MAC times of the filesystem. **MAC** times refer to the **Modified, Accessed, and Created** times that are records created by the filesystem as files are created, edited, or accessed. The downside to only using MAC times for timeline analysis is that the recorded times may not be accurate. For example, this can happen when files are moved from one volume to another, or if a user uses a third-party tool to change the timestamps and the timestamps are dependent on the system time.

We will now use multiple sources to help us to determine the context of what is happening on a system regarding a specific artifact. These additional sources may not be as easily manipulated as the MAC times and can be used to determine any irregularities in the timestamps. For example, through the use of multiple resources found within the forensic image, we can see when the user logs in, launches an executable, and accesses a file associated with the executable. This method of accessing multiple sources helps us to confirm and validate the information provided by the MAC times.

Using multiple frames of reference to the event being investigated allows us to support our hypothesis about the event. Can we determine whether the incident being investigated results from user activity, or is it a system process? Using all of the available sources such as event logs, filesystem logs, or internet history that is captured by the system allows us to get into the small details to see the context of the event.

By gathering data points from multiple sources, you can create what Rob Lee from the SANS Institute calls a super timeline, because of the sheer amount of data points you will have to sort through.

Hard drive capacity is not getting smaller. In fact, it is increasing at a phenomenal rate. Users and developers are using this increased capacity to store more data and to increase the number of logs that can track what occurs in a system. In some investigations, you may not need to examine the content of the files, for example, in an investigation dealing with illicit images, I need not see the visual depiction of the file. To answer the question of whether a user knew about the existence of a specific file, I can use timeline analysis to make that determination.

The commercial forensic (and open source) tools have made many advances when it comes to the creation of timelines. At one time, you had to use many tools to extract data to create a timeline. Now you can use just a single tool to create a timeline.

> **Note**
> In this chapter, we will be discussing date-times, which will be converted into UTC/GMT. Always be aware of which time zone your dataset is operating in and the time zone in which it is stored. I use GMT/UTC as a standard for when I am conducting an examination.

In this chapter, I will demonstrate the use of several tools for you to see the difference in the outputs and discuss where the tools pull the information from.

X-Ways

X-Ways Forensics has a very robust timeline-creation utility built-in, called **event list**. X-Ways compiles multiple sources such as timestamps at the filesystem level, internal timestamps, browser histories, event logs, registry hives, emails, and many other sources. When you start an event list, the data will be presented chronologically and you will have created a timeline. The event list is a very detailed timeline with copious amounts of information, which allows you to see the sequence of events of the incident you are investigating.

> **Note**
>
> As you explore the features of a new tool, remember to validate the tool against a known dataset. For this lab, we will use a forensic image offered by Digital Corpora. You can visit `https://digitalcorpora.org/` and go to the 2008 M–57 Jean scenario for more information.

In this scenario, you are investigating a data leak. Someone has posted a spreadsheet containing the confidential information of an organization onto a competitor's website, and the spreadsheet came from the computer of the CFO, Jean. During her interview, Jean states that she emailed the spreadsheet to the president, Allison, on her request. The spreadsheet is `m57plan.xls` and can be found on the desktop of Jean's account. It has an MD5 hash value of `e23a4eb7f2562f53e88c9dca8b26a153` and a modified time of `2008-JUL-20 01:28:03` GMT, which also corresponds to Jean's statement regarding when she emailed the spreadsheet.

The filename and time frame give us a starting point of where to conduct the timeline analysis. When you are in the user environment of X-Ways Forensics, select the icon for the event list:

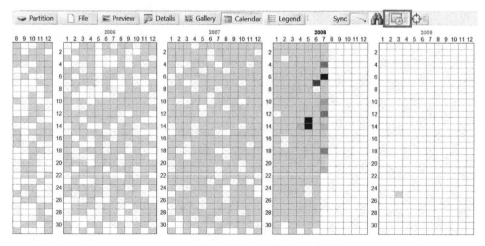

Figure 5.1 – X-Ways

As you can see in the preceding screenshot, when you select the **Calendar** option, it will show you the calendar interface so that you can drill down to a specific day. If I do not filter any of the results on the event list, I have over one million entries that I will need to parse through. My preferred workflow method is to start big and then filter the results to meet the needs of my investigation.

When I filter down to July 20, I have reduced my results to a much more manageable 4,052 events.

Once we filter the results, let's search for the filename and see what activity has occurred. One of the first results shows that at 01:27:42, a link file was created for the spreadsheet. In the following screenshot, you can see the user activity from 01:27 to 01:28. A pre-fetch file (EXCEL.EXE-1C75F8D6.pf) was created for Excel at 01:27, which shows the user starting the Excel program and then opening the spreadsheet, which corresponds to the creation of a link file:

Timestamp ▲	Type	Category	Description	Name	Type
07/20/2008 01:27:27 +0	Value changed	Registry	\Software\Microsoft\Office\9.0\Common\Open Find\Places\Standar...	ntuser.dat	registry
07/20/2008 01:27:27 +0	Key changed	Registry	\Software\Microsoft\Office\9.0\Common\Open Find\Microsoft Outlo...	NTUSER.DAT	registry
07/20/2008 01:27:40 +0	Key changed	Registry	\Software\Microsoft\Windows\ShellNoRoam\MUICache	REGISTRY_USER_NTUSER_S-1-5-21-484763869-79684...	registry
07/20/2008 01:27:40 +0	Creation	Internal file metadata		EXCEL.EXE-1C75F8D6.pf	pf
07/20/2008 01:27:40 +0	Program started	Operating system		EXCEL.EXE-1C75F8D6.pf	pf
07/20/2008 01:27:40 +0	Access	File system		XLINTL32.DLL	dll
07/20/2008 01:27:40 +0	Key changed	Registry	\Microsoft\Windows\CurrentVersion\Installer\UserData\S-1-5-18\Pro...	SOFTWARE	registry
07/20/2008 01:27:40 +0	Key changed	Registry	\Microsoft\Windows\CurrentVersion\Installer\UserData\S-1-5-18\Pro...	REGISTRY_MACHINE_SOFTWARE	registry
07/20/2008 01:27:40 +0	Access	File system		EXCEL.EXE	exe
07/20/2008 01:27:40 +0	Record change	File system		EXCEL.EXE	exe
07/20/2008 01:27:41 +0	Modification	Internal file metadata	C:\Documents and Settings\Jean\Local Settings\Temp	Temp.LNK	lnk
07/20/2008 01:27:42 +0	Modification	Internal file metadata	C:\Documents and Settings\Jean\Local Settings\Temp	Temp.LNK	lnk
07/20/2008 01:27:42 +0	Key changed	Registry	\Software\Microsoft\Internet Explorer\Desktop\Components\0	REGISTRY_USER_NTUSER_S-1-5-21-484763869-79684...	registry
07/20/2008 01:27:42 +0	Creation	File system		m57biz.LNK	lnk
07/20/2008 01:27:42 +0	Access	File system		desktop.ini	ini1
07/20/2008 01:27:42 +0	Access	File system		Desktop.ini	ini1
07/20/2008 01:27:42 +0	Access	File system		Desktop.ini	ini1
07/20/2008 01:27:42 +0	Creation	File system		Temp.LNK	lnk
07/20/2008 01:27:50 +0	Modification	File system		EXCEL.EXE-1C75F8D6.pf	pf
07/20/2008 01:27:50 +0	Record change	File system		EXCEL.EXE-1C75F8D6.pf	pf
07/20/2008 01:27:50 +0	Access	File system		EXCEL.EXE-1C75F8D6.pf	pf
07/20/2008 01:27:59 +0	Key changed	Registry	\Software\Microsoft\Office\9.0\Common\Open Find\Places\Standar...	NTUSER.DAT	registry
07/20/2008 01:27:59 +0	Key changed	Registry	\Software\Microsoft\Office\9.0\Common\Open Find\Places\Standar...	REGISTRY_USER_NTUSER_S-1-5-21-484763869-79684...	registry
07/20/2008 01:27:59 +0	Key changed	Registry	\Software\Microsoft\Office\9.0\Common\Open Find\Places\Standar...	NTUSER.DAT	registry
07/20/2008 01:27:59 +0	Key changed	Registry	\Software\Microsoft\Office\9.0\Common\Open Find\Places\Standar...	REGISTRY_USER_NTUSER_S-1-5-21-484763869-79684...	registry
07/20/2008 01:27:59 +0	Key changed	Registry	\Software\Microsoft\Office\9.0\Common\Open Find\Places\Standar...	ntuser.dat	registry
07/20/2008 01:27:59 +0	Key changed	Registry	\Software\Microsoft\Office\9.0\Common\Open Find\Places\Standar...	ntuser.dat	registry
07/20/2008 01:27:59 +0	Key changed	Registry	\Software\Microsoft\Office\9.0\Common\Open Find\Places\Standar...	REGISTRY_USER_NTUSER_S-1-5-21-484763869-79684...	registry
07/20/2008 01:28:00 +0	Record change	Messaging		RE: Please send me the information now.eml (2)	eml
07/20/2008 01:28:02 +0	Access	File system		VMware Shared Folders.lnk	lnk
07/20/2008 01:28:02 +0	Access	File system		AIM Tunes.url	url
07/20/2008 01:28:03 +0	Last saved	Internal file metadata		m57biz.xls (1)	xls
07/20/2008 01:28:03 +0	Last saved	Internal file metadata		m57biz.xls (1)	xls
07/20/2008 01:28:03 +0	Key changed	Registry	\Software\Microsoft\Office\9.0\Common\Open Find\Microsoft Excel\...	ntuser.dat	registry
07/20/2008 01:28:03 +0	Creation	Internal file metadata	C:\Documents and Settings\Jean\Desktop\m57biz.xls	m57biz.LNK	lnk
07/20/2008 01:28:03 +0	Value changed	Registry	\Software\Microsoft\Office\9.0\Common\Open Find\Microsoft Excel\...	ntuser.dat	registry
07/20/2008 01:28:03 +0	Key changed	Registry	\Software\Microsoft\Office\9.0\Common\Open Find\Microsoft Excel\...	ntuser.dat	registry

Figure 5.2 – Filter results

When you view the event list, you can see where the forensic tool is getting the information that is being displayed. The creation of the pre-fetch file starts with a change in the NT `user.dat` file and follows along from gathering information from the internal file metadata to the operating system artifact. We can follow along and observe what occurs at the user and system levels as the user activity is being recorded.

If you look at timestamp 01:28:00, you can see that Jean sent a message out. In the **Name** column, we can see the subject of the email, and when we double-click on it, we can view the email itself:

Timestamp ▲	Type	Category	Des	Name	Type ▲	Sender	Recipients
07/20/2008 00:01:07 +0	Created	Messaging		RE: which email address are you using?.eml	eml	alex <alison@m57.biz>	Jean User <jean@m57.biz>
07/20/2008 00:01:07 +0	Created	Messaging		RE: background checks.eml	eml	alex <alison@m57.biz>	Jean User <jean@m57.biz>
07/20/2008 00:01:07 +0	Created	Messaging		RE: programmers.eml	eml	alex <alison@m57.biz>	Jean User <jean@m57.biz>
07/20/2008 00:01:08 +0	Created	Messaging		RE: CNN.com Daily Top 10.eml	eml	alex <alison@m57.biz>	Jean User <jean@m57.biz>
07/20/2008 00:01:08 +0	Created	Messaging		RE: which email address are you using?.eml	eml	alex <alison@m57.biz>	Jean User <jean@m57.biz>
07/20/2008 01:22:45 +0	Record change	Messaging		Please send me the information now.eml	eml	tuckgorge@gmail.com (alison@m57...	jean@m57.biz
07/20/2008 01:22:45 +0	Received	Messaging		Please send me the information now.eml	eml	tuckgorge@gmail.com (alison@m57...	jean@m57.biz
07/20/2008 01:22:45 +0	Sent	Messaging		Please send me the information now.eml	eml	tuckgorge@gmail.com (alison@m57...	jean@m57.biz
07/20/2008 01:26:17 +0	Created	Messaging		Please send me the information now.eml	eml	tuckgorge@gmail.com (alison@m57...	jean@m57.biz
07/20/2008 01:26:17 +0	Created	Messaging		RE: Please send me the information now.eml (2)	eml	Jean User <jean@m57.biz>	alison@m57.biz <tuckgorge@...
07/20/2008 01:28:00 +0	Record change	Messaging		RE: Please send me the information now.eml (2)	eml	Jean User <jean@m57.biz>	alison@m57.biz <tuckgorge@...
07/20/2008 01:28:47 +0	Sent	Messaging		RE: Please send me the information now.eml (2)	eml	Jean User <jean@m57.biz>	alison@m57.biz <tuckgorge@...
07/20/2008 05:03:40 +0	Record change	Messaging		Thanks!.eml	eml	tuckgorge@gmail.com (alison@m57...	jean@m57.biz
07/20/2008 05:03:40 +0	Sent	Messaging		Thanks!.eml	eml	tuckgorge@gmail.com (alison@m57...	jean@m57.biz
07/20/2008 05:03:40 +0	Received	Messaging		Thanks!.eml	eml	tuckgorge@gmail.com (alison@m57...	jean@m57.biz
07/20/2008 05:03:58 +0	Created	Messaging		Thanks!.eml	eml	tuckgorge@gmail.com (alison@m57...	jean@m57.biz
07/20/2008 05:04:00 +0	Created	Messaging		RE: Thanks!.eml	eml	Jean User <jean@m57.biz>	alison@m57.biz <tuckgorge@...
07/20/2008 05:04:00 +0	Record change	Messaging		RE: Thanks!.eml	eml	Jean User <jean@m57.biz>	alison@m57.biz <tuckgorge@...
07/20/2008 05:04:00 +0	Record change	Messaging		RE: Obama makes first trip to Afghanistan.eml	eml	Jean User <jean@m57.biz>	alex <alex@m57.biz>
07/20/2008 05:04:00 +0	Record change	Messaging		RE: Obama makes first trip to Afghanistan.eml	eml	Jean User <jean@m57.biz>	alex <alex@m57.biz>
07/20/2008 05:04:00 +0	Record change	Messaging		RE: Obama makes first trip to Afghanistan.eml	eml	Jean User <jean@m57.biz>	alex <alex@m57.biz>
07/20/2008 05:04:23 +0	Created	Messaging		RE: Obama makes first trip to Afghanistan.eml	eml	Jean User <jean@m57.biz>	alex <alex@m57.biz>
07/20/2008 05:04:48 +0	Created	Messaging		RE: Obama makes first trip to Afghanistan.eml	eml	Jean User <jean@m57.biz>	alex <alex@m57.biz>
07/20/2008 05:07:52 +0	Sent	Messaging		RE: Thanks!.eml	eml	Jean User <jean@m57.biz>	alison@m57.biz <tuckgorge@...
07/20/2008 23:41:10 +0	Sent	Messaging		what is going on?.eml	eml	AlisonM57 <alison@m57.biz>	jean@m57.biz
07/20/2008 23:41:11 +0	Record change	Messaging		what is going on?.eml	eml	AlisonM57 <alison@m57.biz>	jean@m57.biz
07/20/2008 23:41:11 +0	Received	Messaging		what is going on?.eml	eml	AlisonM57 <alison@m57.biz>	jean@m57.biz
07/20/2008 23:46:35 +0	Created	Messaging		what is going on?.eml	eml	AlisonM57 <alison@m57.biz>	jean@m57.biz
07/20/2008 23:47:32 +0	Sent	Messaging		are you around today?.eml	eml	AlisonM57 <alison@m57.biz>	jean@m57.biz
07/20/2008 23:47:32 +0	Record change	Messaging		are you around today?.eml	eml	AlisonM57 <alison@m57.biz>	jean@m57.biz
07/20/2008 23:47:32 +0	Received	Messaging		are you around today?.eml	eml	AlisonM57 <alison@m57.biz>	jean@m57.biz
07/20/2008 23:50:58 +0	Created	Messaging		RE: what is going on?.eml	eml	Jean User <jean@m57.biz>	AlisonM57 <alison@m57.biz>
07/20/2008 23:51:00 +0	Record change	Messaging		RE: what is going on?.eml	eml	Jean User <jean@m57.biz>	AlisonM57 <alison@m57.biz>
07/20/2008 23:52:54 +0	Sent	Messaging		Hi Jean.eml	eml	bob@m57.biz	jean@m57.biz
07/20/2008 23:53:19 +0	Received	Messaging		Hi Jean.eml	eml	bob@m57.biz	jean@m57.biz
07/20/2008 23:53:19 +0	Record change	Messaging		Hi Jean.eml	eml	bob@m57.biz	jean@m57.biz
07/20/2008 23:56:37 +0	Sent	Messaging		When is our next meeting?.eml	eml	carol@m57.biz	jean@m57.biz
07/20/2008 23:56:37 +0	Sent	Messaging		RE: what is going on?.eml	eml	Jean User <jean@m57.biz>	AlisonM57 <alison@m57.biz>
07/20/2008 23:56:38 +0	Created	Messaging		are you around today?.eml	eml	AlisonM57 <alison@m57.biz>	jean@m57.biz

Figure 5.3 – Jean's email

We can see that Jean has emailed what appears to be `allison@M57.biz`, but, in reality, it is going to `tuckgorge@gmail.com`. We can then filter by file type, in this case, the `.eml` files, and you can see the results as follows:

Subject	RE: Please send me the information now
Date	07/20/2008 01:28:47 +0
Sender	Jean User <jean@m57.biz>
Recipients	tuckgorge@gmail.com
Attachments	m57biz.xls

I've attached the information that you have requested to this email message.

----- Original Message -----

From: alison@m57.biz [mailto:tuckgorge@gmail.com]

Sent: Sunday, July 20, 2008 2:23 AM
To: jean@m57.biz
Subject: Please send me the information now

Hi, Jean.

I'm sorry to bother you, but I really need that information now --- this VC guy is being very insistent.
Can you please reply to this email with the information I requested --- the names, salaries, and
social security numbers (SSNs) of all our current employees and intended hires?

Thanks.

Alison

E-mail Header
Date: 20 Jul 2008 01:28:47 -0000
From: Jean User <jean@m57.biz>
Sender: Jean User <jean@m57.biz>
To: <tuckgorge@gmail.com>
Subject: RE: Please send me the information now
Importance: Normal
Mime-Version: 1.0
Content-Type: multipart/mixed;
boundary="----=_NextPart_0"

Figure 5.4 – Jean's email header

When you look at the **Sender** and **Recipients** columns, and when the data is sorted
chronologically, you can get a good idea about the email communication between the
attacker and Jean. It appears they have compromised Allison's account, as we can see
the name "Alex" and the email account tuckgorge@gmail.com associated with
the account.

Using the event list feature of X-Ways Forensics allows us to pinpoint when the file was compromised and from what vector. Now we can direct our investigation to Allison's computer to determine whether the attacker compromised her system. Based on these initial results, I believe that the attacker targeted Jean in a phishing attack.

What I like about X-Ways Forensics is its ability to gather the dates and times from traditional sources and combine them with the actual artifacts, in this case, the emails. This gives you another level of granularity and context for your investigation.

The X-Ways Forensics documentation lists the following as sources of information for the event list feature:

Index.dat file(s)	Browser history
LNK file(s)	USNJrnl
Registry	Event log(s)
Metadata of Microsoft Office file(s)	Email message(s)
Recycle Bin file(s)	Shadow copy file(s)
Prefetch file(s)	Restore point(s)
Cookie(s)	MAC timestamp(s)

As you can see, this shows a very diverse list of sources, and when used for analysis, it can provide the investigator with the confidence to rely on the date timestamps they are reporting in their investigation.

I have found that forensic suites are now also including timeline analysis with their products. I have discussed X-Ways Forensics and its ability to create a timeline for analysis with its event list feature. I have included a list of some additional forensic suites that you may use to analyze timeline data. The following list is not inclusive of all of the forensic suites that are available:

- Belkasoft Evidence Center: belkasoft.com/ec
- Autopsy: www.sleuthkit.org/autopsy
- Recon Lab: sumuri.com/software/recon-lab
- Paladin: sumuri.com/software/paladin

X-Ways is not the only tool that you can use to create timelines; there are also a number of open source tools that you can utilize. One of the most common is `Plaso/log2timeline`, which we will discuss next.

Plaso (Plaso Langar Að Safna Öllu)

Plaso (Plaso Langar Að Safna Öllu) is a Python backend and framework for the `log2timeline` tool. `log2timeline` is a forensic tool that pulls out timestamps from a system and creates a database of all the events, also known as a super timeline.

> **Note**
> You can download Plaso at `https://github.com/log2timeline/plaso`.

Plaso will work on most operating systems and was initially designed to replace the Perl version of `log2timeline`. The development has now shifted, and they have created several CLI tools supported by the Plaso backend.

The tools supported by Plaso are activated by the **command-line interface (CLI)**. While the CLI can intimidate the user, if you take your time and proceed slowly, you will be able take the mystique out of the CLI. Many open source tools use the CLI instead of the **graphical user interface (GUI)**. The very core of the CLI consists of two parts: the executable and the modifiers. Once you learn the specific modifiers for the CLI command, you will see that it all falls into place.

Let's talk about the tools included with Plaso:

- `image_export`
- `log2timeline`
- `pinfo`
- `psort`
- `psteal`

image_export

`image_export` will export file content from a device, media image, or forensic image. There are several parameters that you can use to define the information you wish to extract.

In the Windows version of the executable, the executable will end with `.exe`. With macOS, you may see it end in `.sh`.

Using `-h` or `--help` will give you the full list of parameters:

```
C:\tools\plaso>image_export.exe -h
usage: image_export.exe [-h] [--troubles] [-V] [-d] [-q]
                        [--artifact_definitions PATH]
                        [--custom_artifact_definitions PATH] [--data PATH]
                        [--logfile FILENAME] [--partitions PARTITIONS]
                        [--volumes VOLUMES] [--no_vss] [--vss_only]
                        [--vss_stores VSS_STORES]
                        [--artifact_filters ARTIFACT_FILTERS]
                        [--artifact_filters_file PATH]
                        [--date-filter TYPE_START_END] [-f FILE_FILTER]
                        [-x EXTENSIONS] [--names NAMES]
                        [--signatures IDENTIFIERS] [-w PATH]
                        [--include_duplicates]
                        [IMAGE]
```

Figure 5.5 – image_export

Further down the screen, you will see the detailed explanations for the modifiers. Note that I will only cover the most commonly used options; there is additional documentation that we will not discuss here:

- `--names NAMES`: The filter on filenames. This option accepts a comma-separated string denoting all filenames, for example, `x NTUSER.DAT,UsrClass.dat`.

- `-w PATH, --write PATH`: The directory in which extracted files should be stored.

- `--data PATH`: The path to a directory containing the data files.

- `-x EXTENSIONS, --extensions EXTENSIONS`: The filter on filename extensions. This option accepts multiple comma-separated values, for example, `csv`, `docx`, and `pst`.

If you use the following command, it will export the `.xls` file to the `files` folder:

```
image_export --names 'm57plan.xls' C:\tools\plaso\image\
jean.001 -w C:\tools\plaso\export\files
```

You can see the breakdown of the preceding command as follows:

image_export --names 'm57biz.xls' C:\tools\plaso\image\jean.001 -w C:\tools\plaso\export\files

Command	modifier	source	destination

Figure 5.6 – CLI map

Here, with the `image_export` command, we are using the `names` modifier to look for a specific file. In this case, it is `M57plan.xls`. Now, you can tell the executable where to search; in this command, we are searching in the forensic image, `jean.001` (make sure that you include the full path to where the forensic image is located). Next, you can indicate where you want the exported files to be sent. The `-w` modifier will specify the write location.

You will find that the modifiers have some commonality with the commands within the plaso framework.

log2timeline

`log2timeline` is a CLI tool that is designed to extract chronological-based events from files, directories, forensic images, or devices. It will create a database file (`.plaso`) that can be then be analyzed by a variety of tools.

As you can see in the following screenshot, the `-h` modifier (help) will display the options for the command. As before, there are detailed explanations not displayed that will give you additional context for these commands. You should be able to recognize some of them from the previous command we looked at:

```
c:\tools\plaso>log2timeline.exe -h
usage: log2timeline.exe [-h] [--troubles] [-V] [--artifact_definitions PATH]
                        [--custom_artifact_definitions PATH] [--data PATH]
                        [--artifact_filters ARTIFACT_FILTERS]
                        [--artifact_filters_file PATH] [--preferred_year YEAR]
           [--process_archives] [--skip_compressed_streams]
                        [-f FILE_FILTER] [--hasher_file_size_limit SIZE]
                        [--hashers HASHER_LIST]
                        [--parsers PARSER_FILTER_EXPRESSION]
                        [--yara_rules PATH] [--partitions PARTITIONS]
                        [--volumes VOLUMES] [-z TIMEZONE] [--no_vss]
                        [--vss_only] [--vss_stores VSS_STORES]
                        [--credential TYPE:DATA] [-d] [-q] [--info]
                        [--use_markdown] [--no_dependencies_check]
                        [--logfile FILENAME] [--status_view TYPE] [-t TEXT]
                        [--buffer_size BUFFER_SIZE] [--queue_size QUEUE_SIZE]
                        [--single_process] [--temporary_directory DIRECTORY]
                        [--worker_memory_limit SIZE] [--workers WORKERS]
                        [--sigsegv_handler] [--profilers PROFILERS_LIST]
                        [--profiling_directory DIRECTORY]
                        [--profiling_sample_rate SAMPLE_RATE]
                        [--storage_format FORMAT]
                        [--task_storage_format FORMAT]
                        [STORAGE_FILE] [SOURCE]
```

Figure 5.7 – log2timeline

Try using the `info` modifier, as follows:

```
c:\tools\plaso>log2timeline.exe --info
```

You will get a list of all of the supported plugins, parsers, and output modules:

```
******************************* Parser Presets ********************************
      Name : Description
-------------------------------------------------------------------------------
   android : android_app_usage, chrome_cache, filestat, sqlite/android_calls,
             sqlite/android_sms, sqlite/android_webview,
             sqlite/android_webviewcache, sqlite/chrome_27_history,
             sqlite/chrome_8_history, sqlite/chrome_cookies, sqlite/skype
     linux : bash_history, bencode, czip/oxml, dockerjson, dpkg, filestat,
             gdrive_synclog, olecf, pls_recall, popularity_contest, selinux,
             sqlite/google_drive, sqlite/skype, sqlite/zeitgeist, syslog,
             systemd_journal, utmp, webhist, xchatlog, xchatscrollback,
             zsh_extended_history
     macos : asl_log, bash_history, bencode, bsm_log, cups_ipp, czip/oxml,
             filestat, fseventsd, gdrive_synclog, mac_appfirewall_log,
             mac_keychain, mac_securityd, macwifi, olecf, plist,
             sqlite/appusage, sqlite/google_drive, sqlite/imessage,
             sqlite/ls_quarantine, sqlite/mac_document_versions,
             sqlite/mac_notes, sqlite/mackeeper_cache, sqlite/mac_knowledgec,
             sqlite/skype, syslog, utmpx, webhist, zsh_extended_history
   webhist : binary_cookies, chrome_cache, chrome_preferences,
             esedb/msie_webcache, firefox_cache, java_idx, msiecf,
             opera_global, opera_typed_history, plist/safari_history,
             sqlite/chrome_27_history, sqlite/chrome_8_history,
             sqlite/chrome_autofill, sqlite/chrome_cookies,
             sqlite/chrome_extension_activity, sqlite/firefox_cookies,
             sqlite/firefox_downloads, sqlite/firefox_history
      win7 : amcache, custom_destinations, esedb/file_history,
             olecf/olecf_automatic_destinations, recycle_bin, winevtx, win_gen
 win7_slow : mft, win7
   win_gen : bencode, czip/oxml, esedb, filestat, gdrive_synclog, lnk,
             mcafee_protection, olecf, pe, prefetch, sccm, skydrive_log,
             skydrive_log_old, sqlite/google_drive, sqlite/skype,
             symantec_scanlog, usnjrnl, webhist, winfirewall, winjob, winreg
     winxp : recycle_bin_info2, rplog, win_gen, winevt
winxp_slow : mft, winxp
-------------------------------------------------------------------------------
```

Figure 5.8 – info

From the preceding output, you can see that some of the presets include collecting artifacts from many filesystems.

At a very basic level, you can use the following command structure:

```
log2timeline OUTPUT INPUT
```

One idiosyncrasy of log2timeline is that the output file is the first modifier to the executable and then you specify the input:

```
log2timeline C:\tools\plaso\export\files\jean.plaso C:\tools\
plaso\image\jean.001
```

When the command executes, you should see the following output on the screen:

```
C:\tools\plaso>log2timeline C:\tools\plaso\export\files\jean.plaso C:\tools\plaso\image\jean.001
2019-08-07 11:25:34,830 [INFO] (MainProcess) PID:5324 <data_location> Determined data location: C:\tools\plaso\data

2019-08-07 11:25:34,848 [INFO] (MainProcess) PID:5324 <artifact_definitions> Determined artifact definitions path:
C:\tools\plaso\artifacts
Checking availability and versions of dependencies.
[OPTIONAL]      missing: lz4.
[OK]
```

Figure 5.9 – Output

As the command executes, it locates the data folder that contains the dependencies for the executable, and then it searches for the files that contain the information about the artifacts that may be stored within the system. This is a default folder and is installed when you install `plaso`.

We now have a `.plaso` file that we can find in the `files` folder. In some cases, you might not want to create the database file with every option, that is, the kitchen sink. Rather, you may wish to do a targeted examination of the timeline, in which case you would need to employ filters. Using the `-f` modifier will allow you to do that.

> **Note**
> If you want to download some premade filters, you can do so at `https://github.com/mark-hallman/plaso_filters`.

I downloaded the premade filters and created a folder, named `filter`, within the path of the `plaso` installation. As you see from the following screenshot, I have installed plaso in a folder called `tools` at the root of my `C` drive:

```
log2timeline -f filter_windows.txt C:\tools\plaso\export\files\
jeanfilter.plaso C:\tools\plaso\image\jean.001
```

And, as you can see in the following screenshot, the tool was able to locate my filter within the `artifacts` folder and created a new plaso database file:

```
c:\tools\plaso>log2timeline -f filter_windows.txt C:\tools\plaso\export\files\jeanfilter.plaso C:\tools\plaso\image\jean.001
2019-07-19 15:19:35,018 [INFO] (MainProcess) PID:23288 <data_location> Determined data location: c:\tools\plaso\data
2019-07-19 15:19:35,034 [INFO] (MainProcess) PID:23288 <artifact_definitions> Determined artifact definitions path: c:\tools\plaso\artifacts
Checking availability and versions of dependencies.
[OPTIONAL]      missing: lz4.
[OK]
```

Figure 5.10 – filter

So far, we have covered several commands; however, we still have more to cover. The next command in the framework is `pinfo`.

pinfo

`pinfo` is a command line that is used to display information about the plaso database file (`.plaso`).

The `plaso` database file will contain the following information:

- When the user executed the tool
- What options were used when the tool was run
- What information was obtained by the tool during the preprocessing stage
- The database metadata
- What was parsed and the parameters that were used
- How many events were extracted
- Tagged events

To learn more about the preceding options, execute the command with the `-h` modifier. While the options are similar, you will have a far smaller selection than with the other tools, as shown in the following screenshot:

```
c:\tools\plaso>pinfo -h
usage: pinfo [-h] [--troubles] [-V] [--compare STORAGE_FILE]
             [--output_format FORMAT] [-v] [-w OUTPUTFILE]
             [STORAGE_FILE]

Shows information about a Plaso storage file, for example how it was collected, what information
was extracted from a source, etc.

positional arguments:
  STORAGE_FILE          Path to a storage file.

optional arguments:
  -h, --help            Show this help message and exit.
  --troubles            Show troubleshooting information.
  -V, --version         Show the version information.
  --compare STORAGE_FILE
                        The path of the storage file to compare against.
  --output_format FORMAT, --output-format FORMAT
                        Format of the output, the default is: text. Supported
                        options: json, text.
  -v, --verbose         Print verbose output.
  -w OUTPUTFILE, --write OUTPUTFILE
                        Output filename.
```

Figure 5.11 – pinfo

When you use the `pinfo` command in its simplest form, you will get the following results:

```
------------------------------------------------------------
*************************** Plaso Storage Information
Filename: jeanfilter.plaso
Format version: 20190309
Serialization format: JSON
------------------------------------------------------------
*********************************** Sessions ******************
276a7520-999e-428b-a6b4-11fcf9cf987d :
2019-07-19T22:19:36.092703Z
------------------------------------------------------------
```

As you can see in the preceding screenshot, you get the storage information about the file and how many sessions were used to create it.

You can send the results to the standard output, that is, the monitor, or you can use the -w modifier to create a text file with the results. The use of the additional tools on the .plaso file will create the GUID and the date timestamp of when the analysis was conducted. The tool can also provide system information about the source system you are now examining:

```
------------------------------------------------------------
********** System configuration: 276a7520-999e-428b-a6b4-
11fcf9cf987d ********
Hostname: N/A
Operating system: Windows NT
Operating system product: Microsoft Windows XP
Operating system version: 5.1
Code page : cp1252
Keyboard layout: N/A
Time zone: GMT
------------------------------------------------------------
```

After verifying the information in the database file, you can move on to the next command.

psort

psort is a CLI tool that allows you to filter, sort, and conduct analysis on the contents of the plaso database file. Just like with the previous commands, the -h modifier will show you all the options for the command. In the following psort screenshot, you can see the available options, and you should be able to recognize the commonality of the options with all of the commands in the plaso architecture:

```
c:\tools\plaso>psort -h
usage: psort [-h] [--troubles] [-V] [--analysis PLUGIN_LIST]
             [--temporary_directory DIRECTORY] [--worker-memory-limit SIZE]
             [--logfile FILENAME] [-d] [-q] [--status_view TYPE]
             [--slice DATE] [--slice_size SLICE_SIZE] [--slicer] [--data PATH]
             [-a] [--language LANGUAGE] [-z TIMEZONE] [-o FORMAT]
             [-w OUTPUT_FILE] [--fields FIELDS]
             [--additional_fields ADDITIONAL_FIELDS]
             [--profilers PROFILERS_LIST] [--profiling_directory DIRECTORY]
             [--profiling_sample_rate SAMPLE_RATE]
             [STORAGE_FILE] [FILTER]

Application to read, filter and process output from a plaso storage file.
```

Figure 5.12 – psort

Let's discuss some of the new options:

```
-o FORMAT, --output_format FORMAT, --output-format FORMAT
```

Use the -o list to view a list of the available output formats, as follows:

```
****************************** Output Modules **************
Name : Description
------------------------------------------------------------------
dynamic : Dynamic selection of fields for a separated value
output format.
elastic : Saves the events into an Elasticsearch database.
json_line : Saves the events into a JSON line format.
json : Saves the events into a JSON format.
rawpy : 'raw' (or native) Python output.
kml : Saves events with geography data into a KML format.
2tcsv : CSV format used by legacy log2timeline, with 17 fixed
fields.
null : Output module that does not output anything.
4n6time_sqlite : Saves the data in a SQLite database, used by
the tool 4n6time.
l2ttln : Extended TLN 7 field | delimited output.
tln : TLN 5 field | delimited output.
```

```
xlsx : Excel Spreadsheet (XLSX) output
-----------------------------------------------------------------
************************* Disabled Output Modules
*************************
Name : Description
-----------------------------------------------------------------
4n6time_mysql : MySQL database output for the 4n6time tool.
timesketch : Create a Timesketch timeline.
-----------------------------------------------------------------
```

As you are processing with `psort`, you can export your findings outside of the `plaso` database. There are a wide variety of options that you can use to export the data for analysis. One of the more common formats for exporting is `l2tcsv`, which is the legacy format for `log2timeline` and is a `.csv` worksheet.

A potential issue you may run into when creating the `.csv` worksheet is that if the file you create is too large, some tools may not analyze it, nor will you be able to open it with your favorite spreadsheet program.

`--analysis list`: `psort` comes with analysis plugins installed by default (you can still create your own custom plugins) to allow you to go through the database file and extract and analyze the contents. You can use the `--analysis` list modifier to view the complete list of plugins:

```
***************************** Analysis Plugins *****************************
                     Name : Description
---------------------------------------------------------------------------
          browser_search : Analyze browser search entries from events.
                           [Summary/Report plugin]
        chrome_extension : Convert Chrome extension IDs into names, requires
                           Internet connection. [Summary/Report plugin]
             file_hashes : A plugin for generating a list of file paths and
                           corresponding hashes. [Summary/Report plugin]
                  nsrlsvr : Analysis plugin for looking up hashes in nsrlsvr.
                           [Summary/Report plugin]
               sessionize : Analysis plugin that labels events by session.
                           [Summary/Report plugin]
                  tagging : Analysis plugin that tags events according to rules
                           in a tagging file. [Summary/Report plugin]
  unique_domains_visited : A plugin to generate a list all domains visited.
                           [Summary/Report plugin]
                    viper : An analysis plugin for looking up SHA256 hashes in
                           Viper. [Summary/Report plugin]
                virustotal : An analysis plugin for looking up hashes in
                           VirusTotal. [Summary/Report plugin]
         windows_services : Provides a single list of for Windows services found
                           in the Registry. [Summary/Report plugin]
---------------------------------------------------------------------------
```

Figure 5.13 – List of analysis plugins

If we run the command, it will go through the `plaso` database file, tagging the specific events that have been identified in the `tag_windows.txt` file (which is part of the default installation and can be found in the `data` directory):

```
psort -o null --analysis tagging --tagging-file tag_windows.txt
c:/tools/plaso/export/files/jean.plaso
```

On completion of the process, it will show you how many tags were applied to the database:

```
***************************** Analysis report: 0
  String: Report generated from tagging
Generated on:2019-07-20T20:04:46.000000Z
Report text: Tagging plugin produced 9754 tags.
-------------------------------------------------------------
```

Additionally, you can filter out extraneous data through the use of the `--slice` modifier.

> **Note**
>
> 5 minutes is the default value. If you want a longer or shorter time slice, you can add the amount after the `DATE TIME` with `--slice_size <VALUE>`.

If you find the `GET` event, you may want to place that event into context by observing what occurred before and afterward:

```
psort -q --slice '2008-07-20 01:26:17' c:/tools/plaso/
export/files/jean.plaso -w c:/tools/plaso/export/files/
jeansliceoutput.csv
```

The command will create a `csv` file, which contains events 5 minutes before and 5 minutes after the timestamp placed in the CLI.

The final tool in the framework is `psteal`, which we will discuss next.

psteal

`psteal` is the final CLI command in the plaso framework. It combines the `log2timeline` and `psort` commands to extract and process events in a single step. It is very much the kitchen sink approach, or the "I want it ALLLLLL" approach, and it has a limited selection of modifiers when compared to the other CLI commands within the framework.

Once again, -h will provide you with a list of options for the command, which are displayed in the following screenshot:

```
c:\tools\plaso>psteal -h
usage: psteal [-h] [--troubles] [-V] [--preferred_year YEAR]
              [--process_archives] [--skip_compressed_streams]
              [--storage_file PATH] [--partitions PARTITIONS]
              [--volumes VOLUMES] [--credential TYPE:DATA]
              [--status_view TYPE] [--source SOURCE] [--data PATH]
              [--language LANGUAGE] [-z TIMEZONE] [-o FORMAT] [-w OUTPUT_FILE]
              [--fields FIELDS] [--additional_fields ADDITIONAL_FIELDS]
              [--buffer_size BUFFER_SIZE] [--queue_size QUEUE_SIZE]
              [--single_process] [--temporary_directory DIRECTORY]
              [--worker_memory_limit SIZE] [--workers WORKERS]

psteal is a command line tool to extract events from individual
files, recursing a directory (e.g. mount point) or storage media
image or device. The output events will be stored in a storage file.
This tool will then read the output and process the events into a CSV
file.
```

Figure 5.14 – psteal

At a minimum, specify the source and the output. The process will create the plaso database file and place it in the root of the plaso installation. This location allows you to perform additional tagging, filtering, or analysis after the command completes. The naming convention for the database file will be <timestamp>-<source>.plaso.

Here's the command. It creates a csv file that is almost 1 GB in size. However, if I change the output to xlsx, it reduces the size to 35 MB. So, keep in mind that you are processing and analyzing your datasets:

```
psteal --source C:/tools/plaso/image/jean.001 -o l2tcsv -w c:/
tools/plaso/export/files/jean.csv
```

I am using a relatively small forensic image of a 20 GB hard drive. Just imagine if you were using a 500 GB or a 1 TB hard drive and it has been active for an extended period.

Now that we have created our database file and have exported the datasets we find relevant to the investigation, what do we do now? It is time to analyze the datasets to find the evidence that will either approve or disapprove the allegation. The tools you use for analysis can simply be the spreadsheet reader of your favorite Office suite or a commercial open source tool designed for that specific purpose.

It is not possible to cover all the tool options that are available to an examiner in this book. I will highlight several options that are available and summarize the tools for you. Ultimately, the analysis of the data is where the examiner eyeballs the dataset and reviews the findings. Once again, it comes back to the verification/validation of your forensic tools to ensure they are providing accurate results.

Here are a few tools:

- **ELK stack**: This can be found at `https://www.elastic.co`. It is an acronym for three open source projects: Elasticsearch, Logstash, and Kibana. Elasticsearch is the search and analytical engine. Logstash is the data processor and ingest engine, while Kibana is the visualizer. You have the option to download the three engines and install them in the operating system of your choice. You have options for macOS, Windows, and Linux. There is also the option to pay for the cloud environment if you do not wish to host the systems within your environment.

- **TimelineMaker Pro**: This can be found at `www.timelinemaker.com`. It is a commercial product specifically designed for creating timeline charts. With this tool, you can import the CSV files created with the plaso framework.

- **TimeSketch**: This can be found at `https://github.com/google/timesketch`. It is an open source forensic timeline-analysis tool. It is Linux-based. I have installed it in a virtual environment so that I can use it as needed. It can also be worked on collaboratively by different members of your team. You can also import from a variety of plaso framework output options.

- **Aeon Timeline**: This can be found at `www.aeontimeline.com`. It is a commercial product specifically designed for creating visual timelines. It will allow you to view relationships among events. It was initially designed for authors, but it can also be used to analyze super timelines. You can import the CSV files created using the plaso framework.

- **Timeline Explorer**: This can be found at `ericzimmerman.github.io/#!index.md`. Timeline Explorer is an open source platform created by Eric Zimmerman, who wanted a tool to read MAC time and plaso-generated CSV files without the need to use Microsoft Excel. It is not designed to examine very large CSV files; in fact, Zimmerman recommends explicitly that it is best to open smaller, targeted timelines than one giant one.

Media analysis

There are several vectors that you can use timeline analysis on, such as network analysis, media analysis, software analysis, and hardware analysis. Network analysis is where you are analyzing log files, trace files, and the communication content between users and their devices. Media analysis is where you are analyzing physical storage devices such as hard drives, SSD drives, thumb drives, or optical storage disks. You will examine the content, allocated space, and slack space. When performing software analysis, you are reverse-engineering malicious code or analyzing the protection code for potential exports.

So, let's look at media analysis. The primary source of your digital investigation will be the forensic images of storage devices such as hard drives, SSDs, USB devices, optical disks, and mobile devices such as smartphones. Depending on your organization, you may be the person responsible for creating the forensic image, or the forensic image may be provided to you from another part of your organization. Remember, the forensic image is a bit for bit copy of the source device. In most cases, you do not want to use a backup as the source of your digital forensic investigation because a backup will not contain all of the information that is contained on the storage device.

The storage device may contain four different data types that you want to examine:

- **Allocated space**: This is the space on the storage device that a file occupies. The filesystem recognizes the storage space as being used.

- **Unallocated space**: This is the space on the storage device that is not occupied by a file. The filesystem recognizes the storage space as being available for use.

- **Slack space**: When the data is stored in a cluster; if the file does not completely fill a cluster, the remaining space not used by the file is referred to as slack space.

- **Bad blocks/sectors/clusters**: This is the space on the disk that has been marked bad by the filesystem because of a defect. It can also be used by a user to hide data from a casual inspection.

Brian Carrier describes the progression of media analysis as follows:

- **Disk**: Physical storage devices such as a hard disk drive, SSD, or flash media.

- **Volume**: A container comprising a single disk or multiple disks. You may find numerous volumes on a single disk or a volume may span across multiple discs. You may see the term "volume" interchangeably with the term "partition." Brian Carrier defines that a partition is restricted to a single physical disk, whereas a volume is a collection of one or more partitions.

- **Filesystem**: This is used within the boundaries of a volume and tracks file allocation and cluster use.

- **Data unit**: The smallest allocation unit available to the filesystem. In most cases, this will be clusters, or, in a UNIX-based system, it will be blocks.

- **Metadata**: This is the data about data. This includes the modified, accessed, and created date-time stamps, as well as any other information the filesystem and some applications will track about the file.

The goal of media analysis in your digital forensic investigation is to find relevant artifacts that will either prove or disprove the allegations you are investigating. As you conduct the digital forensic investigation, you may find artifacts that will direct your focus to other locations.

We will now discuss some different analysis techniques that you might use during your digital forensic investigation.

String search

A search method you might use during your digital forensic investigation is a string or byte search. This search technique is utilized when you have a keyword list of specific terms that you wish to search for. Most commercial and open source forensic tools allow for string searches and will search the allocated, unallocated, and file slack spaces. You can use specific words, symbols, or strings of letters as the search criteria. Generally, you will want to have some predefined keyword lists before you start your digital forensic investigation. Your keyword lists will fall into one of the following categories:

- **Generic keyword list**: This is a keyword list that you will use in every case. This list can also be further categorized by the subject of the investigation. For example, you may have a keyword list for digital forensic investigations into fraudulent activity and a different keyword list for a digital forensic investigation into illicit images.

- **Case-specific keyword list**: This is a keyword list that you will use for the specific digital forensic investigation. As you prepare to conduct your digital forensic investigation, you will identify keywords based on the participants, locations, and, sometimes, the slang used by the participants. For example, you could have keywords based on usernames, email addresses, physical addresses, phone numbers, credit card numbers, and more.

> **Note**
> You should avoid keyword terms that are generic or have additional meanings. For example, if you were investigating a homicide, the word "kill" seems to be a valid term to search for. Unfortunately, "kill" is also a term used in the programming language(s) you will find in a computer system. This will leave you with a large number of false positives. Ideally, the goal is to have the keyword list to help filter out non-pertinent data so that you can focus your efforts efficiently.

You may encounter different encoding schemes as you are conducting your searches on the forensic images. You may encounter the following encoding schemes:

- **American Standard Code for Information Interchange (ASCII)** is a character-encoding scheme based initially on U.S. English and is limited to 256-character codes.

- Unicode was developed to overcome the limitations of ASCII. Each character has a unique 2-byte value resulting in the ability to define over 65,000 characters.

While keyword searching can be very powerful, there is a downside to this, as it is very literal when searching for content based on the keyword. For example, if you search for a word, it will not find an alternative spelling, that is, if you are searching for ally, the filter will not find ally. Luckily, there is an alternative search methodology known as pattern matching/regular expressions.

A regular expression uses character strings to create a search pattern, and it will find all instances that match the pattern. Here are some common symbols and their meanings when used to create a regular expression.

- **The asterisk symbol (*)**: Match the preceding character(s) for X amount of time. For example, ca*t will cause positive hits for ct, cat, caat, and caaat.

- **The pound sign (#)**: This will match a number (0-9).

- **The backslash (\)**: The following character will be interpreted literally. \ . will be construed as a period.

- **Caret (^)**: Match the start of the text. For example, ^123 will cause the positive hits to start with 123.

- **The dollar sign ($)**: Match the end of the text. For example, 123$ will cause positive hits to end with 123.

- **Plus symbol (+)**: Repeat the preceding character(s) for one or more times. For example, ca+t will cause positive hits for cat, caat, and caaat.

- **Curly brackets {...}**: Repeat the preceding character(s) for X times (depending on the value in the bracket).

- **Brackets [...]**: This will match a single character in the brackets. For example, [b,c,d] will match on b, c, or d.

- **Brackets w/ ^ [^...]**: This will match any single character not in the brackets. For example, [^b,c,d] will match on any character other than b, c, or d.

- **Brackets (range) [..-..]**: This will match any character within the range. [0-9] will match any character from 0 to 9.

- **Dot (.):** The dot can take the place of any character.

- **Question mark (?):** The preceding character may/ may not be present. For example, `.e01?` will return `.e0 (x)` values. x shows it may find any value after `.e0`.

- **Pipe (|):** This matches any one-character set separated by the pipe (|) character. For example, `br (ead|ake|east)` will return matches for bread or brake or breast.

The following are some common examples of pattern matching that you may find helpful.

To search for an IP address, you can use the following regular expression:

```
\d{1,3}\.\d{1,3}\.\d{1,3}\.\d{1,3}
```

The `\d` specifies that the following will match on a digit (number). The curly brackets, `{1,3}`, indicate the number can be from one to three digits. `\.` is specifically looking for the `.` character. The `\d{1,3}` pattern then repeats an additional three times until it has the value for an IPv4 address.

To search for a US phone number, you can use the following expression:

```
((\(\d{3}\) )|(\d{3}-))?\d{3}-\d{4}
```

The `\(` will match the open bracket. `\d{3}` will match on a three-digit number. `\)` will match on the closed bracket. This pattern will give you the area code, `(###)`, in this format. The remaining regular expression will give you the first three digits, `\d{3}`, the dash, `-`, and the final four digits, `\d{4}`, of the US phone number. If the phone number is not formatted as `(###) ###-####` or `###-###-####`, you will not get a hit.

Regular expressions are a powerful tool, but they can also be very complicated to craft. I like to use the regular expression library (which can be found at `http://regexlib.com/Default.aspx`) to help me with my regular expression skills.

So, what happens when the user deletes a file or folder from the media? Let's discuss what happens when the file or folder is deleted next.

Recovering deleted data

When a file is deleted in the FAT filesystem, the data itself does not get changed. The first character of the directory entry will have it changed to a `xE5` and the file allocation table entries are reset to `x00`. When the filesystem reads the directory entries, and it encounters the `xE5`, it will skip that entry and start reading from the subsequent entries.

To recover deleted files, we need to reverse the process the filesystem used to delete the files. Remember, it has not changed the file contents; they still physically reside in their assigned clusters. We now need to reverse-engineer the deletion and recreate the file entry and the entries in the file allocation table. To do this, we need to find the first cluster of the file, the size of the file, and the size of the clusters in the volume:

```
E5 48 4F 52 54 20 20 20  54 58 54 20 18 6B B0 6D   åHORT   TXT .k°m
D3 4E D4 4E 00 00 E9 5E  D4 4E 08 00 27 00 00 00   ÓNÔN..é^ÔN..'...
```

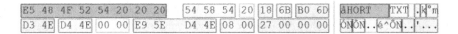

Figure 5.15 – Deleted entry

In the preceding screenshot, we have a directory entry showing that a file has been deleted. We see the `xE5` at the start of the directory entry. (This will require the use of a hex editor to make the changes.) Then, we have to determine the starting cluster, `x00 x08` (which is shown as `x08 x00`), which is cluster number `8`. To determine the file size, look at the last four bytes (remember that the FAT filesystem stores data in little endian, which means that the least-significant byte is on the left, so we would read that value as `x00 x00 x00 x27`, not as it is displayed, `x27 x00 x00 x00`), and when we convert the hexadecimal value to a decimal, we get the value of 39 bytes for the file size.

Now we have to determine how many sectors make up a cluster and what the sector size is. You will need to go to the boot record to get that information. The boot record shows that there are 512 bytes per sector, and there are 8 sectors per cluster, which gives us a cluster size of 4,096 bytes:

Bytes per sector	011	512	15
Sectors per cluster	013	8	114

Figure 5.16 – Boot record

This means that our file will only occupy a single cluster. We then go to the file allocation table and look at the entry for cluster 8 and see that it is zeroed out:

```
00 00 00 00 FF FF FF 0F  0B 00 00 00 0C 00 00 00
0D 00 00 00 0E 00 00 00  0F 00 00 00 10 00 00 00
```

Figure 5.17 – Deleted FAT

To recover the deleted file, perform the following steps:

1. You need to change the entry in the file allocation table from x0000 x0000 to xFFFF FFF8 or xFFFF FF0F. If this were a larger file, you would need to change the file allocation table entry to point to the next cluster until you reach the cluster that contains the end of the file. Should you find an entry marked as allocated before you reach the end of the file, you may be dealing with a fragmented file. Another possibility is when the clusters were made available for use when the file was deleted, the data from a new file was placed in the available space. This would cause the old data to be overwritten with the data from the new file.

2. The next step is to go back to the directory entry and replace xE5 with another character. When replacing the xE5 character of the filename in the directory entry, be careful not to guess what the character is. If you select the incorrect character, you could change the meaning or create a bias with the new filename, and that would be improper. I recommend that when you recover a deleted file, you replace that first character with an underscore or a dash so there is no misunderstanding about the filename.

When recovering a file with a long filename, it is important to relink the long filename to the short filename. This is because when the additional directories are created to accommodate the long filename, the system creates a checksum based on the data of the short filename. When you changed the xE5 value on the short filename entry, you also want to use the same replacement character for the subsequent xE5 entries for the long filename directory entries. The reason for linking the long filename to the short filename is that the short filename directory entry contains information such as the date and times, the starting cluster, and the file size.

As we discussed in *Chapter 4, Computer Systems*, when a file/directory is created on an NTFS volume, the system creates an entry in the $MFT file. The MFT record will contain the metadata about the file/directory; if the contents of the file are nonresident, then the $Bitmap file will be updated to show the clusters occupied by the file are allocated.

When a file/directory is deleted, then the sequence count in the MFT file record's header is incremented by one digit. The allocation status for the record will change from allocated to unallocated. If the file data is nonresident, the system will update the $Bitmap file to show the clusters occupied by the file are now unallocated.

Every MFT file entry will start with the file signature of file, which you can use as a search term to locate MFT file entries in unallocated space. Until the clusters containing the data on the disk are overwritten, we can recover the data.

If the MFT file record is unused, then you can reverse the steps and recover the file. You can decipher the file record, as we discussed in *Chapter 4, Computer Systems*. If the file is resident within the file record, you will recover the data when you retrieve the MFT file record. If the data is nonresident, then you will have to decipher the MFT file record to determine whether the data runs and identify the occupied clusters.

If the system has overwritten the MFT file record, then you cannot recover the deleted MFT file record data or any resident data. You may recover the nonresident data, but that will depend on the size of the files and the fragmentation. Once the MFT record has been overwritten, you will lose any information regarding the data runs and which clusters contain the data.

Summary

In this chapter, we discussed, in detail, timeline creation and timeline analysis with open source and commercial forensic tools. We took an in-depth look at utilizing the commercial forensic tool, X-Ways Forensics, and the open source plaso framework for `log2timeline`. We also touched upon using the kitchen sink approach or using a targeted examination of the dataset. Remember, we are not analyzing the contents of files, just the timelines associated with the files and other events contained within the operating system and filesystems.

In the next chapter, we will discuss the contents of files, specifically, Windows artifacts.

Questions

1. It is important for the examiner to know the time zone in which the evidence was collected.

    a) True

    b) False

2. You can do timeline analysis with X-Way Forensics when you create a(n) _____ list.

    a) Timeline

    b) Date/time

    c) Event

    d) Party

3. Plaso is a framework for how many tools?

    a) One

    b) Three

    c) Five

    d) Seven

4. `Pinfo` will give you what information?

    a) Information about the examiner

    b) Information about the database file

    c) Information about the forensic machine

    d) Information about the suspect

5. Log2timeline is a _____ -based tool.

    a) CLI

    b) GUI

    c) VFD

    d) XYZ

6. `psort` will give you the _____.

    a) Ability to sort

    b) Ability to filter

    c) Ability to connect

    d) All of the above

7. You can do a timeline analysis with an Excel spreadsheet.

    a) True

    b) False

Further reading

You can refer to the following links for more information on the topics covered in this chapter:

- *T. P. P. A. (2019, July 8). Plaso Documentation. Retrieved from The Plaso Project* :`https://buildmedia.readthedocs.org/media/pdf/plaso/latest/plaso.pdf`

- *Carvey, H. (2014). Windows forensic analysis toolkit: Advanced analysis techniques for Windows 8; Waltham, MA: Syngress.* Available at `https://www.abebooks.com/servlet/SearchResults?sts=t&cm_sp=SearchF-_-home-_-Results&an=&tn=Windows+forensic+analysis+toolkit&kn=&isbn=`

6
Windows Artifact Analysis

The world runs on the Microsoft Windows operating system, with Microsoft accounting for nearly 90 percent of the operating system market share (`https://netmarketshare.com/`). In my personal experience, I have examined far more Windows operating systems than any other operating system; macOS would be the next most common operating system with Linux running a distant third. While you have to be prepared to analyze all operating systems, whichever is the most common within the realm you are working in is where you should focus your attention.

This chapter will provide you with an understanding of the Windows operating system and the artifacts you may find. There are entire books written about the Windows operating system; this chapter's goal is to provide you with an understanding of the more common operating system artifacts you may encounter during your investigation. You will start by going through user profiles where most of the user data can be found. Then, we will have a look at the Windows Registry to find out about the Windows settings. You will also look at artifacts to determine the location of user's activities and will learn how to identify which USB devices were used on the system. We will cover all of this in the following topics:

- Understanding user profiles
- Understanding Windows Registry

- Determining account usage

- Determining file knowledge

- Identifying physical locations

- Exploring program execution

- Understanding USB/attached devices

An operating system manages the hardware resources and allows the user to run other applications that are essentially programs within the operating system environment. It can be a treasure trove of artifacts to recreate user or system activity at any given moment in time. When we discuss the Windows operating system, there are multiple versions that could be covered. At the time of writing, the current version of the Windows operating system is Windows 10. That does not mean every system you examine will have Windows 10 installed on it. In fact, it is possible that even in a corporate environment, you could still examine a Windows XP client, although Microsoft released it in 2001 and no longer supports it.

I will focus on Windows 7, 8, and 10 for the rest of this chapter. There may be references to Windows XP because of the legacy support Microsoft is offering to the operating system.

The first item I want to discuss is the different types of user profiles and where the user's data will be stored.

Understanding user profiles

When the Windows operating system is installed, it creates a default folder structure in which to store user and application data. Sometimes, just looking at the folder structure can tell you which version is or isn't installed.

When you are looking for user account profiles, the location can vary depending on the version of the operating system:

- `C:\Documents and Settings\%UserName%`: For Windows XP, WinNT, and Win2000

- `C:\Users\%UserName%`: For Windows Vista, 7, 8, and 10

When the user first logs on to the system, it will create a user profile. That profile will then be used for any subsequent logins and is now the user's environment for their activity on the system. Microsoft defines the different types of user profiles:

- **Local user profile**: This profile is created when the user logs on to a computer for the first time. You will find the profile stored on the hard disk. When changes are made to the profile, the changes will be specific to the user and stored on the local computer.

- **Roaming user profile**: This profile is an administrator-created, network-based profile. The profile will be downloaded to the localhost when the user logs in to the system. When any changes are made to the profile on the localhost, changes will also be made to the server copy when the user logs off from the localhost. This profile type removes the requirement on the part of the user to create a profile when they log on to different hosts on the network. (This will only be found in Enterprise environments.)

- **Mandatory user profile**: This profile is a profile created by the network administrators to lock users down to a specific set of settings when they use a host on the network. The user will not be allowed to make changes to the profile without the administrator's approval. Any changes made by the user to the environment of the localhost will be lost when the user logs off from the localhost.

- **Temporary user profile**: This profile is created when an error occurs when the system is loading the user's profile. When the user logs off, the profile is deleted. You will find the use of temporary profiles on computers running Windows 2000 and later.

Each user profile will have its own registry hive – `NTUSER.DAT` – and is mapped to the system registry key of **HKEY Current User** when the user logs in. This registry hive contains the user's preferences and configuration settings.

Each user profile contains the following folders:

```
\Users\$USER$\Documents
\Users\$USER$\Music
\Users\$USER$\Pictures
\Users\$USER$\Videos
```

The `AppData` folder is a hidden folder that contains user-specific preferences and profile configurations and is further divided into three subfolders:

```
\Users\$USER$\AppData
```

The `Roaming` folder contains data that can be synced within the server environment. Data such as web browser favorites or bookmarks will travel with the user as they log on to different workstations:

```
\Users\$USER$\AppData\Roaming\Microsoft\Windows\Cookies.
\Users\$USER$\AppData\Roaming\Microsoft\Windows\Network
Shortcuts
\Users\$USER$\AppData\Roaming\Microsoft\Windows\Printer
Shortcuts
\Users\$USER$\AppData\Roaming\Microsoft\Windows\Recent
\Users\$USER$\AppData\Roaming\Microsoft\Windows\SendTo
\Users\$USER$\AppData\Roaming\Microsoft\Windows\Start Menu
\Users\$USER$\AppData\Roaming\Microsoft\Windows\Templates
```

The `Local` folder contains data related to the installation of programs. It is workstation specific and will not sync with the server (in a server environment). Temporary files are also stored here:

```
\Users\$USER$\AppData\Local
\Users\$USER$\AppData\Local\Microsoft\Windows\History
\Users\$USER$\AppData\Local\Microsoft\Windows\Temporary
Internet Files
```

The `LocalLow` folder includes low-level access data, such as the temporary files of your browser when running in protected mode.

That completes our discussion on user accounts, so let's move on to the registry, which is the heart and soul of the Windows operating system.

Understanding Windows Registry

The Windows Registry is the very heart of the Windows operating system and will be the source of many of the artifacts we will discuss later in the chapter. I will provide a high-level view of the registry. If you want to dig deeper into the nuts and bolts of the registry, I highly recommend Harlan Carvey's book *Windows Registry Forensics – Advanced Digital Forensic Analysis of the Windows Registry*. Harlan Carvey is also the developer of the tool RegRipper, which is a tool we will use in this chapter.

What is the registry? Microsoft defines the registry as a central hierarchical database. This database is used to store configuration information about users, hardware devices, and applications.

But what does that mean for the forensic investigator? Windows continually references the information in the registry during operations. Information in the registry will contain profiles for each user, installed applications, different document types, and property settings for folders and application icons. The registry will also contain information about the hardware on the system, to include networking information such as the ports that are being used.

Wow. That was a mouthful, but in simple terms, the registry contains information about... almost everything on the computer system.

The components of the registry are found in the `%SystemRoot%\System32\Config` folder and are called hive files. You will find the `SAM`, `SECURITY`, `SOFTWARE`, and `SYSTEM` hives:

- The `SAM` hive is the Security Accounts Manager and contains login information about the users.

- The `SECURITY` hive contains security information and, potentially, password information.

- The `SOFTWARE` hive contains information about application information and the default Windows settings.

- The `SYSTEM` hive includes information on the hardware and system configuration.

There is an additional hive, `NTUser.dat`, which is stored in the root of the user profile. This hive contains information about user behavior and their settings.

Another file in the hive format is the `UsrClass.dat` file, which is found in the `\AppData\Local\Microsoft\Windows` folder of the user account. You will find information concerning **user access control** (**UAC**) configuration and information about the **graphical user interface** (**GUI**) display for the user experience.

The hive comprises subkeys that contain the **Value**, **Type**, and specific **Data** or settings being saved. This will give us a frame of reference as we explore the artifacts contained within the registry.

As you can see in the following screenshot, it is difficult to decipher the meanings of the subkeys and values and what they represent:

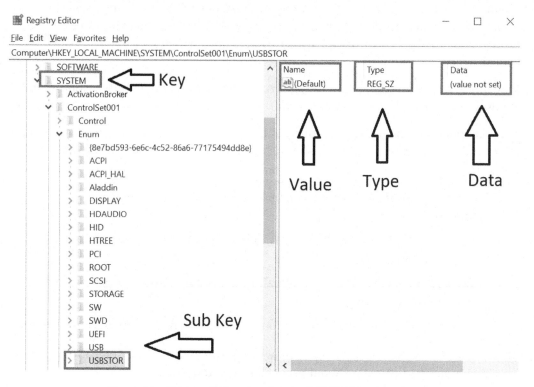

Figure 6.1 – Registry Editor showing the USBSTOR registry key

As we go through the artifacts, I will show you the view you will see with the Registry Viewer and the easier-to-read parsed version created by the forensic tools.

We will use some open source tools during this chapter:

- RegRipper (available for download from `https://github.com/keydet89/RegRipper2.8`), created by Harlan Carvey.

- Eric Zimmerman (whose work is available for download from `https://ericzimmerman.github.io/#!index.md`) has created several open source utilities to parse Windows artifacts.

There are several categories in which we look for artifacts. I like to use the SANS catalog descriptions of the artifacts, which can be found at `https://digital-forensics.sans.org/community/posters` and are listed as follows:

- Account usage
- File knowledge
- Physical location
- Program execution
- USB/drive usage
- Browser usage (which we will discuss in *Chapter 9*, *Internet Artifacts*)

With this understanding of the user profile, we will now discuss the artifacts that determine what actions are associated with the user accounts.

Determining account usage

Identifying the user behind the keyboard is one of the hardest things you have to do when conducting a digital forensic examination. You will have to parse through many artifacts to help make that determination. You will want to gather as much information about the user account in question and see whether you can relate it to the physical person. You will want to gain as much information about that user account and its activity as it relates to the matter you are investigating. We will now go over some artifacts from a Windows-based operating system that will help you make that determination and to identify that account activity starting with the user's last login or password change.

Last login/last password change

This following path will contain information about the user accounts on the system:

C:\windows\system32\config\ SAM\Domains\Account\Users

To navigate to the location that contains the user account information, I will use Eric Zimmerman's Registry Explorer. I have exported the registry hive files from the forensic image so that I can run Registry Explorer and RegRipper.

In the following screenshot, we can see that I have already opened the folder path and the subkeys, and within the Users subkey, there are folders with hexadecimal names and a folder entitled Names. Within the Names subkey, you see a listing of the accounts on the machine:

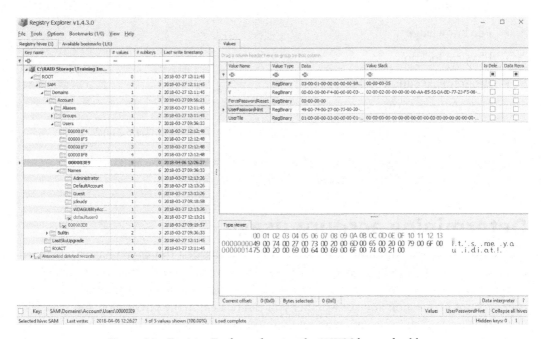

Figure 6.2 – Registry Explorer showing the USERS key and subkeys

It lists the names in English, so they are easily readable. Out of the six accounts being shown, one has been deleted (defaultuser0), and one has the username of jcloudy. The value for the jcloudy subkey will point to the subkeys with the hexadecimal values. Here, jcloudy points to x3E9.

In subkey x3E9, as shown in the following screenshot, I see that I have an **F** and a **V** value and below that, I can see information pertaining to the user's passwords:

	Value Name	Value Type	Data	Value Slack	Is Del...	Data Record...
	Drag a column header here to group by that column					
▼	🔎c	🔎c	🔎c	🔎c	■	■
▶	F	RegBinary	03-00-01-00-00-00-00-00-9A...	00-00-00-05	☐	☐
	V	RegBinary	00-00-00-00-F4-00-00-00-03...	02-00-02-00-00-00-00-00-AA-85-55-DA-BD-77-23-F5-08...	☐	☐
	ForcePasswordReset	RegBinary	00-00-00-00		☐	☐
	UserPasswordHint	RegBinary	49-00-74-00-27-00-73-00-20...		☐	☐
	UserTile	RegBinary	01-00-00-00-03-00-00-00-01...	00-00-00-00-00-00-00-00-00-00-00-00-00-00-00-00-...	☐	☐

Figure 6.3 – Registry subkey X3E9

To make it easier, we can run RegRipper and see whether we can get an easier-to-read output. An example of the output for the `jcloudy` account is as follows:

```
Username        : jcloudy [1001]
SID             : S-1-5-21-2734969515-1644526556-1039763013-1001
Full Name       :
User Comment    :
Account Type    :
Account Created : Tue Mar 27 09:18:58 2018 Z
Name            :
Password Hint   : It's me you idiot!
Last Login Date : Fri Apr  6 12:26:27 2018 Z
Pwd Reset Date  : Tue Mar 27 09:18:58 2018 Z
Pwd Fail Date   : Fri Apr  6 03:30:52 2018 Z
Login Count     : 23
  --> Password does not expire
  --> Password not required
  --|> Normal user account
```

Figure 6.4 – RegRipper output for the jcloudy account

RegRipper parses the data and presents it in an easy-to-read format. And we can see when the account was created, the password hint, the last time the user logged in, and the number of times the user has logged in to the system.

As you look at the username `jcloudy`, you can see the numerals `1001`, and below that, an entry marked `SID`.

SID is the **security identifier** used by the Windows operating system to identify objects within. This is how Windows addresses components internally. At the end of the SID is the **relative identifier** (**RID**), which is the last digits after the SID. For example, if you see `500` as the RID, that would identify the administrator account for that system. The guest account would have an RID of `501`. In this case, as shown in the following diagram, we see the RID of `1001`. This informs me that the `jcloudy` account is user-created, and is not an account created by the system through an automated process:

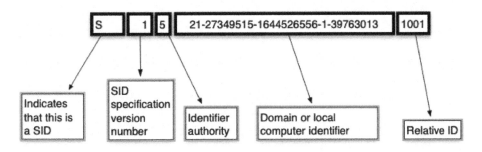

Figure 6.5 – Breakdown of the SID

When doing your exam, the most commonly looked at portion of the SID is the RID. We can associate the RID with a specific user account. As the user creates accounts on the system, the RID will increase by one digit. For example, we could have a user, user X, with an RID of 1005, and if I cannot find accounts 1001 through 1004, it is possible that someone/something deleted those user accounts.

We are going through the registry to find artifacts that support (or do not support) our hypothesis about what occurred. Another source of information to help determine what happened on the system is the event logs.

Windows categorizes events into three different classes:

- **System**: Information generated by the Windows operating system
- **Application**: Information generated by applications on the local machine
- **Security**: Information related to login attempts

In Windows Vista through Windows 10, we can find the event logs at the following path: C:\Windows\System32\winevt\logs

A common excuse that a user gives when they are accused of using the system for criminal or inappropriate reasons is that someone else had access to their system. **Remote Desktop Protocol (RDP)** is a way to access a host from another location. The security log will keep a record of any access using the RDP protocol. You will want to look for event ID numbers 4778 and 4779, which would show you when the service connected/reconnected and when it disconnected.

You can also search for the type of logon into the system. When we examine the security log for event ID 4624, this will tell us the day, time, username, and the means with which the login was successful. As you can see in the following screenshot of Event Viewer, you can use this application to review the exported log files. Once you have loaded the selected log file you want to examine, you can filter the results to only show the events that are relevant to your investigation:

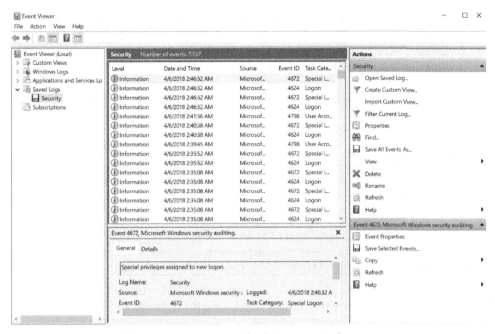

Figure 6.6 – Event Viewer displaying event information

The type of logon is also significant. Was the user sitting at the keyboard or did the user log in from a remote site? Event ID 4624 will identify the login type used by the user. In the following screenshot, you can see the output of Event Viewer showing when the user logged in and the login type. Here, it shows the user's login was type 2, which is "interactive":

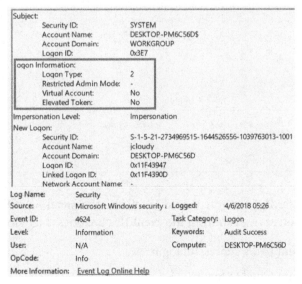

Figure 6.7 – Event Viewer showing the logon type

The following is a list from Microsoft of the other logon types you may encounter, together with their descriptions:

Logon Types	Description
Interactive	Logon to the local host by the user.
Network	A network logon to the local host by the user.
Batch	Allows processes to be started without user input.
Service	Automated process. No user input needed.
Unlock	The local host was unlocked via user input.
NetworkCleartext	Network logon to the local host by the user. The password was sent in cleartext to the authentication package. The password was then encrypted before it was sent on the network.
NewCredentials	The user account was duplicated and received new credentials for the network connection leaving the secure network.
RemoteInteractive	A logon to the local host by the user using a remote application.
CachedInteractive	A network logon to the local host by the user, using the network credentials on the local host.

You may also want to establish the attempted login events to determine whether an attacker compromised the account. The following event IDs will help you make that determination:

- 4624
- 4625
- 4634 | 4647
- 4648
- 4672
- 4720

Due to editorial concerns, I am not allowed to tell you the meaning of the event IDs. Some of the information you may glean from the event IDs includes the following:

- The user account had a successful login.
- The user account failed to log in.

- The user account successfully logged off from the localhost.

- The user account had a successful login using explicit credentials; for example, the command was `run as`.

- The user account had a successful login with elevated permissions; for example, an administrator account.

- The user successfully created a user account.

A full list of Microsoft Windows Event IDs can be found at `https://www.ultimatewindowssecurity.com/securitylog/encyclopedia/`.

If you see many failed logins or if a user was granted administrator rights when they usually do not possess superuser rights, these event ID clues provide you with additional investigative avenues to determine what occurred.

Now that we've examined the user's account activity, next we will discuss the artifacts associated with user account file access.

Determining file knowledge

Some incidents you investigate may deal with contraband images, stolen data, or unlawful access to data. You will have to determine whether the user had knowledge of the file(s) in question, or whether the file(s) existed on the user's system.

We will now talk about some artifacts you can find in the Windows operating system that will help you make that determination.

Exploring the thumbcache

A thumbcache is a database of thumbnail images created when the user is using Windows Explorer in a thumbnail view. Depending on the size of the thumbnail, you may have multiple databases with the same image, but with different sizes. It depends on the view the user selected while in Windows Explorer. The existence of an image found in the database is not substantial proof that the user knew the image was on the system. A thumbnail can be added to the cache without the knowledge of the user. The thumbcache can be found in the user's profile at the following path: `AppData\Local\Microsoft\Windows\Explorer`.

Your commercial forensic tools will process the thumbcache with no issues. If you want to use an open source utility, you can use Thumbcache Viewer (which can be downloaded at `https://thumbcacheviewer.github.io/`).

The following is an example of the output of Thumbcache Viewer:

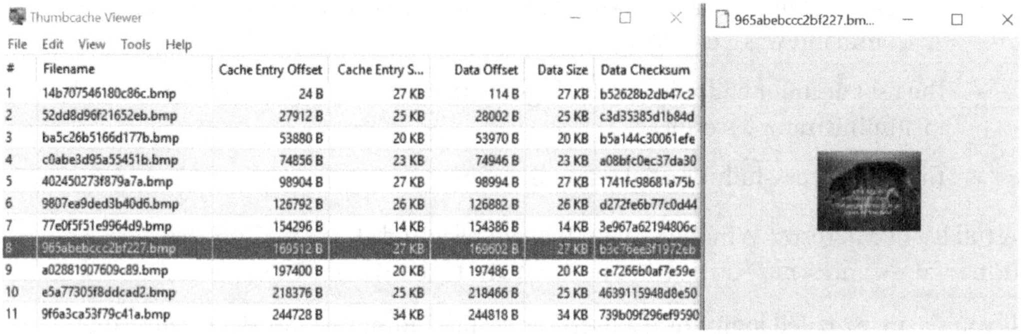

#	Filename	Cache Entry Offset	Cache Entry S...	Data Offset	Data Size	Data Checksum
1	14b707546180c86c.bmp	24 B	27 KB	114 B	27 KB	b52628b2db47c2
2	52dd8d96f21652eb.bmp	27912 B	25 KB	28002 B	25 KB	c3d35385d1b84d
3	ba5c26b5166d177b.bmp	53880 B	20 KB	53970 B	20 KB	b5a144c30061efe
4	c0abe3d95a55451b.bmp	74856 B	23 KB	74946 B	23 KB	a08bfc0ec37da30
5	402450273f879a7a.bmp	98904 B	27 KB	98994 B	27 KB	1741fc98681a75b
6	9807ea9ded3b40d6.bmp	126792 B	26 KB	126882 B	26 KB	d272fe6b77c0d44
7	77e0f5f51e9964d9.bmp	154296 B	14 KB	154386 B	14 KB	3e967a62194806c
8	965abebccc2bf227.bmp	169512 B	27 KB	169602 B	27 KB	b3c76ee3f1972eb
9	a02881907609c89.bmp	197400 B	20 KB	197486 B	20 KB	ce7266b0af7e59e
10	e5a77305f8ddcad2.bmp	218376 B	25 KB	218466 B	25 KB	4639115948d8e50
11	9f6a3ca53f79c41a.bmp	244728 B	34 KB	244818 B	34 KB	739b09f296ef9590

Figure 6.8 – Thumbcache Viewer output

As you can see, the thumbnail does not have the same filename as the source image. To identify the original file that was used to create the thumbnail, we need to look in the Windows Search Indexing database, `Windows.edb`, which can be found at the following path:

```
C:\ProgramData\Microsoft\Search\Data\Applications\Windows\
Windows.edb
```

You will need an additional tool to find the information about the image used to create the thumbnail. You can use ESEDatabaseView (located at `https://www.nirsoft.net/utils/ese_database_view.html`).

The thumbnail name is `96 5a be bc cc 2b f2 27`, which is made up of hexadecimal characters. We need to reverse the values to search the database, so we will want to search for `27 f2 2b cc bc be 5a 96`. The information we are looking for is located in different locations depending on the operating system.

- On a Windows 7 system, you want the table called `SystemIndex_0A`.
- On a Windows 8/10 computer, you want the table called `SystemIndex_PropertyStore`.

Once we input the hexadecimal values into the filter, it reduces the data to a single row:

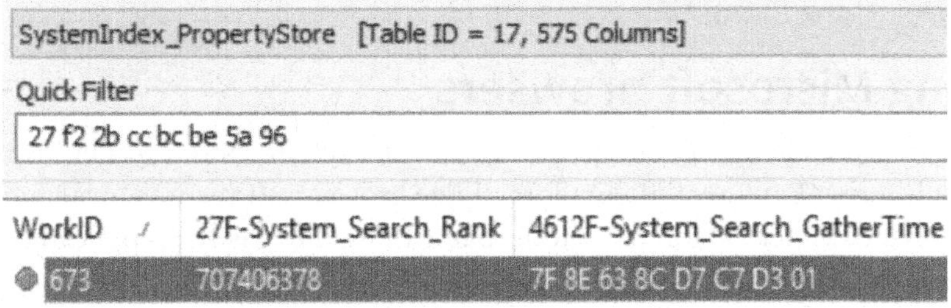

WorkID	27F-System_Search_Rank	4612F-System_Search_GatherTime
673	707406378	7F 8E 63 8C D7 C7 D3 01

SystemIndex_PropertyStore [Table ID = 17, 575 Columns]

Quick Filter

27 f2 2b cc bc be 5a 96

Figure 6.9 – Filtered database results

In the following screenshot, we can see that the file came from the desktop of the user jcloudy. The name of the image is MyTiredHead.jpg:

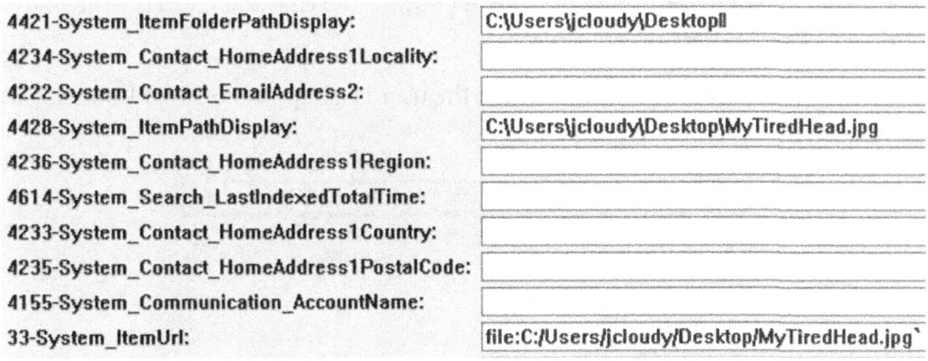

4421-System_ItemFolderPathDisplay:	C:\Users\jcloudy\Desktop\
4234-System_Contact_HomeAddress1Locality:	
4222-System_Contact_EmailAddress2:	
4428-System_ItemPathDisplay:	C:\Users\jcloudy\Desktop\MyTiredHead.jpg
4236-System_Contact_HomeAddress1Region:	
4614-System_Search_LastIndexedTotalTime:	
4233-System_Contact_HomeAddress1Country:	
4235-System_Contact_HomeAddress1PostalCode:	
4155-System_Communication_AccountName:	
33-System_ItemUrl:	file:C:/Users/jcloudy/Desktop/MyTiredHead.jpg`

Figure 6.10 – Filename display in the database

In the following screenshot, we can verify that this is the correct file when we look in the System_ThumbnailCacheID field:

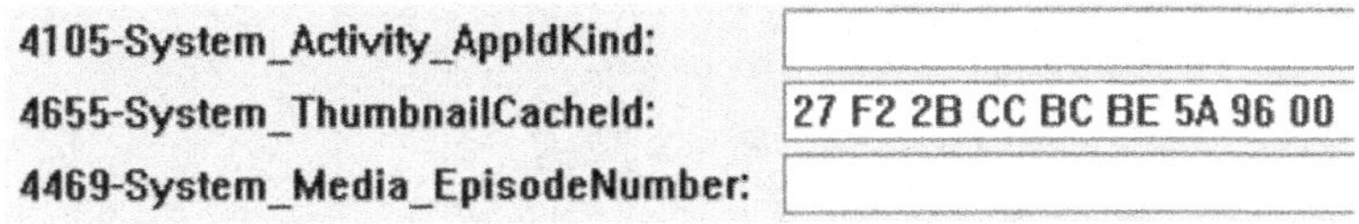

4105-System_Activity_AppIdKind:	
4655-System_ThumbnailCacheId:	27 F2 2B CC BC BE 5A 96 00
4469-System_Media_EpisodeNumber:	

Figure 6.11 – Thumbnail name in the database

That will complete the discussion on the thumbcache. We will now explore the artifacts created by the Edge/Internet Explorer/File Explorer browsers.

Exploring Microsoft browsers

Microsoft uses the same method to record a user's file activity and internet history as they use with the Internet Explorer/File Explorer/Edge browsers. It records local and remote file access. Most commercial forensics tools parse these files easily. Depending on the version, the history file will be located in the following areas:

- IE6-7: `%USERPROFILE%\LocalSettings\History\History.IE5`

- IE8-9: `%USERPROFILE%\AppData\Local\Microsoft\WindowsHistory\History.IE5`

- IE10-11: `%USERPROFILE%\AppData\Local\Microsoft\Windows\WebCache\WebCacheV*.dat`

In the following screenshot, you can see that the user is using version 10/11 because of the existence of the `WebCacheV01.dat` file:

Name ▲	Type
.. = Windows (351)	
. = WebCache (24)	
V01res00001.jrs	jrs
V01res00002.jrs	jrs
V01.chk	chk
V01.log	edblog
V0100016.log	edblog
V0100017.log	edblog
V0100018.log	edblog
V01tmp.log	edblog
WebCacheV01.dat (1)	edb
WebCacheV01.jfm	jfm
V01.log	log
V01tmp.log	log
WebCacheV01.dat	dat
WebCacheV01.dat	hxx
V01.chk	chk
V01.chk	chk

\Users\jcloudy\AppData\Local\Microsoft\Windows\WebCache

Figure 6.12 – File Explorer showing the WebCacheV01.dat file

The `.dat` file is an ESE database. If you want to use a single-use forensic tool, you can export the `.dat` file out of the forensic image and view it with an open source forensic tool such as ESEDatabaseView (located at `https://www.nirsoft.net/utils/ese_database_view.html`). You will want to navigate to the `Containers` table. The following screenshot is the output from X-Ways Forensics:

30.03.18 04:29:48	Visited: jcloudy@file:///C:/Users/jcloudy/Desktop/Larry%20King_%20Time%20to%20Repeal%20the%20'Poorly%20Written'%20Second%20Amendment.html
27.03.18 09:51:12	Visited: jcloudy@file:///C:/Users/jcloudy/OneDrive/Getting%20started%20with%20OneDrive.pdf
06.04.18 03:55:00	Visited: jcloudy@file:///C:/Users/jcloudy/Desktop/AMEN.pdf
03.04.18 06:11:21	Visited: jcloudy@file:///C:/Users/jcloudy/Desktop/The%20Cloudy%20Manifesto.docx
31.03.18 04:19:35	Visited: jcloudy@file:///C:/Users/jcloudy/Desktop/DemLogic.jpg
06.04.18 08:29:08	Visited: jcloudy@file:///C:/Users/jcloudy/Downloads/DemGun.jpg

Figure 6.13 – X-Ways display of the contents of the WebCache

As you can see, we have a date and timestamp and the file path of the file that was viewed. We have one offline HTML file (the first line), which was located on the user's desktop. We see the user opened two PDF files, two JPEG files, one HTML file, and one DOCX file.

There are additional artifacts that show that a user account accessed a file, which we will discuss next.

Determining most recently used/recently used

An **MRU (Most Recently Used)** is a list of recently used files that are stored in the user's NTUSER.DAT hive. When you open an application, and you see the history list of prior files that have been used by the application, you are looking at an MRU. There are a lot of MRU lists stored within the registry file. We will go over some more common locations.

OpenSavePidlMRU from the user's NTUSER.DAT file tracks the last 20 files opened/saved via the Windows Common Dialogue (these are the commonly encountered **Open/Save As** dialog boxes). In the following example, we can see the last 20 files used by the user:

```
OpenSavePidlMRU\*
LastWrite Time: Fri Apr 6 03:56:31 2018
Note: All value names are listed in MRUListEx order.
 My Computer\CLSID_Desktop\LeftUsesBoycotts.pdf
 My Computer\CLSID_Desktop\AMEN.pdf
 My Computer\CLSID_Desktop\UKknifeBan.pdf
 My Computer\CLSID_Desktop\SelfDefenseisMurder.pdf
 My Computer\C:\Users\jcloudy\Desktop\Cloudy thoughts (4apr).
docx
 My Computer\CLSID_Desktop
 My Computer\CLSID_Desktop\Operation 2nd Hand Smoke.pptx
 My Computer\CLSID_Desktop\The Cloudy Manifesto.docx
 My Computer\C:\Users\jcloudy\Desktop\The Cloudy Manifesto.docx
 My Computer\CLSID_Desktop\Huckleberry.png
 My Computer\CLSID_Desktop\DemLogic.jpg
 My Computer\CLSID_Desktop\RedGuns.jpg
```

Another key to look at is `NTUSER.DAT\Software\Microsoft\Windows\CurrentVersion\Explorer\RecentDocs`.

This key contains a list of files that were executed/opened by the user through the Windows Explorer application. You will also have subkeys, based on file extensions, listing those files that were executed/opened. The system will store the entries in chronological order of when the files were executed/opened by the user.

When you are looking at the last entry/modified time of the key, it will correspond to the last entry in the list. This key will keep track of the last 150 files that were opened/executed. The following is the output of the key (I am only showing the top-level entries for brevity's sake):

```
recentdocs v.20100405
(NTUSER.DAT) Gets contents of user's RecentDocs key
RecentDocs
**All values printed in MRUList\MRUListEx order.
Software\Microsoft\Windows\CurrentVersion\Explorer\RecentDocs
LastWrite Time Fri Apr 6 12:27:08 2018 (UTC)
 37 = rootkey.csv
 36 = Hardware and Sound
 10 = DemGun.jpg
 34 = LeftUsesBoycotts.pdf
 33 = AMEN.pdf
 12 = Planning.docx
 32 = UKknifeBan.pdf
 31 = SelfDefenseisMurder.pdf
 30 = Cloudy thoughts (4apr).docx
```

This is an example of the file extension subkeys I described earlier, and it shows the recently used CSV files:

```
Software\Microsoft\Windows\CurrentVersion\Explorer\RecentDocs\.
csv
LastWrite Time Fri Apr 6 12:27:08 2018 (UTC)
MRUListEx = 0
 0 = rootkey.csv
```

This is an example of the file extension subkeys I described earlier, and it shows the recently used DOCX files:

```
Software\Microsoft\Windows\CurrentVersion\Explorer\RecentDocs\.
docx
LastWrite Time Thu Apr 5 08:32:48 2018 (UTC)
```

```
MRUListEx = 0,3,1,2
 0 = Planning.docx
 3 = Cloudy thoughts (4apr).docx
 1 = AIRPORT INFORMATION.docx
 2 = The Cloudy Manifesto.docx
```

This is an example of the file extension subkeys I described earlier, and it shows the recently used HTML files:

```
Software\Microsoft\Windows\CurrentVersion\Explorer\RecentDocs\.
html
LastWrite Time Fri Mar 30 04:32:26 2018 (UTC)
MRUListEx = 1,0
 1 = Cubs' Anthony Rizzo Praises Parkland Kids, Says 'It's too
Easy to Get a Gun'.html
 0 = Larry King_ Time to Repeal the 'Poorly Written' Second
Amendment.html
```

There is also an additional subkey, \Folder, that lists when the user opened folders on the system, which is shown as follows:

```
Software\Microsoft\Windows\CurrentVersion\Explorer\RecentDocs\
Folder
LastWrite Time Fri Apr 6 12:27:08 2018 (UTC)
MRUListEx = 4,5,1,3,2,0
 4 = Downloads
 5 = Hardware and Sound
 1 = The Internet
 3 = OneDrive
 2 = System and Security
 0 = CloudLog (D:)
```

Entries of potential interest include OneDrive and Cloudlog. If I am looking for evidence of specific files, the subject may store the data in cloud storage. When I see artifacts showing the use of cloud storage, it provides additional locations that I will have to locate and acquire the digital evidence to continue my digital forensic investigation.

As you can see, these are great artifacts to see what files were accessed by the user, but what happens when the user deletes a file? That leads us on to our next topic, the Recycle Bin.

Looking into the Recycle Bin

The `Recycle Bin` is Microsoft's effort to protect the user from their own actions. It provides an intermediary step for when a user deletes a file. Windows will move the file into a holding area known as the `Recycle Bin`.

The `Recycle Bin` is a hidden folder stored in the root directory of every fixed disk on the system. The folder name is `$Recycle.Bin`. On an NTFS formatted disk, there will be sub-folders named with the user's SID. These sub-folders are created whenever a user logs on to the system for the first time:

```
$Recycle.Bin
├──S-1-5-18
└──S-1-5-21-2734969515-1644526556-1039763013-1001
```

When a user deletes a file, the original file gets renamed and becomes part of a set of `Recycle.Bin` files. The system will rename the original file with `$R` and then six random alphanumeric characters for the filename. The file extension will remain the same. The system will create a second file, which will start with `$I` and then have the same six alphanumeric characters that the `$R` file has. The `$I` file will also have the same file extension as the `$R` file.

The `$I` file will track the time of deletion and the path to the original file location:

```
Size: 4.9 MB
Moved to recycle bin: 04/05/2018 02:20:17 +0
C:\Users\jcloudy\Desktop\Larry King_ Time to Repeal the 'Poorly
Written' Second Amendment_files
```

As you can see, we have the size of the original file, when the user deleted it, and the original path that includes the filename.

If a user deletes a directory, you will still have the `$R` and `$I` files for the directory. The `$R` file will contain all the subdirectories and all the files with the original names, as shown in the following screenshot:

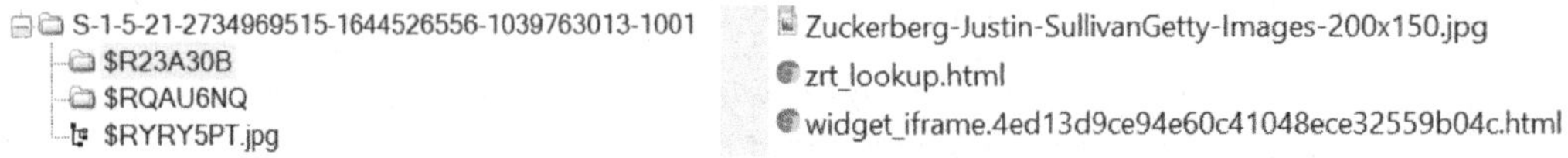

Figure 6.14 – Deleted directory

It is possible for the user to empty the `Recycle Bin`. When that occurs, the filesystem updates the fact that the clusters are now available for use. Until the system overwrites the data, you may recover data from the unallocated clusters. Just be aware that the `$I` (on an NTFS volume) will be resident data in the MFT. NTFS is very efficient in reusing the file entries in the MFT, so it's challenging to recover the information in the $I file.

If the `Recycle Bin` is emptied, you may find other artifacts referencing the file. That brings us to our next topic, link (LNK) files.

Understanding shortcut (LNK) files

A `.lnk` file is used by the Windows operating system as a shortcut or link to files, applications, or resources. It is a simple, easy-to-use method for users to gain access to frequently used documents or applications. The link file will contain useful information for the digital forensic investigator, including the following:

- File MAC times
- File size
- File path
- Volume details

This information will remain even if the destination file has been deleted. The system will create a link file every time the file is double-clicked or when using the **File Open** dialog box. These link files will be stored in the `Recent` folder located at the following path:

```
%Username%\Appdata\Roaming\Microsoft\Windows\
```

Most commercial forensic tools can analyze the link files. An open source option is Eric Zimmerman's LECmd tool (which can be found at `https://ericzimmerman.github.io/`).

When we analyze the contents of the link file, we can see a large amount of information that could be helpful to the digital forensic investigator:

```
Target attributes    A
Target file size     172684
Show Window          SW_NORMAL
Target created       03/30/2018 02:29:57 +0
Last written       04/04/2018 04:59:32 +0
Last accessed       04/04/2018 04:59:32 +0
ID List            Desktop\AIRPORT INFORMATION.docx C=03/30/2018
02:29:58
```

```
              M=04/04/2018 04:59:34 Size=172684
Volume type        Fixed
Volume serial      0xAA920881
Volume name
Local path         C:\Users\jcloudy\Desktop\AIRPORT INFORMATION.
docx
Relative path      ..\..\..\..\..\Desktop\AIRPORT INFORMATION.
docx
Working directory    C:\Users\jcloudy\Desktop
Known Folder       Tracking false
Host name          desktop-pm6c56d
Volume ID          {BC7539BE-7B5B-4E04-9F8D-1C0D9B3AFF21}
Object ID          {30D25F11-3208-11E8-9B15-28E347017777}
MAC Address        28 E3 47 01 77 77
Timestamp          03/27/2018 21:45:39 +0, Seq: 6933
PROPERTYSTORAGE      {446D16B1-8DAD-4870-A748-402EA43D788C}
Size        29
propID         104
```

We can see that the destination file is a Microsoft Word document that was stored on the user's desktop. When we look at the field ID list, we also can see the internal metadata (MAC values) of the file. This can be very important when trying to tie knowledge of the file to a specific user. We can also see the date/time when the link file itself was created. Additional information is the volume type/serial number and hostname, which allow us to tie this link file to the specific location of the destination file. Be aware that this is an option that can be turned off by the user or systems administrator. Another artifact similar to LNK files is the JumpList.

Deciphering JumpLists

JumpLists were introduced with Windows 7 and are very similar to the `Recent` folder (which we discussed with LNK files). It allows the user to access frequently used/recently used files from the Windows taskbar. Even if the user clears out the `Recent` folder, it will not clear out the information stored in the JumpLists. JumpLists can be found at the following paths:

```
%UserProfile%\AppData\Roaming\Microsoft\Windows\Recent\
Automaticdestinations
%UserProfile%\AppData\Roaming\Microsoft\Windows\Recent\
CustomDestinations
```

There are two types of JumpLists:

- Automatic – system-created. Records information about file usage.

- Custom – application-created. Records task-specific information about the application.

In the following screenshot, you can see the `AutomaticDestinations` folder, and inside the folder will be files containing the JumpLists:

Figure 6.15 – JumpList display

The system names the JumpLists based on their JumpLists IDs. For example, in the preceding screenshot, we see **5d696d521de238c3.automaticDestinations-ms**. A search of the JumpLists ID list (which can be found at `https://community.malforensics.com/t/list-of-jump-list-ids/158`) shows that this is the JumpLists ID for the Google Chrome browser.

The following is the information contained in the `ms` file. You can see that the user was using Chrome to view PDF files and offline HTML files. It also contains the date/time the user opened the files:

```
7 04/06/2018 03:56:32 +0 C:\Users\jcloudy\Desktop\
LeftUsesBoycotts.pdf
6 04/06/2018 03:55:00 +0 C:\Users\jcloudy\Desktop\AMEN.pdf
5 04/05/2018 05:51:41 +0 C:\Users\jcloudy\Desktop\UKknifeBan.
pdf
4 04/05/2018 05:48:40 +0 C:\Users\jcloudy\Desktop\
SelfDefenseisMurder.pdf
3 03/30/2018 04:32:25 +0 C:\Users\jcloudy\Desktop\Cubs' Anthony
Rizzo Praises Parkland Kids, Says 'It's too Easy to Get a Gun'.
html
2 03/30/2018 04:29:48 +0 C:\Users\jcloudy\Desktop\Larry King_
Time to Repeal the 'Poorly Written' Second Amendment.html
1 03/27/2018 09:51:18 +0 C:\Users\jcloudy\OneDrive\Getting
started with OneDrive.pdf desktop-pm6c56d
```

Most commercial forensic tools will parse out the JumpLists. An open source option is Eric Zimmerman's JumpList Explorer (located at `https://ericzimmerman.github.io/`). JumpLists are artifacts for files; the next artifact will show which folders the user accessed.

Opening shellbags

Shellbags are a set of registry keys that remember the size and location of the folders and libraries that the user has accessed via the GUI. You may find artifacts showing user interaction with network devices, removable media, or encrypted containers.

You will find them in a registry hive called `USRCLASS.DAT.`, which is located in the users, `AppData\Local\Microsoft\Windows` folder.

Most commercial forensic tools will parse out the shellbags from the `USRCLASS.DAT` file, but the presentation of the artifact will be different. For an open source alternative, I like to use Eric Zimmerman's Shellbag Explorer.

In the following screenshot, you can see the graphical representation of the folders the user accessed via the Windows GUI. This screenshot is taken from Shellbag Explorer:

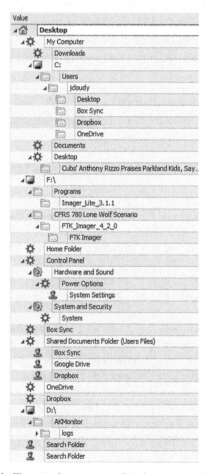

Figure 6.16 – Shellbag Explorer – a graphical representation of shellbags

You cannot determine whether the user accessed any files from within the folder through this artifact. What this artifact shows is that the user accessed the folder. As I look at the display, I see that the user was using three cloud storage services. We have seen prior artifacts for Box Sync and Dropbox, but this is the first reference I have seen regarding Google Drive.

In the following output from RegRipper, we can see the access date and timestamps and the date/time of the first access:

```
Name: Google Drive
Absolute path: Desktop\Shared Documents Folder (Users Files)\
Google Drive
Key-Value name path: BagMRU\7-1
Registry last write time: 2018-04-05 02:05:13.581
Target timestamps
Created on: 2018-03-28 00:43:24.000
Modified on: 2018-03-28 00:43:24.000
Last accessed on: 2018-03-28 00:43:24.000
Miscellaneous
Shell type: Users Files Folder
Node slot: 14
MRU position: 1
# of child bags: 0
First interacted with: 2018-03-28 00:43:25.373
```

This artifact is important if the subject states that they did not know about a file/folder location. This artifact is created by the user's actions. The next artifact can also be used to show user knowledge of a file.

Understanding prefetch

Prefetch is a feature Microsoft introduced to enhance the user experience with the Windows operating system. It allows faster response times by preloading data into the RAM in anticipation of its demand by the user or system. You will find the prefetch files at the following path:

```
%WINDOWS%\PREFETCH
```

The files will have a file extension of `.pf`. The prefetch file will contain information about the executable file it is associated with, such as the list of files used by the executable, the number of times the executable was run, and the last date/time when the executable was run.

Most commercial forensic tools will parse out the prefetch files. For an open source option, you can use NirSoft's `WinPrefetchViewtool` (located at `https://www.nirsoft.net/utils/win_prefetch_view.html`).

In the following screenshot, we are looking at the output of `WinPrefetchView`. You can see the date and timestamp and the process path of the executable (Be aware that due to the method with which the system monitors the prefetch files, you may have to subtract 10 seconds from the created/modified times to get an accurate time.):

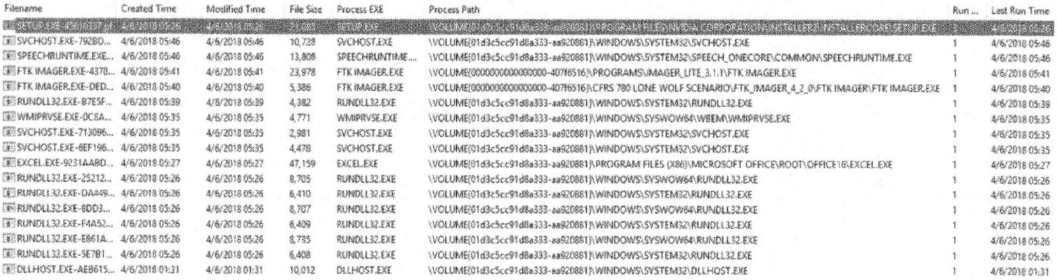

Figure 6.17 – Prefetch files displayed by WinPrefetchView

By using these artifacts, you can determine which applications are being used by the user, which may lead to the discovery of hidden partitions, mobile devices, encrypted containers, or cloud storage.

As operating systems change or are updated, the artifacts may move or be removed. You will have to stay current as changes become known. We will now look at artifacts that help us determine the physical location of the system.

Identifying physical locations

Knowing the physical location of the system may help you prove or disprove the allegations against the subject you are investigating. There was an investigation into a compromise of the organization's network. A former employee was the suspect in the attack because of the threats they made when they were sacked. When the suspect was interviewed, he denied being in the area and stated he was out of state. A judge authorized a search warrant for the suspect's mobile device and laptop computer. When conducting the forensic analysis of the laptop, it was found to have been recently restored to a new version of the operating system. There were also artifacts in the unallocated space that led us to believe the device had been wiped. (All available sectors were overwritten with hexadecimal 00 characters). The suspect had not tampered with the mobile device, and we were able to analyze the device. We were able to map out the Wi-Fi hotspots the device had accessed in the immediate neighborhood during the timeframe the suspect was allegedly out of state. When confronted with the digital evidence, the suspect confessed and admitted he forgot about his mobile device and that it was automatically connecting to Wi-Fi hotspots.

We will now talk about some artifacts you can look at in a system to help determine its physical location at the time of the incident.

Determining time zones

Time zone information on the system allows you to have a starting point with which to correlate activity that is recorded with the date/time that the incident occurred. All the internal date and timestamps will be based on the time zone information recorded in the registry. We can find the time zone information within the system hive. We can find the key at the following path:

```
SYSTEM\CurrentControlSet\Control\TimeZoneInformation
```

This will give us the following output, courtesy of RegRipper:

```
-------------------------------------------
timezone v.20160318
(System) Get TimeZoneInformation key contents
TimeZoneInformation key
ControlSet001\Control\TimeZoneInformation
LastWrite Time Tue Mar 27 09:56:27 2018 (UTC)
  DaylightName  -> @tzres.dll,-111
  StandardName  -> @tzres.dll,-112
  Bias        -> 300 (5 hours)
  ActiveTimeBias -> 240 (4 hours)

  TimeZoneKeyName-> Eastern Standard Time
-------------------------------------------
```

Tzres.dll is the time zone resource DLL. You have the fields of Bias and ActiveTimeBias, which show the values of 300 and 240, respectively, which is the number of minutes offset from GMT. And then you have the time zone common name, which in this case is Eastern Standard Time.

Time zones are not always accurate – the user has the ability to set the time zone to the zone of their choice. The next artifact we will examine may help in locating a physical location.

Exploring network history

Knowing which networks, be they wired or wireless, the suspect has connected to might give you location information about their whereabouts at the time in question. You will find the relevant information in the Software hive or an XML document managed by the operating system. The Wi-Fi document will be found at the following path:

```
C:\ProgramData\Microsoft\Wlansvc\Profiles\Interfaces
```

This directory contains subfolders (using the GUID naming convention) for each interface. The XML document will contain the **SSID (Service Set Identifier)** of the networks the interface has connected to. The following output is consistent with the information you would find in the XML document:

```
<WLANProfile xmlns='http://www.microsoft.com/networking/WLAN/
profile/v1'>
<name>Net 2.4</name>
<SSIDConfig>
<SSID>
<hex>4E657420322E34</hex>
```

```
<name>Net 2.4</name>
<MSM>
<security>
<authEncryption>
<authentication>WPA2PSK</authentication>
<encryption>AES</encryption>
```

As you can see, the SSID of the network is Net 2.4 and it is using
WPA2PSK authentication.

If you go to the registry location, you will find sub hives that will contain networking
information such as the Profiles subkey, which gives us additional information about
the wireless network(s) the subject connected to:

```
SOFTWARE\Microsoft\Windows NT\CurrentVersion\NetworkList
```

The following is the RegRipper output of the networklist sub hive:

```
Launching networklist v.20190128
(Software) Collects network info from Vista+ NetworkList key
Microsoft\Windows NT\CurrentVersion\NetworkList\Profiles
Net 2.4
 DateLastConnected: Fri Mar 30 17:09:01 2018
 DateCreated    : Tue Mar 27 05:15:58 2018
 DefaultGatewayMac: 5C-8F-E0-2A-1C-68
 Type        : wireless
Nla\Wireless
Net 2.4
```

The registry hive gives us a little bit more information, including the MAC address date
and timestamp timestamps of when the last connection was made. There is also an
additional log file we can examine: the WLAN event log.

Understanding the WLAN event log

Microsoft Windows also keeps an event log of wireless connections. The log can be found
at the following path:

```
C:\windows\System32\winevt\Logs\Microsoft-Windows-WLAN-
AutoConfig%4Operational.evtx
```

This log contains SSID information, MAC addresses, and the date and timestamps of the connection. The following event ID numbers may be pertinent to your investigation:

- `11000`
- `8001`
- `8002`
- `8003`
- `6100`

Due to editorial concerns, I am unable to tell you what the codes indicate. In general, the codes will tell you the following:

- Whether there is a wireless network association
- Whether there is a connection to a wireless network
- Whether there is a failed connection to a wireless network
- When the system is disconnected from a wireless network

> **Note**
>
> Everything you ever wanted to know about Microsoft Windows can be found at `https://docs.microsoft.com/en-us/`.

The following output is consistent with what you will see in the event log:

```
3/27/2018 12:15:58 +0
Microsoft-Windows-WLAN-AutoConfig
EventID: 11000
Computer: SYSTEM
Adapter=Broadcom 802.11n Network Adapter DeviceGuid={4B0AE068-
B350-4BD4-85AB-77E0E581863}
LocalMac=EC:0E:C4:20:7F:0E
SSID=Net 2.4 BSSType=Infrastructure Auth=WPA2-Personal
Cipher=AES-CCMP OnexEnabled=0 IhvConnectivitySetting=
ConnectionId=0000000000000002
```

This is an `11000` event ID, which is the start of a wireless connection. So, based on this specific artifact, you can articulate that a connection was made to the wireless network `Net 2.4` on March 27, 2018, at 12:15:58 (GMT) by the computer `SYSTEM`.

If you know where the wireless network Net 2.4 is located, you can associate this computer with that physical location.

Next, we will discuss the artifacts that allow us to determine whether the user executed a specific program.

Exploring program execution

Program execution artifacts indicate programs or applications that were run on the system. The user could cause the execution, or it could be an autostart/run event managed by the system. Some categories overlap with the file knowledge category we discussed earlier in the chapter. I am not going to re-examine those specific artifacts in this section. Just be aware that the artifacts from recent apps, JumpLists, an MRU, and prefetch files will also contain information about program/application activity.

Determining UserAssist

UserAssist is a registry key in the user's NTUSER.DAT file and can be found at the following path:

```
NTUSER.DAT\Software\Microsoft\Windows\Currentversion\Explorer\
UserAssist
```

The key tracks the GUI-based applications that were launched in the system. The system encodes the data in the key with ROT 13 encoding. RegRipper will decode the data automatically. The following represents the output you will see from RegRipper:

```
UserAssist
Software\Microsoft\Windows\CurrentVersion\Explorer\UserAssist
LastWrite Time Tue Mar 27 09:19:59 2018 (UTC)
{CEBFF5CD-ACE2-4F4F-9178-9926F41749EA}
Fri Apr 6 12:40:38 2018 Z
 F:\CFRS 780 Lone Wolf Scenario\FTK_Imager_4_2_0\FTK Imager\FTK
Imager.exe (1)
Fri Apr 6 12:27:04 2018 Z
 {7C5A40EF-A0FB-4BFC-874A-C0F2E0B9FA8E}\Microsoft Office\Root\
Office16\EXCEL.EXE (1)
Fri Apr 6 08:26:06 2018 Z
 Microsoft.Office.OneNote_8wekyb3d8bbwe!microsoft.onenoteim (3)
Thu Apr 5 02:32:31 2018 Z
 Microsoft.Office.WINWORD.EXE.15 (2)
Thu Apr 5 02:05:01 2018 Z
 {6D809377-6AF0-444B-8957-A3773F02200E}\Box\Box Sync\BoxSync.
exe (2)
```

As shown in the preceding output, you can see the date and timestamp of the last execution and the path of the executable. The number in parentheses at the end indicates the number of times the user/system has activated the executable. Next, we will discuss the Shimcache, which also contains information about executed programs.

Exploring Shimcache

This is the default location of the Shimcache: `SYSTEM\CurrentControlSet\Control\Session Manager\AppCompatCache`.

The Shimcache is used to track compatibility issues with executed programs. Some information that is stored in this cache is as follows:

- File path
- `$Standard` Information Attribute Modify Time
- The update time of the Shimcache

The following represents the output you will see from RegRipper:

```
shimcache v.20190112
(System) Parse file refs from System hive AppCompatCache data
*** ControlSet001 *
ControlSet001\Control\Session Manager\AppCompatCache
LastWrite Time: Tue Mar 27 21:45:28 2018 Z
Signature: 0x34
C:\Windows\system32\MRT-KB890830.exe Tue Mar 27 09:38:12 2018 Z
C:\Windows\system32\attrib.exe Fri Sep 29 13:41:33 2017 Z
C:\Program Files\NVIDIA Corporation\DRS\DBInstaller.exe Tue Mar
14 14:07:18 2017 Z
C:\Program Files (x86)\Common Files\Microsoft Shared\Source
Engine\OSE.EXE Sat Mar 3 12:03:10 2018 Z
C:\Users\jcloudy\AppData\Local\Microsoft\OneDrive\Update\
OneDriveSetup.exe Tue Mar 27 09:21:57 2018 Z
```

The artifacts found in Shimcache can provide supporting evidence to the other artifacts found throughout the system, that is, the registry, event logs, filesystem, and so on.

Sometimes, the user will have programs or files contained within a portable device. The next set of artifacts will deal with the use of USB devices.

Understanding USB/attached devices

There are several security risks associated with a USB device. They are small, portable, high-capacity storage devices that can be used to exfiltrate data from an organization, or they can be used to deliver malware to an organization to compromise its security protocols. As a digital forensic investigator, you will want to know whether there were any USB devices attached to the host you are examining. We will now talk about some Windows system artifacts that will allow you to identify USB device usage on the host.

We will now look at the results for two registry keys. The first key can be found at the following path:

```
SYSTEM\CurrentControlSet\Enum\USB
```

This registry key identifies the USB devices attached to the system, as shown in the following output:

```
usbdevices v.20140416
(System) Parses Enum\USB key for USB & WPD devices

VID_0781&PID_5580
LastWrite: Tue Mar 27 09:22:21 2018
SN : AA010215170355310594
LastWrite: Tue Mar 27 12:13:16 2018

VID_0781&PID_5580
LastWrite: Tue Mar 27 09:22:21 2018
SN : AA010603160707470215
LastWrite: Tue Mar 27 21:45:44 2018
```

We can see there were two USB devices attached to the system at different times. We have different volume serial numbers and the last write times from when the system accessed the devices. The volume serial number found in the registry is not the physical device serial number.

> **Note**
> Devices that do not have a unique volume serial number will have an & in the second character of the volume serial number.

The next registry key you want to look at is the following:

```
SYSTEM\CurrentControlSet\Enum\USBSTOR
```

When we look at the values in USBSTOR, we get some additional information about the devices, including the commercial name of the device. We also confirm the serial numbers of the devices with these two entries in the SYSTEM hive:

```
usbstor v.20141111
(System) Get USBStor key info
USBStor
ControlSet001\Enum\USBStor

Disk&Ven_SanDisk&Prod_Extreme&Rev_0001 [Tue Mar 27 09:22:21
2018]
S/N: AA010215170355310594&0 [Tue Mar 27 12:11:44 2018]
Device Parameters LastWrite: [Tue Mar 27 12:11:42 2018]
Properties LastWrite : [Tue Mar 27 09:16:45 2018]
FriendlyName : SanDisk Extreme USB Device

S/N: AA010603160707470215&0 [Tue Mar 27 09:22:21 2018]
Device Parameters LastWrite: [Tue Mar 27 09:22:21 2018]
Properties LastWrite : [Tue Mar 27 09:23:58 2018]
FriendlyName : SanDisk Extreme USB Device
```

In the MountedDevices key in the SYSTEM hive, which can be found in SYSTEM\MountedDevices, we can map the USB device(s) via the serial number to a drive letter on the system:

```
mountdev v.20130530
(System) Return contents of System hive MountedDevices key
MountedDevices
LastWrite time = Tue Mar 27 09:22:21 2018Z

Device: _??_USBSTOR#Disk&Ven_SanDisk&Prod_Extreme&Rev_0001#A
A010603160707470215&0#{53f56307-b6bf-11d0-94f2-00a0c91efb8b}\
DosDevices\D:\??\Volume{3869c27a-31b8-11e8-9b12-ecf4bb487fed}

Device: _??_USBSTOR#Disk&Ven_SanDisk&Prod_Extreme&Rev_0001#A
A010215170355310594&0#{53f56307-b6bf-11d0-94f2-00a0c91efb8b}\
DosDevices\E:\??\Volume{5c3108bf-31c0-11e8-9b10-806e6f6e6963}
```

When we analyze the data, we can see that two USB devices (serial numbers
AA010215170355310594 and AA010603160707470215) were connected to the
system. One was recognized as the D: drive and the second device was recognized as the
E: drive.

Does the question remain as to which user account was responsible for the USB device
usage? To determine the answer to that question, we would have to take the GUID from
each of the USB devices and compare them to the user's NTUSER.DAT file. The GUIDs we
are searching for are 3869c27a-31b8-11e8-9b12-ecf4bb487fed and 5c3108bb-
31c0-11e8-9b10-806e6f6e6963.

RegRipper will also analyze the NTUSER.DAT file and give us the information about the
devices that were used and associated with the user's account:

```
mp2 v.20120330
(NTUSER.DAT) Gets user's MountPoints2 key contents

MountPoints2
Software\Microsoft\Windows\CurrentVersion\Explorer\MountPoints2
LastWrite Time Fri Apr 6 12:35:08 2018 (UTC)
Remote Drives:

Volumes:
Fri Apr 6 12:35:08 2018 (UTC)
  {76d45981-0000-0000-0000-100000000000}
Tue Mar 27 21:45:54 2018 (UTC)
  {3869c27a-31b8-11e8-9b12-ecf4bb487fed}
Tue Mar 27 09:32:09 2018 (UTC)
  {09931f21-7faf-44a9-81d8-1e73c14b9eaf}
  {5c3108bb-31c0-11e8-9b10-806e6f6e6963}
```

As you can see, we find both GUIDs in the registry entry and this shows when the devices
were last mounted. So we can now say that a specific USB device was used on the system
while the jcloudy account was logged in.

Summary

In this chapter, we have discussed how to locate artifacts on a Microsoft Windows-based operating system to determine the subject's culpability in the matter being investigated. You have learned about the different categories of artifacts and what actions of the user/system they represent. Using the knowledge you have gained from this chapter will allow you to quickly determine which accounts were active during the timeframe you are investigating and whether there was a removable storage device involved for the incident under investigation. You have learned about the artifacts to analyze in determining whether a user had knowledge of a specific file or application that was located on the system. We have used several commercial and open source forensic tools to access the artifacts. You now know how to find and analyze digital evidence found on a Microsoft Windows-based operating system.

The next chapter will deal with memory forensics.

Questions

1. Where would you find the registry files?

    a. `%SystemRoot%\System32\Config`

    b. `%SystemRoot%\System32`

    c. `%SystemRoot%\\Config\System32`

    d. `%SystemRoot%\System64\Config`

2. When examining log files, which event ID identifies a successful logon?

    a. 4624

    b. 4625

    c. 4672

    d. 4642

3. A thumbcache is a _____.

    a. Database of toenail images

    b. Database of thumbnail images

    c. Database of deleted thumbnail images

    d. Database of deleted images

4. The user can use Internet Explorer/Edge to view files.

    a. True

    b. False

5. Which of the following will you find in a link (LNK) file?

    a. Volume serial number

    b. Router name

    c. Date of deletion

    d. Volume details

6. Which of the following Microsoft Windows operating systems uses JumpLists?

    a. Windows 98

    b. Windows ME

    c. Windows 7

    d. Windows 2000

7. In which registry hive would we find artifacts relating to USB devices?

    a. NT USER.DAT

    b. SYSTEM

    c. SOFTWARE

    d. SECURITY

The answers can be found in the rear of the book under *Assessments*.

Further reading

Refer to the following links for more information on topics covered in this chapter:

- Altheide, C., Carvey, H. A., and Davidson, R. (2011). *Digital forensics with open source tools*. Amsterdam: Elsevier/Syngress (available at `https://www.amazon.com/Digital-Forensics-Open-Source-Tools/dp/1597495867`)

- Carvey, H. A. (2005). *Windows forensics and incident recovery*. Boston: Addison-Wesley (available at `https://www.amazon.com/Digital-Forensics-Open-Source-Tools/dp/1597495867`)

- Bunting, S. (2012). *EnCase computer forensics: the official EnCE: EnCase certified examiner; study guide*. Indianapolis, IN: Wiley (available at `https://www.amazon.com/EnCase-Computer-Forensics-Official-EnCE/dp/0470901063`)

7

RAM Memory Forensic Analysis

RAM is a vital source of digital evidence that, historically, has been neglected and ignored. As our knowledge of digital evidence grew, examiners began to realize the source of potential digital evidence that existed in RAM. Ultimately, you have an additional multi-gigabyte source of information that needs to be examined and may contain digital artifacts that do not exist in the traditional locations of the system.

In this chapter, we will cover the fundamentals of memory. We will then look at the different sources of memory and learn to capture RAM using RAM capture tools. By the end of this chapter, you will be able to understand the various methods and tools that can process volatile memory.

We'll be covering the following topics in this chapter:

- Fundamentals of memory
- Random access memory
- Identifying sources of memory
- Capturing RAM
- Exploring RAM analyzing tools

Fundamentals of memory

What information does **random access memory (RAM)** contain? It will give you the information about the current running state of the system before you shut it down. It will contain information about any running programs; these could be legitimate processes, and it could contain running malware processes as well. If attackers have compromised the host, the malware may be a resident in the RAM.

You will also find information related to network connections the host has with other peers. This could be a legitimate use of peer-to-peer file sharing, or it could show a link to the attacker's host. These connections are breadcrumbs for you to follow if you are investigating a network intrusion or suspect someone may have compromised the host. The user could also be sharing illicit images, and the connection to other computers will give you leads for you to follow and to investigate additional users for the same crime.

If the user is using cloud services, we may never find the data they are creating on the physical disk in the system. We may only see the evidence of the data being hosted in the cloud in the form of RAM.

RAM is the kitchen table of the computer system. Any action the user/system takes within the system will access the RAM. Every mouse click and every keyboard button that's pushed will be processed through the RAM, and you can recover entire files, passwords, and the text that was placed into the clipboard. All of these are potential sources of digital evidence. Sometimes, you can recover the encryption keys for closed encrypted containers that have been created by the user.

In 2004, Rajib K. Mitra was convicted of jamming police radios. The investigation resulted in the seizure of multiple pieces of digital evidence. The lead detective, Cindy Murphy, learned in 2009 that it was possible to recover encryption keys that may have existed only in RAM. Detective Murphy was able to go back and reexamine the evidence and was able to identify the encryption keys Mitra had used to secure his encrypted container. When Detective Murphy opened the encrypted container, she found many illicit images, which led to Mitra being convicted of the possession of the images.

How is analyzing RAM different from analyzing a hard drive? RAM is a snapshot of a live running system, whereas a hard drive examination is static. We have shut the system down, and we are examining data on the physical device. RAM is much more transient, and if you were to take a forensic image of RAM at two different points of time, you will get different results. Capturing the data in RAM will lead to the loss of potential evidence. You are changing evidence when you collect RAM.

So, let's talk about what RAM is.

Random access memory?

RAM is used to temporarily store working data/code on an active computer system. Unlike on traditional storage devices, that is, a hard drive, data can be read/written on RAM at extremely fast speeds. Current technology allows the RAM chips to be created around an integrated circuit chip with metal oxide semiconductor cells. The data stored within the RAM chips is considered to be volatile. We lose volatile data when the computer system is no longer powered on. This is a significant reason the *pull the plug* tactic when responding to a scene involving activated computer systems is no longer recommended.

You may run into two different types of RAM: **static RAM (SRAM)** and **dynamic RAM (DRAM)**. SRAM is considered faster and more efficient with respect to energy use, whereas DRAM is cheaper to produce than SRAM. You will typically find SRAM being used as cache memory for the CPU, and DRAM chips being used for memory chips for the computer system.

The following is a representation of a DRAM chip you may come across in your investigations:

Figure 7.1 – DRAM image

Do not confuse RAM with **read-only memory (ROM)**. ROM permanently stores data within the memory chips and is not volatile.

Consider the following: a 32-bit Microsoft Windows-based computer system has a limitation of 4 GB of RAM, while a 64-bit Microsoft Windows-based computer system has a limitation of 128 GB of RAM. That is a considerable amount of potential evidence that, historically, has not been analyzed.

For the CPU to access the data/execute code being stored in the memory chips, there must be a unique location identifier to that data; that is, an address. When we start examining raw memory dumps, we will be dealing with the physical address, which is an offset of the memory dump.

Data stored in RAM is stored in pages that are 4 kilobytes in size, and as the system processes add/read data to the pages in RAM, they are utilizing virtual addressing.

All the operating systems access RAM in the same general manner. Let's talk about some concepts that are common to an operating system:

- **Privilege separation**: Privilege determines what a user, user account, and the process is allowed to access. It is a form of access control and when used by the operating system, it helps provide system stability by isolating users and the CPU kernel's actions. The operating system operates in trusted mode, that is, kernel mode, while the user applications operate in untrusted mode, that is, user mode, when executing commands in the system.

- **System calls**: To access resources controlled by the operating system's kernel, the user application must request access. This is done through a system call to the kernel. It is a bridge between the application and the operating system to allow the untrusted mode to become trusted for a specific instance.

- **Process management**: Program code is executed in memory. The operating system is responsible for managing the processes. Current operating systems operate as multi-programming systems, which allows for multiple processes to be executed simultaneously. As we analyze the memory dumps, we are looking at which processes were being executed at the time of capture and analyzing the data that was being stored within RAM.

- **Threads**: A process can have multiple threads. It is the basic unit of using the system's resources, such as CPU. When we analyze the memory dumps, we are looking for the processes timestamps and starting addresses, which will help identify the code in the process.

The contents of RAM may include artifacts of what is or has occurred on the system. This can include the following:

- Configuration information
- Typed commands
- Passwords
- Encryption keys
- Unencrypted data
- IP addresses
- Internet history
- Chat conversations

- Emails

- Malware

As you can tell, the potential to acquire significant evidence is enhanced with the collection of RAM. Where do we find data that is stored in RAM? There are several different sources, all of which we will discuss next.

Identifying sources of memory

What happens if you are not the investigator on the scene when the digital evidence is collected in the RAM, and they do not collect volatile data? Is it possible to still access the RAM, despite having the system shut down? While you cannot analyze the RAM, it is possible to examine other sources may contain the same data that was stored in the RAM. This option may not always be viable, depending on the specific set of circumstances surrounding the seizure of the digital evidence.

You need to know that there are potential additional sources that will contain the same or similar data that was in RAM. They are as follows:

- **Hibernation file (hiberfill.sys)**: Hibernation is the process of powering down the computer while still maintaining the current state of the system. In Windows, the RAM is compressed and stored in a `hiberfill.sys` file. This will allow the system to power down completely, but when the system is reactivated, the contents of the `hiberfill.sys` file will be placed back into RAM.

> **Note**
>
> If you are examining a laptop, hibernation is usually initiated by closing the laptop. In a desktop, this will be user-initiated. The file header for the `hiberfill.sys` file can be hibr, HIBR, wake, or WAKE. When the system is repowered, the header of the file is zeroed out. The `hiberfill.sys` file is a compressed file and will have to be decompressed before you can analyze it.

When analyzing the `hiberfill.sys` file, the last modification date/timestamp will show when the contents of RAM was added to the file.

> **Note**
>
> Another option if you are on scene and cannot do a live capture of the RAM can be to place the system into hibernation, which will then create the `hiberfill.sys` file where the current state of the system is saved.

- **Pagefile (pagefile.sys)**: Paging is a method of storing/retrieving data being used in the RAM chips with a virtual memory file stored on a traditional storage device. While not as fast as using RAM alone, it allows programs to exceed the capacity of the physical memory. When using paging, the system will transfer data in pages. The data stored in the pagefile is typically the least requested data being used in memory. When the requests for that data are processed, it then places the data back into the physical memory.

> **Note**
>
> In the Windows operating system, the paging file, `pagefile.sys`, is stored at the root of the operating system volume. Be aware that the user can change this location. Typically, the page file can be one to three times larger than the amount of physical memory on the system.

- **Swapfile (swapfile.sys)**: With the release of Microsoft Windows 8, Microsoft introduced the `swapfile.sys` file. It is very similar to the page file we just discussed, but with some differences. The Swapfile was created so that the operating system can use it for paging operations with suspended Metro/modern Windows applications. When the application is suspended, the system will write the application data in its entirety into the swap file. This frees up space in the physical memory, and when the application is resumed, it moves the data back into physical memory.

- **Crash dump (memory.dmp)**: If you have used any version of Microsoft Windows, you might have experienced a system crash or a **blue screen of death** (**BSoD**). When that occurs, it may create a dump of memory to store information about the state of the system at the time of the crash.

Depending on the settings, you may get one of the following:

- **Complete memory dump**: The data contained within the physical memory. (Not very common because of issues with the capacity of the physical memory chips.)
- **Kernel memory dump**: Will only contain pages of data that were in kernel mode.
- **Small dump files**: Contains information about running processes/loaded drivers at the time of the crash.

The `SYSTEM` hive will contain the key to determine which memory dumps may exist on the system you are examining. The key you'll want to explore is as follows:

```
SYSTEM\CurrentControlSet\Control\CrashControl\CrashDumpEnable
```

The dump files will be in a proprietary format and will need a third-party tool to convert them (available at https://www.comae.com). So far, we have discussed the locations that will provide sources of RAM. Ultimately, you will want to capture the data within the RAM chips, which is our next topic.

Capturing RAM

When the decision is made to capture the RAM from the system, several factors need to be considered before moving forward. The most significant issue is that you will be changing the state of the system when you collect the volatile data.

The **Scientific Workgroup on Digital Evidence (SWGDE)** has explored the collection of volatile data and offers the following considerations:

- The application used to collect the data in memory will overwrite some contents of the memory.
- The larger the tool and associated files are, the more data it overwrites.
- The system may load the USB device driver into memory.
- The system may load the USB device driver into the registry.
- The application that's used to collect the data in memory will show up in some **Most Recently Used (MRUs)**.

There is the potential that the collection of RAM may cause a system lockup or instability in the system. The digital forensic investigator must be aware of how the tool being used may affect different operating systems.

After calculating the risk versus the reward, you have decided to go forward and collect the contents of the RAM. What do you need to accomplish this task? You have to decide which tool works best in the environment that you will create the memory dump from. One consideration regarding your tool selection will be how big of a footprint the tool will leave on the system.

Preparing the capturing device

To successfully image the RAM, you will need three things:

- A capturing device (such as a USB device)
- Access to the system
- Administrator privileges

> **Note**
> Remember that the amount of RAM installed on the system will dictate the size of your external storage device. If the system has 16 GB of RAM, your external storage device will need to be greater than 16 GB. The memory dump will be the same size as the amount of installed RAM.

You will want to prepare your external storage device before responding to the scene. Your device should be formatted as an NTFS partition. This will alleviate any file size issues you might encounter if the device were formatted in FAT 32.

We will now discuss some tools you can use to create a raw forensic image of the RAM.

Exploring RAM capture tools

I am going to briefly discuss some tools that you can use to capture RAM. There are additional commercial and open source tools available. We could write an entire book (and there are some) about some tools that are used for memory forensics. The goal here is to give you an overview and the skills necessary to accomplish a successful memory dump, but be aware that you can go into much greater detail than I will go into in this chapter.

The following tools are all open source and freely available.

Using DumpIt

DumpIt (available at `https://www.comae.com`) was originally developed by MoonSols. Comae now maintains the project. It is a combination of `Win32dd` and `Win64dd` in one executable. No options are asked of the end user. This tool is fast, small, and portable. It leaves the least significant form of footprint on the RAM.

DumpIt is the simplest of all the tools to use. Once you have created your external device and have responded to the scene, you need to follow these steps:

1. Insert your thumb drive into the target host.

2. Type `cmd` (as shown in the following screenshot):

Figure 7.2 – Search bar

3. Right-click on **Command Prompt** so that you can run it as an administrator (as shown in the following screenshot):

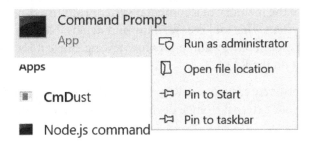

Figure 7.3 – Image administrator

4. Once Command Prompt comes up, navigate to the folder on your USB device that contains the executable. You will then type in the cmd command and execute it.

5. The system will then present you with a screen showing the amount of physical memory and the amount of space on the device. It will then ask you if you want to continue. Select yes, as shown in the following screenshot:

```
P:\Dumpit>dumpit
    DumpIt - v1.3.2.20110401 - One click memory memory dumper
    Copyright (c) 2007 - 2011, Matthieu Suiche <http://www.msuiche.net>
    Copyright (c) 2010 - 2011, MoonSols <http://www.moonsols.com>


    Address space size:      34883502080 bytes (  33267 Mb)
    Free space size:        125729640448 bytes ( 119905 Mb)

    * Destination = \??\P:\Dumpit\FORENSIC-20190820-202139.raw

    --> Are you sure you want to continue? [y/n] _
```

Figure 7.4 – DumpIt screen

6. The amount of RAM installed will dictate the amount of time it will take to create the dump of the RAM. Once the process has been completed, the program will notify you that it was successful:

```
* Destination = \??\P:\Dumpit\FORENSIC-20190820-202139.raw

--> Are you sure you want to continue? [y/n] y
+ Processing... Success.
```

Figure 7.5 – Dumpit successful

DumpIt is not the only tool available. There are additional open source alternatives, such as FTK Imager, which we will discuss next.

Using FTK Imager

FTK Imager Lite (available at `http://accessdata.com`) is a GUI-based utility that allows a user to dump the memory of a computer system running either a Windows 32-bit or 64-bit operating system. This tool is easy to use and deployable on a thumb drive. This tool also allows us to mount binary dump files for viewing. Since it is GUI-based, it leaves a significant footprint on the RAM.

FTK Imager is also relatively easy to use. Remember that it is GUI-based, so as you launch the executable from your external storage device, it will overwrite more data in memory than a CLI-based tool.

Once you have responded to the scene, you will need to do the following:

1. Insert your thumb drive into the target host.

2. If **File Explorer** does not automatically launch, use the Windows + *E* keyboard shortcut to open it.

3. Launch FTK Imager, left-click on **File**, and select **Capture Memory...**, as shown in the following screenshot:

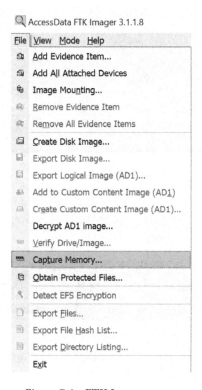

Figure 7.6 – FTK Imager menu

4. The **Memory Capture** window will appear as shown in the following screenshot. Here, you can fill in the destination path:

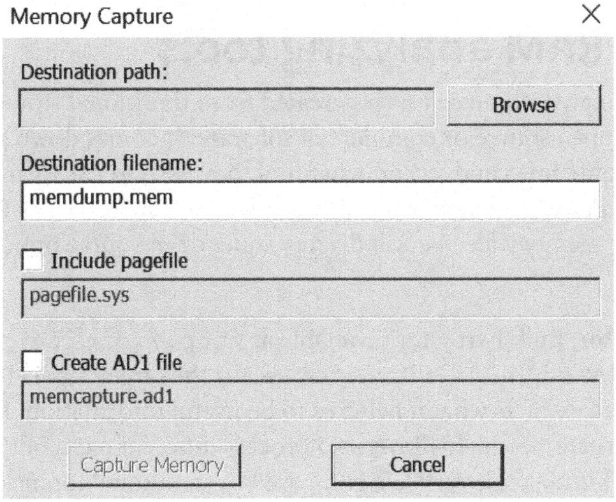

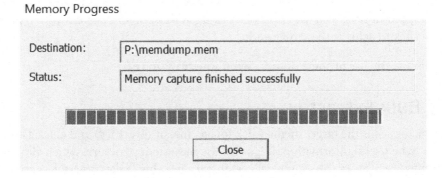

Figure 7.7 – FTK Imager memory capture

However, ensure that you select your external storage device.

5. You also have the option to choose the `pagefile`. There is no reason not to. Check that box and then left-click on **Capture Memory**.

6. Once the tool has finished, you will receive the success notification, as shown in the following screenshot. This will store the memory file on your external storage device:

Figure 7.8 – FTK Image successful

No matter which tool you used to collect the memory, once you have collected it, you need to get a hash value of the file you just created. You do not want to use the suspect system because any commands you issue will change the state of the evidence. You will want to use your forensic laptop or your forensic workstation at your laboratory to generate the hash value.

Now that you have created a memory dump of the RAM, what tools will you use to analyze it? Let's talk about some tools that can be used to analyze RAM.

Exploring RAM analyzing tools

Just like when we analyze forensic images created from traditional storage devices, you have the choice of open source or commercial software. It comes down to the examiner's preferences (and sometimes budget) on what tool they wish to use to analyze the dataset. We will go over some available tools, but this is not an all-inclusive list. Most commercial tools will analyze a memory file; we will discuss some open source options that are available here:

- **Bulk Extractor**: Bulk Extractor (available at `http://digitalcorpora.org/downloads/bulk_extractor`) scans the target media (disk image, file, directory) and extracts what it believes to be useful information. It ignores the filesystem structure, which allows it to process different parts of the source dataset in parallel. This makes it very fast compared to traditional forensic tools. As Bulk Extractor finds data it believes to be relevant, it creates a histogram of the artifacts.

- **Volatility**: Volatility (available at `https://www.volatilityfoundation.org`) is an open source framework for incident response and malware analysis. Volatility supports a wide variety of memory dumps from multiple operating systems. Volatility is very powerful and has numerous plugins.

- **VOLIX II v2**: VOLIX II (available at `https://www.fh-aachen.de/en/people/schuba/forschung/it-forensik/projekte/volixe`) is a GUI frontend for Volatility. It allows you to combine commands to enhance usability and speed. It saves you the effort of working at the CLI and enables you to point and click to achieve the same result.

We will discuss the use of some of these open source options.

Using Bulk Extractor

Bulk Extractor scans the target media (disk image, file, or directory) and extracts what it believes to be useful information. It ignores the filesystem structure, which allows it to process different parts of the source data set in parallel. This makes it very fast compared to traditional forensic tools. As Bulk Extractor finds data it believes to be relevant, it creates a histogram of the artifacts.

Let's take a look at how it works:

1. Bulk Extractor's documentation lists the following information about its output:

alerts.txt	Processing errors recorded in a text file.
ccn.txt	Processes credit card numbers recorded in a text file.
ccn_track2.txt	Processes credit card "track 2" information, which has been found in some bank card fraud cases recorded in a text file.
domain.txt	Processes Internet domains found on the drive, including dotted-quad addresses found in the text recorded in a text file.
email.txt	Processes email addresses recorded in a text file.
ether.txt	Processes Ethernet MAC addresses found through IP packet carving of swap files and compressed system hibernation files and file fragments recorded in a text file.
exif.txt	Processes EXIFs from JPEGs and video segments. This feature file contains all the EXIF fields, expanded as XML records recorded in a text file.
find.txt	Processes the results of specific regular expression search requests recorded in a text file.
identi-fied_blocks.txt	Processes block hash values that match hash values in a hash database that the scan was run against recorded in a text file.
ip.txt	Processes IP addresses found through IP packet carving recorded in a text file.
rfc822.txt	Processes email message headers including the Date, Subject, and Message-ID: fields recorded in a text file.
tcp.txt	Processes TCP flow information found through IP packet carving recorded in a text file.
telephone.txt	Processes US and international telephone numbers recorded in a text file.
url.txt	Processes URLs, typically found in browser caches, email messages, and pre-compiled into executables recorded in a text file.
url_searches.txt	Processes a histogram of terms used in internet searches from services such as Google, Bing, Yahoo, and others recorded in a text file.
url_services.txt	Processes a histogram of the domain name portion of all the URLs found on the media recorded in a text file.
wordlist.txt	Processes a list of all "words" extracted from the disk, useful for password cracking recorded in a text file.
wordlist_*.text	Processes the wordlist with duplicates, removed, formatted in a form that can be easily imported into a popular password-cracking program recorded in a text file.
zip.txt	Processes information regarding every ZIP file component found on the media. This is exceptionally useful as ZIP files include internal structure and ZIP is increasingly the compound file format of choice for a variety of products such as Microsoft Office recorded in a text file.

Figure 7.9 – Bulk Extractor output options

2. You will need to left-click on tools and select **Run bulk_extractor...** to start analyzing your memory dump, as shown in the following screenshot. When you run Bulk Extractor, the viewer will present itself:

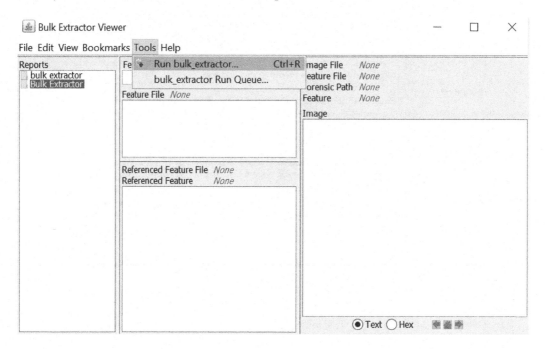

Figure 7.10 – Bulk Extractor menu – the run bulk extractor option

It will then present you with the **Run bulk_extractor** menu.

3. Direct the tool to the location of your image file and the output directory you wish to use. As shown in the following screenshot, you can see the numerous scanners that the Bulk Extractor tool is using to look for artifacts within the memory file:

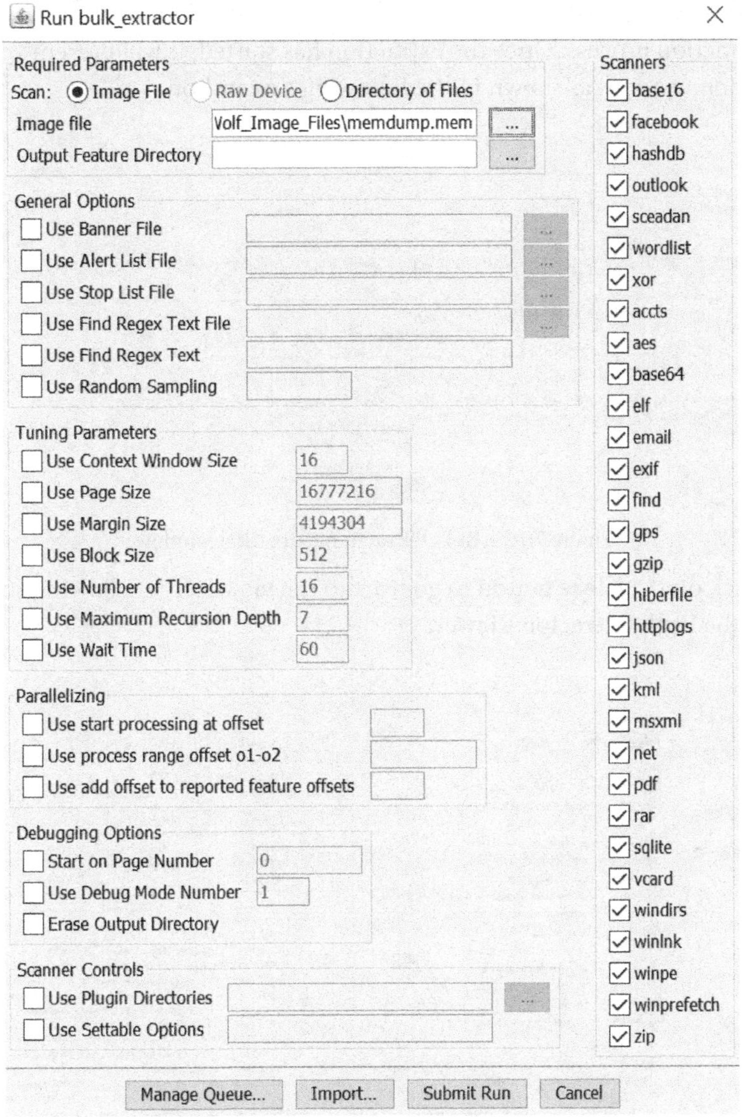

Figure 7.11 – Bulk Extractor menu options to run

You can check or uncheck a given specific artifact search as your needs dictate.

4. Once you are satisfied with the setup, left-click on the **Submit Run** button to start the extraction process. Once the extraction has started, it will present you with the extraction window, as shown in the following screenshot:

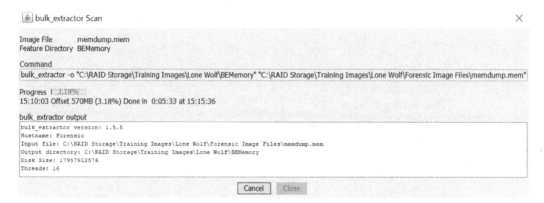

Figure 7.12 – Bulk Extraction extraction window

5. Left-click on the **Close** button to go back to the viewer. The following screenshot shows the **Bulk Extractor Viewer**:

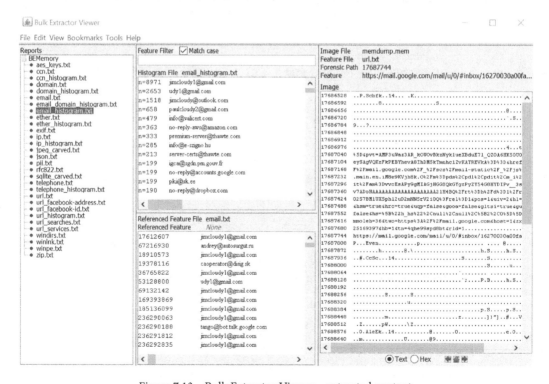

Figure 7.13 – Bulk Extractor Viewer – extracted content

On the left-hand side, we can see the specific artifacts that were recovered by the tool. In the preceding screenshot, I selected the email_histogram.txt file, which gives us a list of times it found a particular email address. By looking at the histogram window, I can see that it found the jcloudy1 email address over 8,000 times. As you go through the email list, you may find emails of evidentiary interest for you to follow up while using traditional media.

Bulk Extractor is a quick and efficient tool that's used to extract data strings that you can use to follow up with your investigation. The next tool we will discuss is Volix II.

Using Volix II

Volix is a GUI frontend for the Volatility framework. It makes it a bit easier for those who are not comfortable using the **command-line interface (CLI)**. Once the program has been downloaded and you have started it for the first time, it will present you with the following screen:

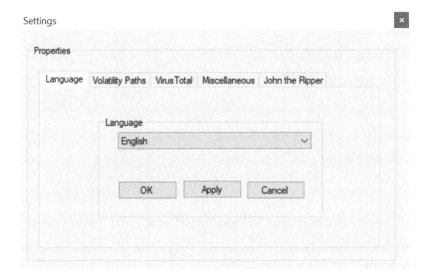

Figure 7.14 – Volix settings

Then, you will be pointed to the location of the Volatility framework. You can use either the standalone executable or the binary files to run the Python scripts. Here, I have already downloaded the standalone executable and have pointed Volix to it.

The other options you can select include the language you wish to use Volix in. If you have a Virus Total API key, you can insert it in on that page. This will compare the data captured from RAM and see if it matches any malware being tracked by Virus Total.

You also have the option of pointing Volix to the John the Ripper executable. If you want to decode/decrypt potential passwords that may be stored in RAM, follow these steps:

1.   Once you've selected **Case**, choose **New**. It will ask you the location of the memory file you wish to analyze, as shown in the following screenshot:

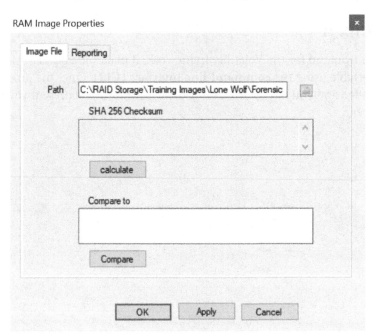

Figure 7.15 – Volix RAM location

2.   If you click on **Reporting**, you can specify the path for the report file that Volix will generate.

3.   Once you select **OK**, the Volix wizard screen will appear. You now have the option of going through a questionnaire to determine what options you wish to run on the memory file. You can also select one of the pre-created scripts to search for that specific artifact, such as **Virus detection** or **Decrypt SAM Hashes**, as shown in the following screenshot:

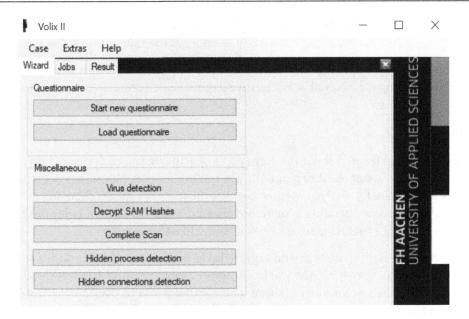

Figure 7.16 – Volix wizard

4. I selected the complete scan. You can see the results in the following screenshot:

Figure 7.17 – Volix scan results

From the preceding screenshot, you can see I have selected `getsids`. In the center screen, it has pulled out the SIDs that were in memory at the time of collection.

How many artifacts you ask it to search for at once will dictate the length of time for the application to complete. Overall, it is a relatively quick search compared to other tools.

Summary

In this chapter, you learned about the cornucopia of artifacts you can recover from RAM. You learned about the different tools you can use for the collection process and the tools you can use for analysis. Remember that the tools are always changing with the technology and as new operating systems are released, your primary tool may not collect RAM. Always have a backup plan in case something like that occurs.

You now have the skills to identify and capture RAM in a manner that conforms to best practices. As you analyze the RAM you have captured, you may find artifacts showing the user's activity on the system, such as social media artifacts and recovering passwords or encryption keys.

You may even find information relating to the user's use of email, which will lead us into our next chapter, which is all about email forensics.

Questions

1. Which of the following are sources of RAM?

   a. Physical memory

   b. `Pagefile.mem`

   c. Swap `file.page`

   d. ROM

2. Which file is created when the computer goes to sleep?

   a. `Page file.sys`

   b. `Swap file.sys`

   c. `Hiberfill.sys`

   d. `Hibernation.sys`

3. When should you capture RAM?

a. Every hour

b. Every week

c. Every digital forensic investigation

d. When you deem it important

4. In general, how many items do you need in order to collect RAM?

a. 1

b. 2

c. 3

d. 4

5. DumpIt is a GUI tool.

a. True

b. False

6. It is acceptable to install DumpIt on the suspect computer.

a. True

b. False

7. Which of the following are analysis tools?

a. DumpIt

b. FTK Imager

c. Volatility

d. MD5 hash

Further reading

Ligh, M. H., Case, A., Levy, J., & Walters, A. (2014). The Art of Memory Forensics: Detecting Malware and Threats in Windows, Linu. John Wiley & Sons. (Available at `https://www.amazon.com/Art-Memory-Forensics-Detecting-Malware/dp/1118825098`.)

8
Email Forensics – Investigation Techniques

Email is just one portion of the global internet that has become a daily resource in the consumer and corporate realms. It has become one of the primary communication tools used by nearly every citizen of the industrialized world. Now that email has become part of everyone's everyday lives, it is very common that criminals will use this vector to commit crimes and to collaborate with their other co-conspirators.

It can be difficult for the digital forensic investigator to trace an email from its destination back to the source. The digital forensic investigator will have to be educated in the methods and delivery systems of the email life cycle. When the digital forensic investigator is successful in identifying the source of the email, that will lead to additional forensic investigations of the digital evidence that was found at the source.

Where can you find digital evidence relating to an email investigation? The local machine will have the destination version of the email, the email server(s), the device that was used to access the email, such as a cell phone, and logs from the internet service provider. The digital forensic investigator will have to be knowledgeable about which tools can analyze emails and the compound files of the email box that are used by some email suites. Knowledge of how to present this information to a non-technical person will be paramount for them to convey the relevance of the data that was recovered. By the end of this chapter, you will understand the protocols that are used to send and receive emails, how to decode the email headers, and how to analyze client and web-based emails.

We will cover the following topics in this chapter:

- Understanding email protocols
- Decoding emails
- Understanding client-based email analysis
- Understanding WebMail analysis

Understanding email protocols

An email protocol is a standard that is used to allow two computer hosts to exchange email communication. When an email is sent, it travels from the sender's host to an email server. The email server can forward the email through a series of relays until it arrives at an email server close to the recipient's host. The recipient will receive a notification stating that an email is available; the recipient will then reach out to the email server to get the email.

Users typically use an email client to access emails. An email client can use different protocols to access the email. We will now discuss some email protocols you may come across when conducting a digital forensics investigation.

Understanding SMTP – Simple Mail Transfer Protocol

SMTP is the protocol for email transmission. It is an internet standard based on RFC 821 but was later updated to RFC 3207, RFC 5321/5322.

> **Tip**
>
> **RFC** stands for **Request for Comments**. This is used on internet/
> communications technology to create standards. An RFC may come from
> different bodies, such as the Internet Architecture Board/Internet Engineering
> Task Force, or even from an independent researcher. It was initially designed
> to track the development of the original ARPANET but has now evolved
> into a source of official documentation regarding internet specifications and
> communication protocols.

Mail servers use SMTP to send and receive email messages from all points of the internet.
Typically, you will find an SMTP server utilizing **Transmission Control Protocol (TCP)**
port 25 on the network. The path from the sender to the recipient is outlined in the
following diagram:

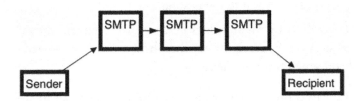

Figure 8.1 – SMTP map

When the user sends an email, it will travel from the host to a series of SMTP servers until
it reaches the destination SMTP server. The recipient will have to use a different protocol
to retrieve the email, which is our next topic.

The next protocol we will discuss is POP3.

Understanding the Post Office Protocol

POP3 is the standardized protocol that allows users to access their inbox and download
emails. POP3 is specifically designed only to receive emails; the system does not allow
users to send emails. This protocol allows the user to be offline when drafting, reading,
or replying and, at the user's request, can access the online mailbox on demand. Be aware
that the email you are conducting your digital forensic examination on may be the only
copy. The user has the option to not leave a copy of the email on the server. Once the email
has been downloaded, the system can remove it from the server to reduce storage use.

You will find POP utilizing port 110 on the network.

In the following diagram, you can see the general functionality of the SMTP-POP process:

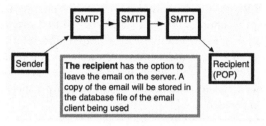

Figure 8.2 – SMTP-POP map

Here, you can see the path the email takes, which is as follows:

1. The email originates from the sender.

2. The SMTP server forwards it to the destination.

3. The recipient collects the email from the server. The recipient can decide if a copy of the email stays on the server or whether the email will be deleted when the user downloads the email from the server.

When we look at the next protocol, we will discuss functions similar to SMTP, but with some significant differences. We will discuss these differences in the next section.

IMAP – Internet Message Access Protocol

IMAP is the **Internet Message Access Protocol** and is a standard protocol used by an email client to access emails on an email server. The protocol was designed with the goal of complete inbox management with multiple clients. In most cases, email messages will be left on the server until the user deletes them. IMAP is a newer protocol than POP, but both are still prevailing email standards in use today. The most significant difference between IMAP and POP is that POP retrieves the contents of the mailbox and IMAP was designed as a remote access mailbox protocol.

In the following diagram, you can see the general functionality of the SMTP-IMAP process:

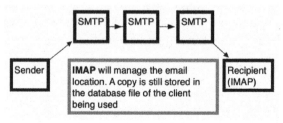

Figure 8.3 – IMAP map

Here, you can see the path the email takes:

1. The email originates from the sender.

2. The SMTP server forwards it to the destination.

3. The recipient collects the email from the server. A copy of the email stays on the server until the user explicitly deletes it.

All three protocols we just discussed are typically used in the email client-server relationship. Users also have another option when it comes to accessing emails known as web-based email, which is the topic of the next section.

Understanding web-based email

Web-based email is a service the user accesses with a web browser. Some standard webmail providers are Gmail, Yahoo Mail, and Outlook/Hotmail. Some internet service providers also provide an email account that can be accessed with a web browser.

User deleted emails stored on a web-based email server typically remain on the server until the system deletes them. A characteristic feature of web-based email is that when the user deletes an email, it is moved from the inbox into a `Deleted/Trash` folder and can still be accessed. After the email remains in the `Deleted` folder for a set timeframe, then the system will permanently delete it from the user's inbox.

With that, we have gone over the different methods of how a user may access email services. However, once you have the email dataset available for examination, you may find the contents of the email encoded. How do you decode the contents of the email to determine whether a crime/violation has/has not been committed?

In the next topic, we will decode the email header so that you can make an informed choice about your investigative endeavors.

Decoding email

An email has many globally unique identifiers for a digital forensic investigator to identify and to track down. The mailbox and domain name, along with the message ID, will allow a digital forensic investigator to serve judicially approved subpoenas/search warrants on the vendor to follow any investigative leads.

In this section, we will break down the email header one section at a time so that you can make a decision regarding how to conduct your investigation. We will start off by discussing the email envelope.

Understanding the email message format

The vast majority of email users are only familiar with basic email information, such as this:

```
Subject background checks
Date 07/19/2008 23:39:57 +0
Sender alison@m57.biz
Recipients jean@m57.biz
```

We are back to dealing with our friend Jean, and from looking at the email, we can see several fields commonly associated with an email. Here, we know the subject, background checks, the date and time when the email was sent, the sender, and the recipient. We also have the content of the email, as shown here:

```
Jean,
One of the potential investors that I've been dealing with has
asked me to get a background check of our current employees.
Apparently they recently had some problems at some other
company they funded.
Could you please put together for me a spreadsheet specifying
each of our employees, their current salary, and their SSN?
Please do not mention this to anybody.
Thanks.
(ps: because of the sensitive nature of this, please do not
include the text of this email
in your message to me. Thanks.)
```

As we look at the email, it appears that the email was sent to *Jean* from *Alison*. Alison is requesting a spreadsheet of employee confidential information. Based on the basic examination of this email, there is nothing to contradict what it initially appears to be.

The user has created the information in the *to* and *from*, as well as the *subject* and the *content* of the email. The system bases the date and time off of the system time, which can be set by the user.

Underneath the typical email information, there is another layer of information that is particularly useful when you are conducting your investigations. This is referred to as the *email header*, and it contains information about the source, transmission, and destination of a specific email.

Most email clients would require an additional command to view the email header. For example, Gmail requires you to *click Show original* to see the email header. The following is the email header for the email Jean received from Alison:

```
-----HEADERS-----
Return-Path: <simsong@xy.dreamhostps.com>
X-Original-To: jean@m57.biz

Delivered-To: x2789967@spunkymail-mx8.g.dreamhost.com

Received: from smarty.dreamhost.com (sd-green-bigip-81.
dreamhost.com [208.97.132.81])
 by spunkymail-mx8.g.dreamhost.com (Postfix) with ESMTP id
E32634D80F
 for <jean@m57.biz>; Sat, 19 Jul 2008 16:39:57 -0700 (PDT)

Received: from xy.dreamhostps.com (apache2-xy.xy.dreamhostps.
com [208.97.188.9])
 by smarty.dreamhost.com (Postfix) with ESMTP id 6E408EE23D
 for <jean@m57.biz>; Sat, 19 Jul 2008 16:39:57 -0700 (PDT)

Received: by xy.dreamhostps.com (Postfix, from userid 558838)
 id 64C683B1DAE; Sat, 19 Jul 2008 16:39:57 -0700 (PDT)

To: jean@m57.biz
From: alison@m57.biz
subject: background checks
Message-Id: <20080719233957.64C683B1DAE@xy.dreamhostps.com>
Date: Sat, 19 Jul 2008 16:39:57 -0700 (PDT)
```

The email header shows where the email originated from and what servers it touched upon. Starting from the bottom, we can see the `Message-Id` field:

```
Message-Id: <20080719233957.64C683B1DAE@xy.dreamhostps.com>
```

The `Message-Id` field is a unique identification for every email that has been sent. When a user sends an email, it will receive its message ID at the first email server it touches. The design of a message ID is that it will be globally unique, which means there should not be another email with the same message ID. If you find different emails that contain the same message ID, you are dealing with one of two scenarios:

- The email server is not compliant with the standard.

- A user has altered the email.

When you look at the message ID, you will see a string of random alphanumeric characters, including the @ symbol and a domain name. Sometimes, the arbitrary string of alphanumeric characters may contain a date/timestamp. If we look at the preceding example, we can see the numbers 20080719233957, which can be translated to *2008 07 19* – the year, month, and day. *23:39:57* is the time in hours, minutes, and seconds (GMT) when the email touched the first server.

Continuing from the bottom to the top, we can see the first Received line. This email transverses three different email servers. As the email crosses a server on its journey to its destination, each email server will attach a Received line on top of the preceding Received line. You can follow the email path from source to destination. In the email, we are examining the first server the email touched, which is as follows:

```
Received: by xy.dreamhostps.com (Postfix, from userid 558838)
 id 64C683B1DAE; Sat, 19 Jul 2008 16:39:57 -0700 (PDT)
```

This is the first server the email touched; we have the domain name, dreamhostps.com, along with a user ID. The next logical step would be to subpoena the ISP and try to identify the subscriber with user ID 558838. The term Postfix identifies the email server. Postfix is a free, open source mail transfer agent and could be a commercial email server or an email server maintained by a potential bad actor.

The next two Received lines identify the subsequent servers on the path to the destination:

```
Received: from smarty.dreamhost.com (sd-green-bigip-81.
dreamhost.com [208.97.132.81])
 by spunkymail-mx8.g.dreamhost.com (Postfix) with ESMTP id
E32634D80F
 for <jean@m57.biz>; Sat, 19 Jul 2008 16:39:57 -0700 (PDT)
Received: from xy.dreamhostps.com (apache2-xy.xy.dreamhostps.
com [208.97.188.9])
 by smarty.dreamhost.com (Postfix) with ESMTP id 6E408EE23D
 for <jean@m57.biz>; Sat, 19 Jul 2008 16:39:57 -0700 (PDT)
```

In both cases, we now have IP addresses of the specific servers (and server names) that touched the email.

What's interesting is when we look at the Return-Path field:

```
Return-Path: <simsong@xy.dreamhostps.com>
```

The `Return-Path` is the address where undeliverable messages will be sent. The `Return-Path` will also override the `From` field that the user will see. You will see this being used in email mailing lists, where you can reply to the user of the post and not to the list.

There are optional fields that you may come across in your investigations. These fields typically start with an *X–*, as shown here:

```
X-Priority: 3
X-Mailer: PHPMailer 5.2.9 (https://github.com/PHPMailer/
PHPMailer/)
Message-Id: <ff176aaf06e2f6958ada6e2d3c43b095@
x3.netcomlearning.com>
X-Report-Abuse: Please forward a copy of this message,
including all headers, to abuse@mandrill.com
X-Report-Abuse: You can also report abuse
here: http://mandrillapp.com/contact/
abuse?id=30514476.1925a088d66f450cb25a4034f3ec6942
X-Mandrill-User: md_30514476
```

These fields are not part of the email protocol standard. They can contain information about a virus scan, spam scans, or information about the server. As you can see, it provides information about contact information regarding abuse, such as, spam. You may also see an optional field called `X-Originating-IP` that may contain the IP address of the sender when the message was sent. An email provider can strip that information and replace it with a server address, which is what happens when a message is sent from Gmail.

A note about IP addresses. There are two different types of IPv4 addresses: public and private. You may see both in the email header. If you see a private IP address, you cannot identify the provider (unless you are investigating within the organization). Private IPv4 addresses run from the following addressing schemes:

- 10.X.X.X
- 127.X.X.X
- 172.16.X.X
- 192.168.X.X

We will discuss email attachments in the next section.

Email attachments

MIME is the acronym for **Multipurpose Internet Mail Extensions**, which is the internet standard for allowing emails to accept text other than ASCII, binary attachments, multipart message bodies, and non-ASCII base header information. When you are viewing the header, you will see MIME indicated with the following:

```
MIME-Version: 1.0
```

An example of this is as follows:

```
MIME-Version: 1.0
Content-Type: text/html; charset=us-ascii
Content-Transfer-Encoding: 7bit
```

Here, we can see the content type, which is HTML, and with the following line, we see it is using 7-bit coding. If there was an attachment, we would also see Base64 encoding, which converts the binary data into ASCII text.

The system will separate the body of the email based upon the data type for each segment. For example, a JPEG image will accompany one segment; it will store ASCII text in a different segment. Each segment will start with a MIME header that includes the keyword _PART_.

Now that we have discussed the email and header, we need to look at some of the clients the user may use to access the emails.

Understanding client-based email analysis

There are many email clients a user has access to in order to retrieve, read, and send emails. Depending on the environment, consumer versus commercial, you may run into different email clients. In the consumer market, you will find that Microsoft Outlook/ Outlook Express will prevail because it is preinstalled on the system. Microsoft Outlook comes with the Microsoft Office suite. There are also freeware options available such as the Thunderbird email client.

You can conduct an email examination by exporting the container used by the client and opening it with the email client installed on your forensic computer. Another option is to utilize specialized commercial forensic software that is created for email examinations. The more common forensic suites will typically be able to analyze the more common email client containers.

We will discuss some more common email clients in the following sections.

Exploring Microsoft Outlook/Outlook Express

Outlook stores email information in several file types, such as pst, .mdb, or .ost. We will find the PST file on the user's hard disk at the following path:

```
\Users\$USER$\AppData\Local\Microsoft\Outlook
```

The OST file is an offline file that may also be stored on the user's hard drive in the same path as the PST file. You will find the MDB file on the server. Typically, this file is found when you are investigating a corporate environment.

The system will store all the content used with the Outlook client in the PST/OST file. Be aware that the user can change the default location, as well as the naming convention. You do not need a login to access the PST/OST file.

If you need to carve out a PST/OST file from the unallocated space of the storage device, you may have to deal with fragmentation because of the potential size of the PST/OST file.

Microsoft has replaced Outlook Express with Windows Live. The next section will provide details about this client.

Exploring Microsoft Windows Live Mail

Starting with Windows Vista and Windows 7, Windows Live became the default email client shipping with the Windows operating system. (Note that it has been discontinued and that Windows Mail is now included with Windows 10 instead.) The client stores email messages in the following path:

```
\Users\$USER$\AppData\Local\Microsoft\Windows Live Mail
```

Users can use this client to access their web-based emails as well. Windows Live Mail will download the contents of those accounts and then create the folder structure within the user's path.

The client will store the emails as an .eml file under the Windows Live Mail folder, as shown here:

```
Windows Live Mail (96)
 |   ├──Calendars (21)
 |   |   ├──DBStore (11)
 |   |   |   ├──LogFiles (4)
 |   |   |   └──Backup (3)
 |   |   |       └──new (3)
 |   |   └──little9@hotmail.com (10)
 |   |       └──DBStore (10)
```

```
|   |           ├──Backup (3)
|   |           |  └──new (3)
|   |           └──LogFiles (4)
|   ├──Outbox (0)
|   ├──Sentinel (2)
|   ├──little9@hotmail.com (1)
|   ├──Hotmail (54)
|   |   ├──Inbox (30)
|   |   ├──Drafts (0)
|   |   ├──Junk email (2)
|   |   ├──Sent items (15)
|   |   ├──Deleted items (6)
```

As you can see, this user was using Hotmail with the Windows Live Mail application. You can see the email address, little9@hotmail.com, and see that 54 emails are being stored in the user's folders.

The emails are in the standard text format, .eml, which can be read by any forensic tool. Alternatively, you can use a text editor. The next client is also popular and free: Mozilla Thunderbird.

Mozilla Thunderbird

Thunderbird is a free, open source email client provided by Mozilla. Thunderbird will store emails within a .MBOX file. The MBOX format is a generic term for a family of file formats that is used to store emails. It will store all of the emails, based on folders, and a single database file. By default, the MBOX file can be found in the following path:

```
$USERNAME$\AppData\Roaming\Thunderbird\Profiles
```

The following is the folder structure you will see when Thunderbird is installed:

```
u2xziaos.default-release (106)
├──minidumps (0)
├──crashes (1)
|   └──events (0)
├──extensions (1)
├──calendar-data (4)
├──storage (12)
|   └──permanent (12)
|       └──chrome (12)
|           └──idb (11)
|               └──3870112724rsegmnoittet-es.files (0)
├──ImapMail (16)
```

```
|    └──imap.mail.yahoo.com (15)
└──Mail (4)
    └──Local Folders (4)
```

The profile name is created by Thunderbird. The release version of the software the user has installed can also be seen here. As we analyze the folder structure, we will see that it contains information about crashes and stores data in a minidump when a crash occurs. There may also be calendar data and mailboxes.

Here, the user is using the IMAP protocol to access their Yahoo mail account, and there are 15 items stored within the folder.

When we look in the folder, we will see the following files:

- `Archive.msf`
- `Archives.msf`
- `Bulk Mail.msf`
- `Draft.msf`
- `Drafts.msf`
- `INBOX`
- `INBOX.msf`
- `msgFilterRules.dat`
- `Sent-1.msf`
- `Sent.msf`
- `Templates.msf`
- `Trash.msf`

The **MSF** files are **Mail Summary files**, which is one part of the email. The email client, Thunderbird, stores the email data in two different parts. The first part is the MBOX file, which does not have a file extension. The MSF files are the index files for Thunderbird and contain email headers and a summary. Thunderbird uses these files as an index to locate the email stored in the MBOX.

In the following screenshot, you can see three emails are being stored in the MBOX. When X-Ways parses out the inbox, the emails will have a `.eml` file extension:

☐ ▼ Name ▲	▼ Type
☐ 🗀.. = imap.mail.yahoo.com (15)	
☐ 🗀. = INBOX (3)	mbox
☐ 📄 Banks.eml	eml
☐ 📄 New sign in on thunderbird.eml	eml
☐ 📄 Re: midgets.eml	eml

Figure 8.4 – Thunderbird inbox

The MBOX format is used by many email clients, including Apple Mail, Opera Mail, and Thunderbird. Most commercial and open source forensic suites will process the MBOX and provide access to emails.

While the user can access their email from a client, there is another popular option that allows the user to access their email without using a client: webmail.

Understanding WebMail analysis

Web-based email has become increasingly popular as we transition from the twentieth to the twenty-first century. It provides ease of access, requires little to no configuration from the user, and is available from any computer. In the simplest terms, WebMail is just another internet artifact for conducting browser analysis (we will cover internet artifacts in *Chapter 9, Internet Artifacts*).

The service provider maintains the user's email and may provide additional services, such as address books and calendars. Users have the option of using a client to access web-based email, but I have found that those users are in the minority. When content is being hosted by the service provider, that provides additional obstacles to the digital forensic investigator. The only artifacts relating to the content may be in the user's internet history, and that may be fragmented. If a digital forensic investigator wants to access the content of a user's web-based email, they will have to serve a search warrant (in the United States; your jurisdiction may have different requirements) on the service provider. You may be unable to access or recover any deleted emails from the account. It will depend on the specific set of circumstances for each service provider.

If the digital forensic investigator wants to investigate the user's use of web-based email, then they will have to analyze the temporary internet files or the internet *cache* on the user's system. The temporary internet files/cache contains images, text, or any component of the web page the user has viewed in their browser.

Their browser saves this information in the temporary internet `files/cache` location to enhance the user experience. It does this by having a faster response time when presenting pages to the user. Instead of continually redownloading the content, you can reach back into the cache and present that information to the user.

Gmail is very popular and when its web application was first deployed, it changed the way WebMail was presented to users. No longer were static web pages displaying the content of the email and the user's email folders. Gmail dynamically created content on the fly for each user. No longer were image files and text being saved to the user's local storage device; instead, Gmail used **Asynchronous JavaScript (AJAX)** and XML files. This new method did not allow for a web page to be rebuilt by investigators.

You can still recover artifacts within the internet cache and other potential sources such as RAM or the pagefile on the user's local storage device. You will need to conduct keyword searches for email addresses or keyword searches for terms related to your investigation.

Before I look into the cache, I want to look into the internet history of the installed browser to see if the user has accessed web-based email. For the Chrome browser, you will find the history stored in an SQLite database named `History` at the following path:

```
$USER$\AppData\Local\Google\Chrome\User Data\Default
```

The analysis of the `History` database shows the user accessed the Gmail web-based service, as shown in the following screenshot:

```
        08/28/2019   Inbox (2) -
  19    22:19:39     badguyneedslove@gmail.com - https://mail.google.com/mail/?pc=topnav-about-n-en
        +0           Gmail
```

Figure 8.5 – Email – History

We have a date/time stamp, along with the email address. The artifact also shows that the user had two unread emails in the inbox when they accessed the service.

I found this from the internet cache for the Google Chrome browser, which can be found at the following location:

```
$USER$\AppData\Local\Google\Chrome\User Data\Default\History
Provider Cache
```

As you can see from the following screenshot showing the Chrome cache, the content is not easily decipherable and does not give us a lot to follow up with:

GB/download/20Thunderbird — Download Thunderbird — Mozilla:❒ ❒ ◆ ◆   ❒ ❒ ❒ ❒
◆❒ https://www.google.com/search?q=thunderbird&rlz=1C1CHBF_enUS864US864&oq=thunderbird&aqs=chrome..69i57j0l5.9899j0j8&sourceid=chrome&ie=UTF-82❒ thunderbird
◆ ❒ * ❒ https://accounts.google.com/ServiceLogin?service=mail&passive=true&rm=false&continue=https://mail.google.com/mail/&ss=1&scc=1&ltmpl=default&ltmplcache=2&em
Google:❒ ❒ Û◆ ❒ ❒   ◆❒ ❒ k❒ ❒ ❒ ❒   Û◆ ❒ * https://www.google.com/gmail/2*Gmail - Free Storage and Email from Google:❒ ❒ Û◆ ❒ ❒   ❒ ❒ ❒ ❒ ❒   □❒ ◆❒
en#inbox?compose=GTvVlcSKkwxGgHJTLbmhqKzczCTgBmGGzPvwmqptDGQssRWwIVbLFkZqQgQfMHBKkXsqjtjxGvqCP2-Inbox (2) - badguyneedslove@gmail.com - Gmail:❒
◆ ❒ * https://mail.google.com/mail/2*Gmail - Free Storage and Email from Google:❒ ❒ Û◆ ❒ ❒   ◆❒ ❒ ◆❒ ❒ ❒   pxÔ
◆❒ https://accounts.google.com/signup/v2/webcreateaccount?service=mail&continue=https%3A%2F%2Fmail.google.com%2Fmail%2F%3Fpc%3Dtopnav-about-n-en&flowName=
Google Account:❒ ❒ pxÔ◆   ❒ ❒ ◆❒ ❒ ¼ ◆❒ https://accounts.google.com/signup/v2/webgradsidvphone?service=mail&continue=https%3A%2F%2Fmail.google.com%2Fma

Figure 8.6 – Chrome cache displayed

If we keep searching for the email address we found in the cache, **badguyneedslove@ gmail.com**, we may find other artifacts, such as the following:

```
{"endpoint_info_list":[{"endpoint":"smtp:badguy27@
yahoo.com","c_id":"d24c.2d00","c_name":"Joe Badguy
Smith"},{"endpoint":"smtp:badguyneedslove@gmail.
com","c_id":"e80f.5b71","c_name":"John Badguy
Smith"},{"endpoint":"smtp:yahoo@mail.comms.yahoo.net","c_
id":"624f.10f0","c_name":"Yahoo! Inc."}]}
```

This artifact, which can also be found within the cache, gives us another email address, badguy27@yahoo.com, to follow up. The content of the email still remains out of reach.

Let's look at the Firefox cache and see whether it can give us a better look at the cache and history.

The cache and history for the Firefox browser can be found at the following location:

```
$USERS$\AppData\Local\Mozilla\Firefox\Profiles\<profile>\cache2
```

Firefox will store the internet history and cache underneath the user's profile. The folder structure you will see may look like this:

```
Mozilla (1,505)
└─Firefox (1,505)
  └─Profiles (1,504)
    ├─55abhq00.default-release (1,504)
    │ ├─safebrowsing (50)
    │ │ └─google4 (10)
    │ ├─jumpListCache (5)
    │ ├─startupCache (236)
    │ ├─cache2 (1,162)
    │ │ ├─entries (1,160)
    │ │ └─doomed (0)
    │ ├─thumbnails (0)
```

```
    |   ┌──OfflineCache (1)
    |   └──safebrowsing-updating (49)
    |       └──google4 (9)
    └──cqr6ioib.default (0)
```

It looks like the visual depiction of the content of the Firefox cache is not much better:

```
"matches": [
    {
      "lookupId": "badguyneedslove@gmail.com",
      "personId": [
        "114987255021342983529"
      ]
    }
  ],
  "people": {
    "114987255021342983529": {
      "personId": "114987255021342983529",
      "metadata": {
        "lastUpdateTimeMicros": "1567030765000",
        "identityInfo": {
          "originalLookupToken": [
            "badguyneedslove@gmail.com"
```

It does not provide a wealth of information, but it does supply breadcrumbs for us to follow up and conduct additional investigative efforts with.

In the world of forensics, the artifacts you rely upon can quickly change with new updates to the software or changes in the operating system. Be flexible with your investigative techniques so that you can jump into the latest technology to make your investigation successful. Once you have identified that the subject of your investigation is using web-based email, your best course of action is to serve the service provider with the appropriate judicial paperwork to freeze the account and get the required content.

Summary

In this chapter, we have gone over standard email protocols; the system uses SMTP for sending emails, while POP and IMAP are used for receiving emails. IMAP also includes features that can be used to manage the user's inbox. We went over the email header and the components that make up the header. WebMail and email clients were also discussed.

You now have the skills necessary to read an email header and determine the servers that were used to transmit the email, as well as what protocols the system used to send and receive the email. When conducting a digital forensic examination, you can now identify artifacts from typical email clients and web-based email.

In the next chapter, you will learn that some web-based emails have similarities among them.

Questions

1. Which of the following is not an email protocol?

    a. HTML

    b. POP

    c. SMTP

    d. IMAP

2. Which of the following will allow the user to manage their inbox?

    a. COC

    b. POP

    c. FreeBSD

    d. IMAP

3. The email header is created by user input information.

    a. True

    b. False

4. Thunderbird stores emails in which file?

    a. Inbox

    b. Outbox

    c. MBOX

    d. Letterbox

5. Which email client uses a PST file?

   a. Thunderbird

   b. Gmail

   c. Yahoo Mail

   d. Outlook

6. Windows Live Mail was replaced with which client?

   a. Outlook Express

   b. Outlook

   c. Windows Mail

   d. Windows Email

7. You will always find the content of web-based email in the user's cache.

   a. True

   b. False

You will find the answers at the back of this book, under *Assessments*.

Further reading

- *Jones, R. (2006). Internet forensics: Beijing: OReilly* (can be purchased at `http://shop.oreilly.com/product/9780596100063.do`)

9
Internet Artifacts

The internet has become a staple in commercial and consumer environments. Digital communication between users is a daily activity. It is uncommon for a household not to have a device connected to the internet in some manner. They give students in elementary school devices to connect to the internet to enhance their education. Email addresses, URLs, social media, and file sharing are all vectors of activities a user can partake of. It is up to the user to decide whether their online activities are going to meet social norms and be accepted, or whether they will cross the line and conduct criminal activity. Your job as a digital forensic investigator will be investigating their activities in the digital realm.

In this chapter, we will be discussing some of the common browsers and social media sites and the artifacts they provide. We will also discuss P2P file sharing tools and some cloud computing services and their artifacts.

We'll be covering them in the following topics:

- Understanding browsers
- Social media
- P2P file sharing
- Cloud computing

Understanding browsers

What is a browser? It is a program or application a user can use to access websites via the **World Wide Web (WWW)**.Which is the best browser is an ongoing debate and can be a very personal choice for a user. The user has options in which they can personalize the browser to enhance their experience when accessing the WWW. As a result, this creates many artifacts that any digital forensic investigator can use to recreate the user's activity. There will be logs, history files, and cache files that a digital forensic investigator can examine and identify unethical or criminal activity.

Like all technology, browsers are continuously being updated and changed. User experience is typically the key to the changes, but lately, security has also been a driving factor. While the security enhancements are not specifically designed to frustrate or hamper digital forensic investigations, they have that effect.

We will now discuss some common browsers you may encounter during your investigations. This is not an all-inclusive list, and there will be browsers that you may encounter that we will not discuss.

As of July 2019, according to W3Counter, the Chrome browser has a 55 percent market share, followed by Safari at 12 percent, Internet Explorer/Edge at 8 percent, and Firefox at 6 percent. Chrome is the leader in the browser wars, and you can find the Chrome browser in many operating systems. We will now discuss the Chrome browser and the artifacts you may run into during your investigations.

Exploring Google Chrome

Google Chrome was released in 2008 and was very popular with users. It provided a fast and efficient user experience and has also experienced very few exploits. Chrome stores much of the data within different databases and also provides us with the option of syncing data across multiple platforms. This means you may come across artifacts that were generated with a different device. So, let's get into the details of the Chrome browser.

Understanding bookmarks

The first artifact we will want to look at is the user's bookmarks. The bookmarks allow the user to save web pages they find interesting and may give insight into the user's activity. You can find the bookmarks file at the following path:

```
%USERS%/AppData/Local/Google/Chrome/User Data/Default/Bookmarks
```

The file will *not* have a file extension, and it is a JSON (JavaScript Object Notation is an open standard file and data interchange format) formatted file.

You can open the file in any text reader and it will show you the contents, as shown in the following screenshot of a JSON BBC bookmark:

"date_added": "13105251021405925",
"id": "110",
"meta_info": {
    "last_visited_desktop": "13197567715245509"
},
"name": "BBC News",
"sync_transaction_version": "592",
"type": "url",
"url": "http://news.bbc.co.uk/"
, {
"date_added": "13105251021408611",
"id": "111",
"meta_info": {
    "last_visited_desktop": "13197950930217586"
},
"name": "CNN",
"sync_transaction_version": "592",
"type": "url",
"url": "http://www.cnn.com/"

Figure 9.1 – JSON BBC bookmark

Here, we can see the following fields:

- Date added
- Last visited desktop
- The name of the bookmark
- The URL

But the presentation of information is not very graphical. An alternative method is to use a free text viewer such as Notepad++ (available at `https://notepad-plus-plus.org/`) and use the JSON plugin. That will make the folder structure easier to read, as depicted in the following screenshot:

JSON
├─ checksum : d5686c72fcf309b5fa2e90a0bebc96ed
├─ roots
│ ├─ bookmark_bar
│ │ ├─ children
│ │ ├─ date_added : 13181512829205642
│ │ ├─ date_modified : 13210451812960795
│ │ ├─ id : 1
│ │ ├─ name : Bookmarks bar
│ │ └─ type : folder
│ ├─ other
│ └─ sync_transaction_version : 604
├─ synced
└─ version : 1

Figure 9.2 – JSON root folder

The preceding screenshot shows that there are three folders underneath the root directory: bookmark_bar, other and synced. When the bookmark_bar folder is expanded, it reveals the existence of additional children folders, as depicted in the following screenshot:

Figure 9.3 – JSON children

The first folders are only labeled with numbers starting with zero. When we expand the 1 folder, the name of the folder is revealed to be News, along with the date/time stamps or when it was added and modified. When the children folder is opened, the bookmarks are now available for viewing, as shown in the following screenshot:

Figure 9.4 – JSON bookmarks

The date/time stamps are encoded in Google Chrome Value. To decode the date/time stamp, I enjoy using the open source tool DCode (which is available at `https://www.digital-detective.net/dcode/`). DCode can also be used to decipher numerous different types of date/time stamps.

As shown in the following screenshot, you can see the tool has translated the Google Chrome Value into a more readable format:

Figure 9.5 – DCode tool used for translating Google Chrome value

The BBC News bookmark was added on Saturday, April 16, 2016, at 03:30:21 UTC.

The mere presence of an incriminating bookmark may not be enough to act upon. To support the hypothesis, the user visited the web page indicated by the bookmark; you may have to look at additional artifacts. One such artifact is the history file, which we will examine next.

Understanding the Chrome history file

The Google Chrome history file will be found at the following path:

```
%USERS%/AppData/Local/Google/Chrome/User Data/
```

The file will not have a file extension, and it is a SQLite database. Most forensic tools will view the contents of the database. The history database contains quite a lot of information about the user's activity:

- Downloads:

  This will include the path of where the downloaded file was saved, the location the file was downloaded from, the start/stop times of the download, and the size of the file downloaded.

- Keyword search will track the search terms that the user entered into the URL address bar.

- Typed URLs will track the URLs the user typed into the address bar.

- History:

  This will track the URLs visited by the user, the number of times the URL was visited, and the date/time the URL was visited.

As we examine the history file, the following text depicts the user's activity.

```
C:\Users\IEUser\Downloads\Thunderbird Setup 68.0.exe
 https://www.thunderbird.net/en-GB/download/     08/29/2019
 16:14:38 +0     08/29/2019 16:14:40 +0     1
```

The user downloaded a file named Thunderbird Setup 68.0.exe and saved it in the Downloads folder of the IEUser. We also have the start time of 16:14:38 UTC and know that the download completed at 16:14:40 UTC.

The user also conducted two keyword searches, as follows:

```
gmail           https://www.google.com/search? q=gmail&
 (REDACTED)          08/28/2019 22:17:04 +0
thunderbird     https://www.google.com/search?q=thunderbird&
 (REDACTED)     08/29/2019 16:14:29 +0
```

The user searched for the terms Gmail and Thunderbird. The search engine Google was used for the search, with the search for the term Gmail. The search was conducted on August 28, 2019 and the Thunderbird search was conducted on August 29, 2019. (I have redacted a portion of the URL(s) to help with formatting.)

The following is a listing of the websites the user visited:

```
08/28/2019 22:22:08 +0      (2 unread) - badguy27@yahoo.com -
Yahoo Mail   https://mail.yahoo.com/d/ (REDACTED)

08/28/2019 22:22:36 +0      Banks - badguyneedslove@gmail.com -
Gmail        https://mail.google.com/mail/ (REDACTED)

08/29/2019 16:14:29 +0      thunderbird - Google Search
https://www.google.com/search?q=thunderbird&rlz=1C1CHBF_
(REDACTED)

08/29/2019 16:14:33 +0      Thunderbird — Download Thunderbird —
Mozilla   https://www.thunderbird.net/en-GB/download/     1
```

From the history file, we can see that the user searched for the term Thunderbird and that seconds later, the user went to the Thunderbird download page. Before the user searched for the term Thunderbird, the user visited two different web-based email accounts. We can see the user visited Yahoo mail and Gmail the night before. Based on this analysis, we have identified distinct and different email addresses the user may be using or, at a minimum, has access to.

Next, in terms of browser artifacts, are cookies.

Cookies

A cookie is a dataset created by a website and stored on the user's system. Cookies are designed to track the user's activity, such as adding an item to a shopping cart or recording the pages the user has visited. Be aware that just because a cookie is on the system, it is not conclusive evidence that the user knowingly visited the site. You will need to find other artifacts as supporting evidence of the user's activity.

The Google Chrome cookie file can be found at the following path:

```
%USERS%/AppData/Local/Google/Chrome/User Data/Default
```

The file will not have a file extension, and it is a SQLite database. Most forensic tools will view the contents of the database. The following screenshot is the output of X-Ways Forensics:

creation_utc	host_key	name	value	path	expires_utc	is_secure	is_httponly	last_access_utc	has_expires	is_pe
13211504229653934	.google.com	_ga		/gmail/about	13274576231000000	0	0	13211504229653934	1	1
13211504229654926	.google.com	_gid		/gmail/about	13211590631000000	0	0	13211504229654926	1	1
13211504361869670	.google.com	APISID		/	13274576361869670	0	0	13211568843104513	1	1
13211504373193089	mail.google.com		COMPASS	/mail/u/0	13212368374193089	1	1	13211504554421139		

Figure 9.6 – Cookies

While the data is readable, the format leaves a lot to be desired. A third-party application, Chrome Cookies View (available at `http://www.nirsoft.net/utils/chrome_cookies_view.html`), will parse the data in a format that is easy to read, as shown in the following screenshot:

Host Name	Path	Name	Value	Secure	HTTP Only	Last Access... ∕	Created On	Expires
.google.com	/gmail/about	_ga		No	No	8/28/2019 22:17	8/28/2019 22:17	8/27/2021 22:17
mail-ads.google.com	/mail/u/0	COMPASS		Yes	Yes	8/28/2019 22:19	8/28/2019 22:19	9/7/2019 22:19
www.yahoo.com	/	flash_enabled		No	No	8/28/2019 22:21	8/28/2019 22:21	9/27/2019 22:21

Figure 9.7 – Cookie View

Now, the columns and the data are lined up and formatted correctly. The tool also converts the date/timestamp from Google Chrome time into UTC time. Cookies are one part of tracking the user's activities, but the cache may also contain artifacts that are useful for your investigation.

Cache

We discussed the cache earlier in *Chapter 8, Email Forensics – Investigation Techniques*, and we still have the same issue in that when we examine the content, it is difficult to decipher. There is a third-party tool called Chrome Cache View (available at www.nirsoft.net/utils/chrome_cache_view.html) that converts the data into a readable format. The following screenshot is an example of the output you may see:

gmail.html	https://www.google...	text/html	0	8/28/2019 15:17	8/28/2019 15:17			sffe	HTTP/1.1 302			private	172.217.14.100
s2	https://www.google...	text/javascript	14,685	8/28/2019 15:17	8/27/2019 14:47	8/27/2019 14:27	8/26/2020 14:47	sffe	HTTP/1.1 200	br	data_3 [253952]	public, max-age=31536000	172.217.14.100
about.html	https://mail.google...	text/html	0	8/28/2019 15:17	8/27/2019 21:40		8/28/2019 21:40	sffe	HTTP/1.1 301			public, max-age=86400	172.217.11.165
about.html	https://www.google...	text/html	0	8/28/2019 15:17	8/28/2019 04:21		8/29/2019 04:21	sffe	HTTP/1.1 301			public, max-age=86400	172.217.14.100
about.html	https://www.google...	text/html	15,504	8/28/2019 15:17	8/28/2019 15:17	7/19/2019 00:30	8/28/2019 15:17	dffe	HTTP/1.1 200	gzip	data_3 [303104]	private, max-age=3000	172.217.14.100

Figure 9.8 – Cache view

When you select the items of interest, Chrome Cache View allows you to export the information into a much easier to read format, as follows:

```
====================================================
Filename          : gmail.html
URL               : https://www.google.com/gmail
Content Type      : text/html
File Size         : 0
Last Accessed     : 8/28/2019 15:17
Server Time       : 8/28/2019 15:17
Server Last Modified:
Expire Time       :
Server Name       : sffe
Server Response   : HTTP/1.1 302
Content Encoding  :
Cache Name        :
```

```
Cache Control      : private
ETag               :
Server IP Address  : 172.217.14.100
URL Length         : 28
=======================================================
```

This is much easier to read and understand. You are still being shown all the same information, but the presentation is much better.

You have the filename and the date/time they visited the web page. Of interest is the server IP address. If you find data within the cache such as illicit images, this may lead you to the server where the original images were hosted.

Now, we will discuss passwords and how they are stored within the Chrome browser.

Passwords

Passwords can be key to unlocking different files or encryption. Most users will reuse the same passwords for multiple different accounts. Your ability to recover the user's previously used passwords can be a treasure trove of information. Chrome has the option for a user to save passwords.

You will find the password information in the `Logon Data` file, which can be found at the following path:

```
%USERS%/AppData/Local/Google/Chrome/User Data/Default
```

The file will not have a file extension, and it is a SQLight database. It does not contain the actual password for the user accounts; instead, it stores information about each account, which is used to encrypt the passwords. There is a third-party utility, Chrome Pass (available at `https://www.nirsoft.net/utils/chromepass.html`), which will decrypt the passwords.

The Google Chrome browser is the current number one browser used today. You may encounter multiple browsers on a user's system. The next browser we will talk about is Internet Explorer, the default browser for the Microsoft Windows operating system.

Exploring Internet Explorer/Microsoft Edge

Internet Explorer is the web browser of the Microsoft Windows operating system. Microsoft has included the browser with Windows since 1995. Internet Explorer was the number one browser during the 1990s, but with the release of Firefox in 2004 and Google Chrome in 2008, its popularity has dropped. Internet Explorer is still included with Windows 10 but has been replaced with Microsoft Edge.

So, let's jump in and look at the artifacts you may recover from the user's activity in the Internet Explorer Edge browser.

Bookmarks

Unlike the Google Chrome browser, Internet Explorer saves bookmarks in a URL format. The default path Internet Explorer keeps the bookmarks in is as follows:

```
%USER%/Favorites
```

All commercial and open source forensic tools can read the URL format. The following screenshot depicts the typical data structure you will find:

Miniature Schnauzer Dog Breed Information.url	url	2.5 KB	09/02/2019 18:01:11 +0	09/02/2019 18:01:13 +0
schnauzers - Bing images.url	url	1.1 KB	09/02/2019 18:01:30 +0	09/02/2019 18:01:30 +0
Salt and Pepper Miniature Schnauzer - Bing images.url	url	1.3 KB	09/02/2019 18:01:47 +0	09/02/2019 18:01:47 +0
Christen's Miniature Schnauzers - Las Vegas, NV.url	url	180 B	09/02/2019 18:02:11 +0	09/02/2019 18:02:11 +0

Figure 9.9 – IE bookmarks

As you examine the bookmarks stored in the `Favorites` folder, you can also view the created and modified timestamps. These are the date/time stamps for when the URL file was created/modified.

When you examine the URL file, you may find content similar to the following:

```
[DEFAULT]
BASEURL=http://christensminischnauzers.com/
[{000214A0-0000-0000-C000-000000000046}]
Prop3=19,2
[InternetShortcut]
URL=http://christensminischnauzers.com/
IDList=
```

As you can see, it contains the URL, which is the point of interest if the website is dealing with contraband, or the user's activity, which support your hypothesis about the events you are investigating.

Next, we'll check the user's history and see if we can find any interesting artifacts.

IE history

Internet Explorer will track the user's activity for 20 days. This is the default setting and can be changed by the user. As we discussed in *Chapter 6, Windows Artifact Analysis,* Internet Explorer will also track some user activity in the operating system. Internet Explorer is an integral part of the Windows operating system, and even if the user prefers a different browser, there still may be artifacts of interest within the Internet Explorer history.

Edge and Internet Explorer version 10 and higher use an ESE database called WebCacheV01.dat that can be found at the following path:

```
%User%\AppData\Local\Microsoft\Windows\WebCache
```

To analyze the WebCacheV01.dat file, we will use ESEDatabaseview (we first used it in *Chapter 6, Windows Artifact Analysis,*). Export the database out of the forensic image to analyze it.

The first table you will want to look at is the Containers table, and you should see something similar to what is depicted in the following screenshot:

ContainerId	LastAccessTime	Name	Directory
1	132119207925900830	Content	C:\Users\IEUser\AppData\Local\Microsoft\Windows\Temporary Internet Files\Content.IE5\
2	132115040805283385	feedplat	C:\Users\IEUser\AppData\Local\Microsoft\Feeds Cache\
3	131594261121527040	ietld	C:\Users\IEUser\AppData\Roaming\Microsoft\IETldCache\
4	132119207924265464	History	C:\Users\IEUser\AppData\Local\Microsoft\Windows\History\History.IE5\
5	132119207926189424	Cookies	C:\Users\IEUser\AppData\Roaming\Microsoft\Windows\Cookies\
6	132119207925419840	iecompat	C:\Users\IEUser\AppData\Roaming\Microsoft\Windows\IECompatCache\
7	132119207925516038	iecompatua	C:\Users\IEUser\AppData\Roaming\Microsoft\Windows\iecompatuaCache\
8	132119207913683684	DNTException	C:\Users\IEUser\AppData\Roaming\Microsoft\Windows\DNTException\
9	132119207925131246	EmieSiteList	C:\Users\IEUser\AppData\Local\Microsoft\Internet Explorer\EmieSiteList\
10	132119207925131246	EmieUserList	C:\Users\IEUser\AppData\Local\Microsoft\Internet Explorer\EmieUserList\
11	132119207944659440	DOMStore	C:\Users\IEUser\AppData\Local\Microsoft\Internet Explorer\DOMStore\
12	132119207959858724	MSHist012019082820190829	C:\Users\IEUser\AppData\Local\Microsoft\Windows\History\History.IE5\MSHist012019082820190829\
13	132115041147334574	iedownload	C:\Users\IEUser\AppData\Roaming\Microsoft\Windows\IEDownloadHistory\
14	132119207959762526	MSHist012019082920190830	C:\Users\IEUser\AppData\Local\Microsoft\Windows\History\History.IE5\MSHist012019082920190830\
15	132119207959762526	MSHist012019082620190902	C:\Users\IEUser\AppData\Local\Microsoft\Windows\History\History.IE5\MSHist012019082620190902\
16	132119207959954922	MSHist012019090220190903	C:\Users\IEUser\AppData\Local\Microsoft\Windows\History\History.IE5\MSHist012019090220190903\

Figure 9.10 – ESE database showing the Containers table

There are 16 tables in the database, and the containers of interest are tables 12, 14, 15, and 16. When you look at the names of the tables, they start with MSHist01, followed by numbers.

The numbers tell us if the history file is a daily or a weekly file. In the following diagram, you can see the breakdown of the table name:

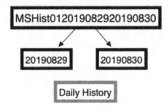

Figure 9.11 – Daily history folder naming convention

The name contains the period of time the history covers. As shown in the preceding diagram, the data it contains spans from August 29, 2019, to August 30, 2019. In the following diagram, we can see the breakdown for a weekly timeframe:

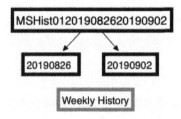

Figure 9.12 – Weekly history naming convention

This data spans the time period August 26, 2019, to September 2, 2019.

For the `MSHist01` files, the file path shown under the `Directory` field is for legacy purposes. If you follow the path shown, you will find a file called `container.dat` that does not contain any information.

> **Note**
>
> For the rest of the entries, the file path will contain data corresponding to the specific table and may be relevant to your investigation.

Let's look at the contents of table `12`, as shown in the following screenshot:

EntryId	SyncTime	ExpiryTime	ModifiedTime	AccessedTime	Url
1	132115734791679663	132138198789360361	132115482789355131	132115734791679663	:2019082920190830: IEUser@file:///C:/Program%20Files/Windows%20Mail/MSOERES.dll
2	132115734793861687	0	132115482789355131	132115734793861687	:2019082920190830: IEUser@:Host: Computer
3	132115735348103202	132138195053033732	132115483347995798	132115735348103202	:2019082920190830: IEUser@file:///C:/Users/IEUser/Downloads/EnableWinMailWin7/msoe_64.zip
4	132115735669898689	132138195374936623	132115483669890000	132115735669898689	:2019082920190830: IEUser@file:///C:/Program%20Files/Windows%20Mail/msoe.dll
5	132115736325813786	132138196030768150	132115484325730216	132115736325813786	:2019082920190830: IEUser@file:///C:/Users/IEUser/Downloads/EnableWinMailWin7/msoe_32.zip

Figure 9.13 – Contents of table 12

Table `12` is a daily history file, and it shows five entries for that day. When we look at the URL, it is not showing up as internet history, but is depicting the files the user accessed with File Explorer. The user accessed the `Windows Mail` folder and the `Download` folder. It lists the specific filenames at the end of the path.

The date and time values are a decimal conversion of the hexadecimal Windows 64-bit (Big Endian).

To convert the values, you will need to do the following:

- Take the decimal number, `132115734791679663`
- Convert it into hex, `1D5 5E8F 917F 6EAF`

Then, you need to use DCode to get the date/timestamp:

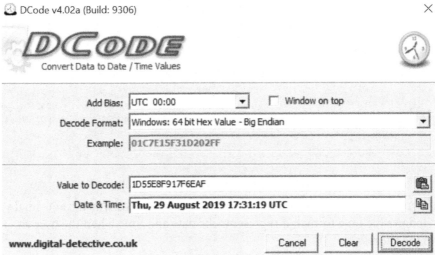

Figure 9.14 – DCode tool used to convert Windows Time value

We have the user's history, but does it show that the user willingly and knowingly visited the sites listed in the history? Is it possible there are references to websites the user never visited? The answer to those questions is yes. With pop-ups, and ads, it is possible to have a reference in the history file that the user never visited.

To help show the intent of the user, we want to see an artifact showing the user's actions explicitly. That is the next artifact will talk about – typed URL.

Typed URL

When the user types a URL into the address bar, a record is created in the user's `NTUSER.dat` file. The following output is from `RegRipper`:

```
TypedURLs
Software\Microsoft\Internet Explorer\TypedURLs
LastWrite Time Tue Sep  3 17:29:58 2019 (UTC)
  url1 -> http://bankrobbery.com/
  url2 -> http://yahoo.com/
  url3 -> http://gmail.com/
```

The most recent typed URL is `url1`. The system will only list each URL one time. If the user enters the same URL, the system will move the URL to the top of the list to become the most recent URL. With Internet Explorer version 10, the maximum number of URLs is 50.

There is a registry key of typed URLs time; see `TypedUrlTime` in the following screenshot:

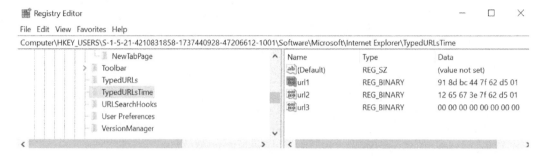

Figure 9.15 – TypedURLsTime registry entry

The URL number corresponds to the same value in typed URLs. The hexadecimal value is in the Windows file time format; it represents the date and time when the user entered the URL into the address bar.

Another source of information is the cache, which we will discuss next.

Cache

The `WebCacheV01.dat` file we analyzed in the *IE history* section also handles the cache files. You can use `ESEDatabaseViewer` to analyze the database, but there is another option you can use called Internet Explorer Cache Viewer (available at `https://www.nirsoft.net/utils/ie_cache_viewer.html`).

The following screenshot (cache view) shows the output of the viewer:

Filename	Content Type	URL	Last Accessed	Last Modified	Expiration Time
acquire-80[1].png	image/png	https://f6ef4eacbe624ae1083a-b3d937de523d4a3...	9/2/2019 11:27	12/5/2018 13:05	9/2/2019 11:42
update_2_19_0_1...	text/html	https://f6ef4eacbe624ae1083a-b3d937de523d4a3...	9/2/2019 11:27	8/22/2019 09:59	9/2/2019 11:42
AAGEZpS[1].jpg	image/jpeg	http://static-global-s-msn-com.akamaized.net/i...	9/2/2019 11:23	9/2/2019 04:57	9/7/2019 04:56
AAesHLQ[1].png	image/png	http://static-global-s-msn-com.akamaized.net/i...	9/2/2019 11:23	8/30/2019 00:28	9/4/2019 00:28
AAGHCg4[1].jpg	image/jpeg	http://static-global-s-msn-com.akamaized.net/i...	9/2/2019 11:23	9/2/2019 10:27	9/7/2019 10:27

Figure 9.16 – The output of cache view

The tool will give you the filename and the URL of where the file came from, along with the date/time stamps. The system stores these files in the following path(s):

- For a Windows 7-based system:

```
%USER%/AppData/Local/Microsoft/Windows/Temporary Internet
Files\Content.IE5
```

```
Temporary Internet Files
├──Content.IE5
│    ├──OPDYBC4P
│    ├──S97WTYG7
│    ├──Q67FIXJT
│    ├──4MNQZMD8
│    ├──SCD1EGFC
│    ├──34UZLM61
│    ├──V2I5AL1G
│    └──5S4OGUTD
```

- For a Windows 8/10-based system:

```
%USERS%/AppData/LocalLow/Microsoft/Windows/AppCache

Windows
    └──AppCache
        └──0Z1ZMDEH
%USERS%/AppData/Local/Microsoft/Windows/INetCache
INetCache
│    ├──Low
│    │    ├──IE
│    │    │    ├──4TENJ512
│    │    │    ├──9SKPYC9A
│    │    │    ├──QMIGA2MM
│    │    │    └──EP19S3JV
```

- For the Microsoft Edge browser:

```
%USER%/AppData/Local/Packages/Microsoft.
MicrosoftEdge_8wekyb3d8bbwe/AC

MicrosoftEdge
│    │    ├
│    │    ├──Cache
│    │    │    ├──9CG3K1S3
│    │    │    ├──IHCXX8UB
│    │    │    ├──OOW222LO
│    │    │    └──CENY1YGT
```

The system will randomly generate the naming of the subdirectories using alphanumeric characters.

The next artifact we will discuss is cookies.

Cookies

Edge and Internet Explorer save the cookie files as simple text files. `WebCacheV01.dat` also tracks the cookie files, as shown in the following screenshot:

ContainerId	LastAccessTime	Name	PartitionId	Directory
1	132119207925900830	Content	M	C:\Users\IEUser\AppData\Local\Microsoft\Windows\Temporary Internet Files\Content.IE5\
2	132115040805283385	feedplat	M	C:\Users\IEUser\AppData\Local\Microsoft\Feeds Cache\
3	131594261121527040	ietld	M	C:\Users\IEUser\AppData\Roaming\Microsoft\Windows\IETldCache\
4	132119207924265464	History	M	C:\Users\IEUser\AppData\Local\Microsoft\Windows\History\History.IE5\
5	132119207926189424	Cookies	M	C:\Users\IEUser\AppData\Roaming\Microsoft\Windows\Cookies\
6	132119207925419840	iecompat	M	C:\Users\IEUser\AppData\Roaming\Microsoft\Windows\IECompatCache\
7	132119207925516038	iecompatua	M	C:\Users\IEUser\AppData\Roaming\Microsoft\Windows\iecompatuaCache\
8	132119207913683684	DNTException	M	C:\Users\IEUser\AppData\Roaming\Microsoft\Windows\DNTException\
9	132119207925131246	EmieSiteList	M	C:\Users\IEUser\AppData\Local\Microsoft\Internet Explorer\EmieSiteList\
10	132119207925131246	EmieUserList	M	C:\Users\IEUser\AppData\Local\Microsoft\Internet Explorer\EmieUserList\
11	132119207944659440	DOMStore	M	C:\Users\IEUser\AppData\Local\Microsoft\Internet Explorer\DOMStore\
12	132119207959858724	MSHist012019082820190829	M	C:\Users\IEUser\AppData\Local\Microsoft\Windows\History\History.IE5\MSHist012019082820190829\
13	132115041147334574	iedownload	M	C:\Users\IEUser\AppData\Roaming\Microsoft\Windows\IEDownloadHistory\

Figure 9.17 – Content of the Containers table

Table 5 contains the information about the cookies and is displayed in the following screenshot:

EntryId	AccessCount	SyncTime	CreationTime	ExpiryTime	ModifiedTime	AccessedTime	Url	Filename
36	18	132119208683123513	132119208683098265	132435432680000000	132119208683098265	132119208683123513	Cookie:ieuser@yahoo.com/	IF0DA7EK.txt
41	2	132115040834588257	132115040834204478	132452000840000000	132115040834204478	132119208375537727	Cookie:ieuser@www2.bing.com/	QZVGRJVN.txt
21	17	132119208820850307	132119208820850307	132460487960000000	132119208820850307	132119222099087060	Cookie:ieuser@www.msn.com/	Q01C9WT2.txt
47	3	132115044434921485	132115044434921485	132115908430000000	132115044434921485	132115044436696825	Cookie:ieuser@www.mozilla.org/	YP2ZL4QD.txt
45	4	132115040938396120	132115040938396120	132192800940000000	132115040938396120	132119208561572465	Cookie:ieuser@www.google.com/	U095JS89.txt
88	1	132119208810386393	132119208810378061	132750792850000000	132119208810378061	132119208810386393	Cookie:ieuser@www.bing.com/images	6MC65DME.txt
38	6	132115040768554247	132115040768554247	132452000760000000	132115040768554247	132119222095615988	Cookie:ieuser@www.bing.com/	IT9CA013.txt
60	20	132119208680379897	132119208680379897	133696008670000000	132119208680379897	132119208686590905	Cookie:ieuser@www.akc.org/	0W6YLVUJ.txt
24	8	132119208661351321	132119208661342905	132461352650000000	132119208661342905	132119208661351321	Cookie:ieuser@w55c.net/	XTF8XNNC.txt
50	1	132119208020635033	132119208020550601	132434568060000000	132119208020550601	132119208020635033	Cookie:ieuser@tvpixel.com/	QLCX0KXB.txt

Figure 9.18 – Content of the Cookies table

Just like when we examine the history, the date/time stamps are decimal conversions of the hexadecimal Windows file time. It also contains the URL and the filename being stored on the system.

The cookie files are stored in the following path(s):

- For Internet Explorer:

```
%USER%/AppData/Roaming/Microsoft/Windows/Cookies/
```

- For Microsoft Edge:

```
%USER%/AppData/Local/Packages/Microsoft.
MicrosoftEdge_8wekyb3d8bbwe/AC/MicrosoftEdge/Cookies
```

When we look at the contents of the folder, we find that it is full of text files, with the filenames of the random alphanumeric character format that Windows uses. The following output is typical of what you may find:

```
Name            Created                  Modified
06PC9CZM.txt    09/03/2019   17:29:48    09/03/2019   17:29:48
09BHTXJM.txt    09/02/2019   18:00:59    09/02/2019   18:00:59
09WSNIHD.txt    09/03/2019   17:29:27    09/03/2019   17:29:27
0W6YLVUJ.txt    09/02/2019   18:01:08    09/02/2019   18:01:08
0WBQAB4E.txt    09/02/2019   18:23:51    09/02/2019   18:23:51
16SUYNBJ.txt    09/03/2019   17:29:51    09/03/2019   17:29:51
1983DVP6.txt    09/02/2019   18:23:46    09/02/2019   18:23:46
28Z2GM8G.txt    09/03/2019   17:29:49    09/03/2019   17:29:49
2CM18GNC.txt    09/03/2019   17:29:38    09/03/2019   17:29:38
```

For an effective analyzation, you will have to work through the WebCacheV01.dat file to determine which cookie file is associated with each entry in the database.

The following is an example of the content of a cookie text file:

```
MR
0
c.msn.com/
1024
3308281856
30796639
4095225949
30760429
```

This cookie is from the MSN website, and as we discussed previously, it tracks the user's visits and any of the preferences that may be enabled at the time of the visit.

Examining the cookies of the browser will never be the smoking gun, but you could use it to support your hypothesis regarding what occurred during your investigation.

Exploring Firefox

Firefox is an open source browser developed by the Mozilla foundation. Mozilla released Firefox in 2004 and is a browser you may encounter during your investigations. We will cover some more common artifacts you may encounter during your examination.

Profiles

One feature offered by Firefox is the use of multiple profiles. A user has the option to create multiple profiles for the browser to segregate their activity. The path where you can find the profiles is as follows:

```
%USER%/AppData/Local/Mozilla/Firefox
```

I have found three user profiles and they are displayed as follows:

```
Firefox
└─Profiles
  ├─tszci9zh.Badguy
  │ ├─thumbnails
  │ ├─safebrowsing
  │ │ └─google4
  │ ├─startupCache
  │ ├─cache2
  │ │ ├─entries
  │ │ └─doomed
  │ └─OfflineCache
```

This is the BadGuy profile:

```
  ├─fd8rnyou.BagGuy Needs Love
  │ ├─startupCache
  │ ├─cache2
  │ │ ├─entries
  │ │ └─doomed
  │ ├─thumbnails
  │ ├─safebrowsing
  │ │ └─google4
  │ └─OfflineCache
```

The user of this profile is BadGuy Needs Love:

```
  ├─30nh3g6c.default-release
  │ ├─startupCache
  │ ├─cache2
  │ │ ├─doomed
  │ │ └─entries
  │ ├─thumbnails
  │ ├─OfflineCache
```

```
|    ├──safebrowsing
|    |   └──google4
|    └──jumpListCache
```

The final profile is the default user.

Firefox creates the profile with a random alphanumeric eight-digit prefix, followed by the username. If the user has not created any additional profiles, you will only see the default – release and default username. Here, the user has created two additional profiles:

- Badguy
- Badguy Needs Love

Inside each folder structure, Firefox will save data appropriate to each profile.

There is also a profiles.ini file, which can be found at the following path:

```
%USER%/AppData/Roaming/Mozilla/Firefox/profiles.ini
```

The contents of the profile.ini file is as follows:

```
[Install308046B0AF4A39CB]
Default=Profiles/tszci9zh.Badguy
Locked=1

[Profile2]
Name=Badguy
IsRelative=1
Path=Profiles/tszci9zh.Badguy
Default=1

[Profile1]
Name=default
IsRelative=1
Path=Profiles/9wofgs9f.default

[Profile0]
Name=default-release
IsRelative=1
Path=Profiles/30nh3g6c.default-release

[General]
Startwithlastprofile=1
Version=2
```

```
[Profile3]
Name=BagGuy Needs Love
IsRelative=1
Path=Profiles/fd8rnyou.BagGuy Needs Love
```

The `Startwithlastprofile` field shows which profile will start when the application starts. Here, it shows that the `BadGuy` profile is the default profile.

We will now move on and look at the cache.

Cache

Firefox stores the cache files under each profile. The file path will remain the same, as we discussed in the previous section:

```
%USER%/AppData/Local/Mozilla/Firefox/Profiles/%Profile%

Firefox
└──Profiles
    ├──tszci9zh.Badguy
    │   ├──thumbnails
    │   ├──safebrowsing
    │   │   └──google4
    │   ├──startupCache
    │   ├──cache2
    │   │   ├──entries
    │   │   └──doomed
    │   └──OfflineCache
```

Firefox will store the cache in the `cache2` profiles. You can use the open source application `MZcacheview` (available at `https://www.nirsoft.net/utils/mozilla_cache_viewer.html`) to view the contents. The results are very similar to what we have seen in the previous browsers.

Cookies

Unlike Internet Explorer, Firefox does not save the browser cookies in single files. Firefox uses a SQLite database to store this information. You can find the cookie database at the following path:

```
%USER%/AppData/Roaming/Mozilla/Firefox/Profiles/%Profile%
```

Note the change in the path. Instead of being stored in the `Local` folder, we are now in the `Roaming` folder.

You can use the third-party open source application MZCookiesView (available at `https://www.nirsoft.net/utils/mzcv.html`) to view the file or any SQLite database reader.

The next artifact we will discuss is the history file.

History

Mozilla Firefox tracks the browser history in the SQLite database file called `places.sqlite`. Firefox also tracks the users typed URLs in this database You can use any SQLite database tool to read the file, or you can use the third-party open source MZHistoryView (available at `https://www.nirsoft.net/utils/mozilla_history_view.html`). You can find the history database at the following path:

```
%USER%/AppData/Roaming/Mozilla/Firefox/Profiles/%Profile%
```

The following screenshot shows the typical output you would see with this tool:

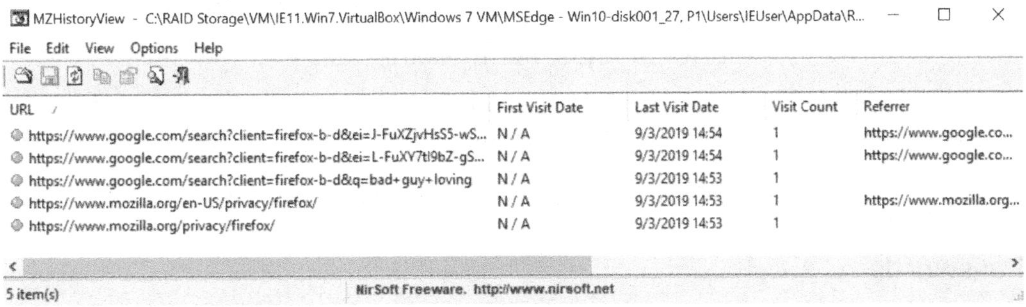

Figure 9.19 – Firefox history is shown in MZHistoryView

> **Note**
>
> The image Firefox history only shows a few entries. If this was an actual investigation, depending on how long they used the Firefox browser, you could find thousands of entries in the history file.

An example of the typed URL is in the third record. If you double-click on the entry, it will bring up the `Properties` window, as shown in the following screenshot:

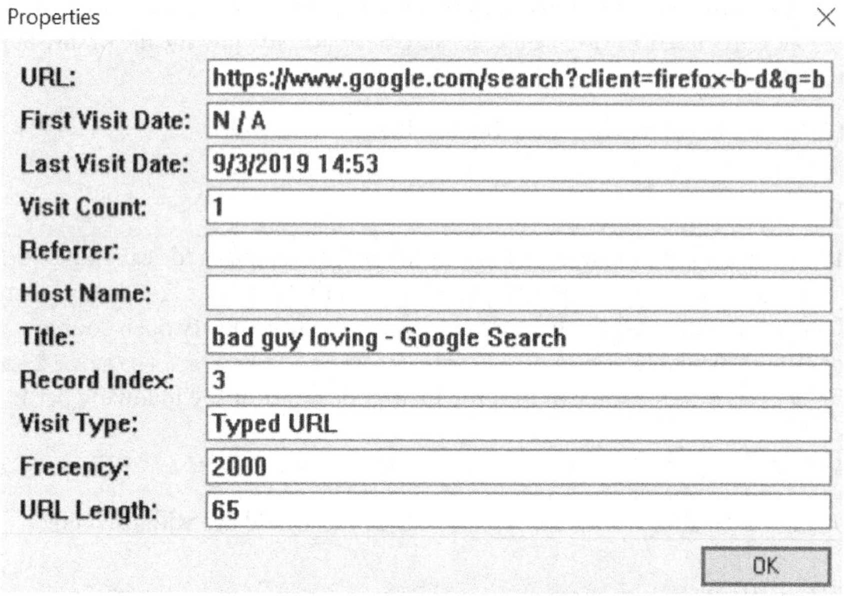

Properties   ✕

URL:	https://www.google.com/search?client=firefox-b-d&q=b
First Visit Date:	N / A
Last Visit Date:	9/3/2019 14:53
Visit Count:	1
Referrer:	
Host Name:	
Title:	bad guy loving - Google Search
Record Index:	3
Visit Type:	Typed URL
Frecency:	2000
URL Length:	65

OK

Figure 9.20 – Typed URL is shown in record 3

From the preceding screenshot, we can determine that the user did a Google search for the phrase bad guy loving on September 3, 2019.

Passwords will be the next artifact we will discuss.

Passwords

Mozilla Firefox offers the user the opportunity to save their passwords. Firefox uses two files, key#.db (I have seen files named key3 and key4; be aware you may come across additional numbers) and logins.json, to store the passwords in an encrypted format. We can decode the passwords using the open source third-party tool Password Fox (available at https://www.nirsoft.net/utils/passwordfox.html).

You can find the files at the following path:

```
%USER%/AppData/Roaming/Mozilla/Firefox/Profiles/%Profile%
```

In the following screenshot, you can see the typical output of Password Fox:

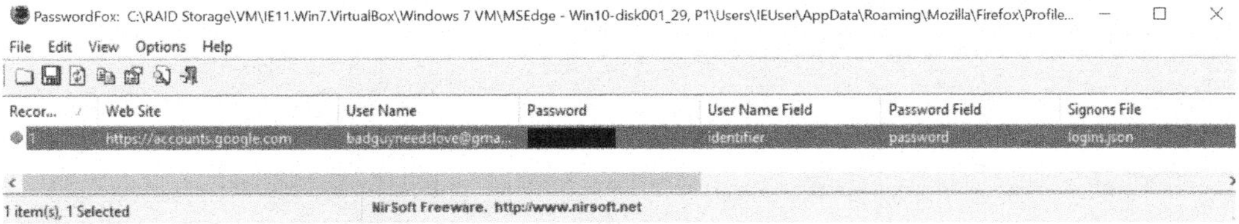

Figure 9.21 – Password shown in PasswordFox

I have redacted the password in the following screenshot, but it is beneficial when you gain access to the user's passwords and to access the accounts (with proper authorization, of course.) If you double-click on the record, it will bring up the Properties window, as displayed in the following screenshot, showing password properties:

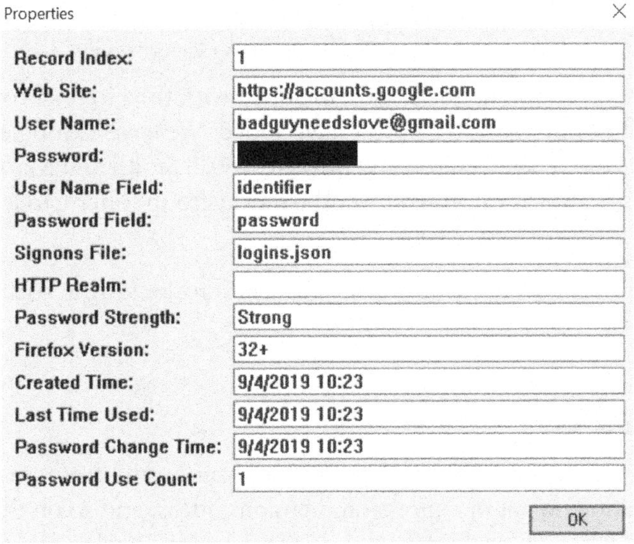

Figure 9.22 – Password properties in Password Fox

As we analyze the content, it appears this is the user's Gmail account, and we have the date/time stamps for when the password was created, changed, and used.

Bookmarks

Mozilla Firefox saves the user's bookmarks in an SQLite database file. You can find the database file at the following path:

```
%USER%/AppData/Roaming/Mozilla/Firefox/Profiles/%Profile%
```

You can use the third-party open source tool FavoritesView (available at `https://www.nirsoft.net/utils/faview.html`) to do this. The following screenshot shows the output of the FavoritesView application:

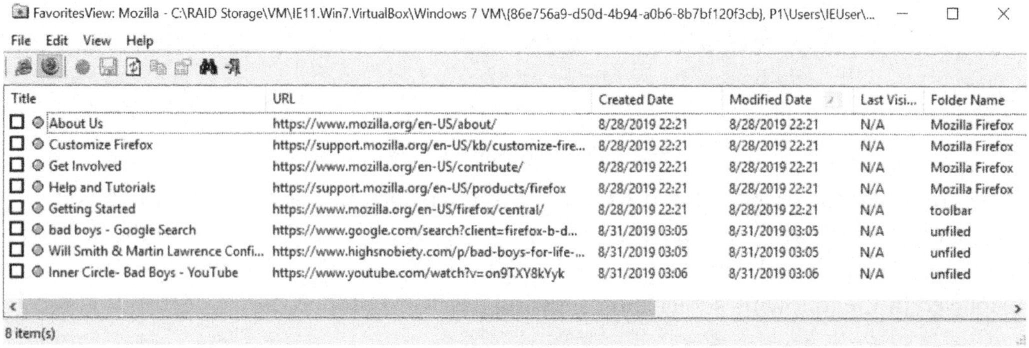

Figure 9.23 – Favorites are shown in FavoritesView

You can see the default bookmarks that are included with the Firefox browser. The last three entries are the bookmarks that users have added. We have a Google search for the term `bad boys`. A web page referencing the actors Will Smith and Martin Lawrence and the final entry is a YouTube video from the music group Inner Circle for their video Bad Boys.

That completes our analysis of the browsers. We will start looking at social media in the next section.

Social media

What is social media? Social media is the use of applications or programs to create and share information, forms of expression, opinions, ideas, and so on through virtual communities through the global internet. Users can access social media through web-based technology such as a mobile device application. In some situations, the user can sync data from one platform to another. These platforms/applications rarely require a fee from the user and are very simple to use.

While a majority of social media users use the services in a manner the service provider intended, some use these new communication media for nefarious purposes. It is a very unusual investigation where social media does not play a part in the investigation.

The user's social media communication leaves a digital trail of breadcrumbs for the investigator to follow. Sometimes, the investigator can determine the user's location at the date/time when the incident being investigated occurred. Alternatively, they may find communications between the suspect and victim that led to the incident being investigated.

As a digital forensic investigator, you will have to be aware of the existence of social media and what potential artifacts exist in digital evidence. A significant challenge when searching social media is that the majority of the social media artifacts will not be saved to the user system. The applications store the data in the service provider's cloud, which is a fancy way of saying the data will be on the service provider's servers.

Because of the vast diversity and sheer amount of social media applications, there is not a simple checklist that will cover all situations. The digital forensic investigator must be flexible in their investigation techniques when dealing with new social media technology or changing social media technology.

The goal of this section is to familiarize you with some current social media applications and to provide you with a general plan for your investigation. Remember, when conducting an analysis dealing with social media, there may be two locations for you to find digital evidence relating to your investigation: the user system and the service provider. Do not neglect to serve the appropriate judicial paperwork on the service provider; typically, they will give you extensive information regarding your investigation.

The popularity of specific social media ebbs and flows as the users' demographic changes. Some younger users are disinclined to use Facebook with their friends because their parents and grandparents also use Facebook. Some social media applications may be restricted to geographical locations; for example, KaKaoTalk is very popular in the Republic of Korea but has very few users in the United States. The following is a short description of some popular social media applications you make come across during your investigations:

- Facebook: The most extensive social media application with nearly 2,000,000,000 users. It combines commercial advertisers and consumer users with their content. It is easy to use. Users can upload images, recorded videos, live videos, and voice/video/text chat via the messenger application.

- Instagram: A photo and video sharing social media application. Users can share photos and recorded videos and live videos. Users can also chat and comment with other users via the app.

- Snapchat: A video/photo-sharing social media application. Initially, when a user sent a "snap" after the recipient viewed the image, it would be deleted from the system. Now, users have the option of saving "snaps."

- Twitter: Social media application used for news, politics, sports, entertainment, and so on. Twitter allows 280-character tweets, with longer tweets being linked in the following messages.

- WhatsApp: A messaging application that allows users to engage in voice/video chat.

- Tinder: A location-based social media application used as a dating service. Users "swipe right" or "swipe left" on profiles they like/dislike. If both parties "like" each other, then they can chat using the app.

- GroupMe: This is a group messaging application. Users can use their cell phone number or use their Facebook or Twitter account to log in to the app. Users can share photos, videos, locations, and text.

- Kik: Instant messaging social media application. The service provider is based in Canada. It allows anonymous communication between individuals. Users can share text, photos, and videos. It is estimated that nearly 40 percent of teenagers in the United States use the application. (While this book was going through the editing and post production processing, Kik has ceased operation as a social media venue)

- Tumblr: A blogging/social networking application. Users can post pictures/videos to a blog page.

- Reddit: This is a news aggregation and discussion social media application. It contains almost every topic imaginable, including illegal activities. In July 2019, it was the number five most visited website in the United States.

This is not a complete list of social media applications you may come across, nor would I attempt to create such a list. Social media applications will change as technology changes, and as the users' choices grow, new social media applications will come to the forefront. As a digital forensic investigator, it will be impossible for you to know all the facets of all the social media applications. You need to understand what social media applications are being used and how they are being used by consumers and criminals. Some social media applications will not have the means to be accessed via the localhost; the service provider will restrict them to being accessed by a mobile device only. How can you determine if the subject of the investigation is using a social media platform? The web browser history will be essential in that regard; they may access their profile/account via a web browser, or there may be email communication between the user and the service provider. One of the more popular social media applications you may come across is Facebook.

Facebook

Facebook is a social media platform that a user can access via the web browser. Analyzing those artifacts may give you the username or the Facebook user ID. Let's say you analyze an URL, such as the one displayed here:

```
https://www.facebook.com/photo.php?fbid=10215539711464494&set
=a.1627301761019&type=3&source=11&referrer_profile_
id=1190817474
```

As you examine the URL, the portion relevant to our organization is the profile ID, which is as follows:

```
profile_id=1190817474
```

When you add the numbers to the end of the Facebook.com, it will take you to the user's Facebook page. The profile ID is a unique number and will redirect you to the user's Facebook username, as shown in the following screenshot:

Figure 9.24 – Facebook URL

Once you have obtained the user's Facebook profile ID number and their username, that information can then be given to the service provider as part of the judicial paperwork. This can be used to access the content being stored on the service provider's servers.

Another tool that you can use is Bulk Extractor (which we discussed in *Chapter 7, RAM Memory Forensic Analysis*). When you run Bulk Extractor, it will also find the profile ID numbers, as shown in the following screenshot:

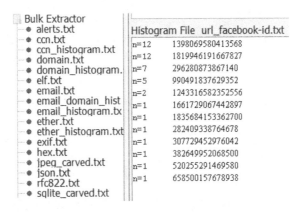

Figure 9.25 – Bulk Extractor output for Facebook

You can run Bulk Extractor against the forensic image or a captured memory file to find artifacts relating to social media. Another very popular social media application you may come across is Twitter.

Twitter

We can filter the results from the domain histogram, as shown in the following screenshot. Here, we can see the user accessed the Twitter web page:

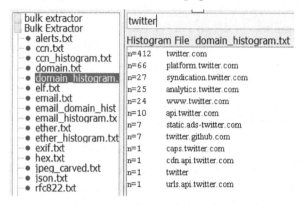

Figure 9.26 – Bulk Extractor output for Twitter

Twitter users have a "handle" and a UID (user ID) when they sign up for the service. Users can change their handle whenever they desire, but the UID will remain the same. If we have a user with the handle of @badguyneedslove and then they change it @badguy27, the UID will stay the same.

Searching for the term twid in the forensic image will identify the UID for the account. You can also take the user's Twitter handle and use the following website: http://gettwitterid.com.

This will give you the UID when you input the Twitter handle, as shown in the following screenshot:

Figure 9.27 – Twitter ID

We entered the Twitter handle of `badguyneedslove`, and it gave us the Twitter ID of `1170432764291665920`, as well as the full name of the user (which may or may not be accurate. Remember this is user-supplied information.).

Not all of the information you want or need for your investigation will be found on the user's device; you may have to reach out to the service provider to get information being stored on the service provider's servers.

Service provider

A majority of the information you need for your investigation will be in the care and custody of the service provider. They will have the subscriber information such as, name, address, age, usage dates/times, and IP addresses. This content is hosted on the service provider servers. This seized computer system or mobile device may not have all the information you want as you conduct your investigation. Serve the service provider with the appropriate judicial paperwork to get that information. The judicial framework will be based on where the service provider is located. You will have to meet all the requirements of the service provider's judicial system.

`Search.org` maintains a service provider list and contact information of the legal department that will receive the completed judicial paperwork. Some service providers also provide that information on their website. For example, the service provider Kik has created a specific web page (located at `https://lawenforcement.kik.com/hc/en-us`) that contains all the information needed by the investigator to serve them with additional paperwork.

Investigating a user's activity on social media can be difficult. You may have to use third-party software or manually parse through the hexadecimal data stored on the storage device. Even with all of that effort, it may come down to the retention policies of the service provider for you to get the information you need to make your investigation successful. Another aspect of the internet that has the potential for criminal use is peer-to-peer file sharing, which is our next topic.

Peer-to-Peer file sharing

Peer-to-Peer (**P2P**) file sharing allows users to share files with others in the P2P community. Users will share videos or music files with the community, but you can find almost any file type you can imagine. P2P has legitimate and illegitimate uses, depending on the user's search criteria. It is a popular method of sharing illicit images and videos with other users in the P2P community. There are several P2P applications the user can choose from. I cannot give a detailed analysis on all potential P2P applications, but we will go over some more common P2P applications you may run into during your investigations.

P2P applications allow the user to become a node on the network. When the user installs the application, they can designate which files/folders they want to make available to the P2P network. The application will then create an index of the shared files/folders to share on the P2P network. When the user searches the P2P network and finds a file they wish to download, the application will identify all the nodes possessing that file. The application will then connect to the nodes and start downloading pieces of the file from all the available nodes.

When the P2P application shares the files/folders, it tracks the filename and the file type, and creates a SHA-1 hash value for the file. This will be a variation of the SHA-1 hash value used by the commercial and open source forensic tools. The P2P version of the SHA-1 creates a hash value using the Base32 numbering system, while the forensic tools use the Base16 numbering system. The Base16 numbering system uses the alphanumeric characters 0 – 9 and A – F, while the Base32 numbering system uses that alphanumeric characters A – Z and 2 – 7. Chris Hurst posted how to use Python to convert Base32 values into Base16 (available at `https://github.com/qbittorrent/qBittorrent/wiki/How-to-convert-base32-to-base16-info-hashes`). The following is the Python code that Chris Hurst provided:

```
>>> import base64
>>> b32Hash = "WRN7ZT6NKMA6SSXYKAFRUGDDIFJUNKI2"
>>> b16Hash = base64.b16encode(base64.b32decode(b32Hash))
>>> b16Hash = b16Hash.lower()
>>> print (b16Hash)
```

After you spend some time working in the field of digital forensics, you will learn the artifacts you may find depends on the operating system, the P2P application, and if the user modified any of the default settings.

We will now look into some of the common P2P applications you may encounter during your digital forensic investigations.

Ares

Ares Galaxy is an open source P2P application utilizing the decentralized network configuration (available at `sourceforge.net/projects/aresgalaxy/`). Ares creates entries in the user's local profile path, as shown here:

```
%USER%\AppData\Local\Ares\
```

In the `Data` folder, you will find two files, `ShareH.net` and `ShareL.dat`. These files track the filename, the hash value, the date/time stamp of when the file was downloaded, and the sharing status of the file. These files are encrypted but can be decrypted using the Magnet Forensics AXIOM forensic tool (available at `https://www.magnetforensics.com`).

Ares creates entries in the user's `NTUSER.dat` file, as shown here:

```
\ntuser (ROOT)\Software\Ares
```

When we run `RegRipper` against the `NTUSER.dat` file, we get the following output:

```
Software\Ares
LastWrite Time Sat Sep  7 21:48:04 2019 (UTC)
Stats.LstConnect: Mon Sep  8 15:51:07 2019 UTC
Personal.Nickname: Badguy27
General.Language: English
PrivateMessage.AwayMessage: This is an automatic away message
generated by Ares program, user isn't here now.
Search Terms: Badguy movies
```

The application stores the last date/timestamp application connected, the nickname of the user (this can also be an auto-generated field based on the account username of the operating system), and the last 25 search terms entered by the user.

Depending on the version of Ares the user has installed, it may change the `location/` information in the `NTUSER.dat` file.

eMule

eMule is an open source P2P application utilizing the decentralized network configuration and was released in 2002 as an alternative to eDonkey2000 (available at `www.emule-project.net`). When the user installs eMule, it creates an `eMule` folder, containing two subfolders, `incoming` and `temp`, as shown here:

```
Downloads
└──eMule
     ├──Incoming
     └──Temp
```

As files are being downloaded, the file parts are stored in the `temp` folder and when all the pieces have been downloaded, the completed file is moved into the `incoming` folder. These folders are shared by default and cannot be disabled by the user.

eMule stores its configuration files in the user's local profile, as follows:

```
%USER%\AppData\Local\eMule
```

In the `config` subdirectory, you will find the `preferences.ini` file. Contained within will be the user's nickname and the location of the incoming and temporary directories, as follows:

```
AppVersion=0.50a
Nick=http://emule-project.net
IncomingDir=C:\Users\IEUser\Downloads\eMule\Incoming
TempDir=C:\Users\IEUser\Downloads\eMule\Temp
```

If the user does not specify a nickname, the default nickname is the URL email, that is, `project.net`.

Also of interest will be `shareddir.dat` and `sharedfiles.dat`. `shareddir.dat` will contain the user-created shared directories, as follows:

```
%USER%\Downloads\
```

In this case, the user is also sharing their `Downloads` folder. The `sharedfiles.dat` file will contain a list of files being currently shared. The output may be similar to what is shown here:

```
C:\Users\IEUser\Downloads\aresregular246_installer.exe
C:\Users\IEUser\Downloads\bad-guy-pictures-145577-3671477.png
C:\Users\IEUser\Downloads\eMule0.50a-Installer.exe
C:\Users\IEUser\Downloads\Shareaza_2.7.10.2_x64.exe
```

The file indicates the user is sharing three executables and a PNG image.

In the `preferences.dat` File, you will find the unique identification number assigned to each user on the network. It is a 16-byte hexadecimal value, as shown in the following screenshot:

```
Offset     0  1  2  3  4  5  6  7   8  9 10 11 12 13 14 15    ANSI ASCII
00000000  14 C2 B6 08 E8 AA 0E 5A  EA 26 35 5C BB 56 F5 6F  Â¶ è² Zê&5\»Võo
00000016  4C 2C 00 00 00 00 00 00  00 01 00 00 00 FF FF FF  L,           ÿÿÿ
00000032  FF FF FF FF FF FF FF FF  FF FF FF FF FF 0A 00 00  ÿÿÿÿÿÿÿÿÿÿÿÿÿ
00000048  00 0A 00 00 00 1F 03 00  00 58 02 00 00          X
```

Figure 9.28 – eMule User ID

The user identification number is highlighted. Also, note that in every identification number, in 6th and the 15th byte, you will find the values x/0E and x/6F.

The AC_SearchStrings.dat file will store the last 30 searched terms entered by the user. In the following screenshot, eMule Search Terms shows the user only searched for the term charlie chaplin:

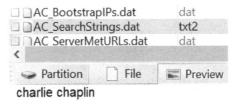

Figure 9.29 – eMule Search Terms

The known.met file contains a list of files that have been downloaded by the application and files that have been shared by the application. You may find filenames indicative of contraband images that are no longer on the user's system. The application will delete entries as the the.met file increases in size to prevent the file from becoming too large. In the following screenshot, you can see the contents of the .met file:

Filename	File Size	Last Written (UTC)	Last Shared (UTC)	File Hash
eMule0.50a-Installer.exe	3,389,035	9/7/2019 20:35	9/7/2019 21:40	3D366ED505B977FC61C9A6EE01E96329
bad-guy-pictures-145577-3671477.png	77,384	9/7/2019 19:25	9/7/2019 21:40	C6829ED8112C9FAF77D4A11A4AFC971E
Shareaza_2.7.10.2_x64.exe	7,437,220	9/7/2019 20:36	9/7/2019 21:40	E465DB484C7EE2F5737AF018B92A5E69
aresregular246_installer.exe	4,981,533	9/7/2019 20:33	9/7/2019 21:40	B34892C391BB1C961BBB494C70B2EA9B

0 / 4 selected | 4 selected records exported successfully

Figure 9.30 – MetViewer

The file will contain the filename, file size, and date/time stamps for when this file was shared and the hash value of the files. I used the third-party open source forensic tool eMule MET Viewer (which is available at https://www.gaijin.at/en/software/emulemetviewer).

The last P2P application we will look at is Shareaza.

Shareaza

Shareaza is an open source P2P application that utilizes the decentralized network configuration and was released in 2004 (available at `http://shareaza.sourceforge.net/`). The application will create a `Shareaza` folder in the `Local` and `Roaming` folders of the user's profile. The following is the folder structure(s) you will see in the user profile:

```
%USER%\AppData\Local\Shareaza
%USER%\AppData\Local\Shareaza\Incomplete

%USER%\AppData\Roaming\Shareaza
%USER%\AppData\Roaming\Shareaza\Collections
%USER%\AppData\Roaming\Shareaza\Data
%USER%\AppData\Roaming\Shareaza\Torrents
```

In the `Data` folder, you will find a file called `Profile.xml`, which will contain user-created and application created artifacts. The user can complete personal information such as name, location, and gender, and that will be included in the XML file.

Shareaza also creates entries in the user's `NTUSER.dat` file. It will create a Shareaza key with many subkeys. In the `Download` subkey, you will find the entries `CollectionPath` and `IncompletePath`. `CollectionPath` is where the completed files will be stored; `IncompletePath` is where the incomplete files are stored. In the following screenshot, we can see entries:

CollectionPath	REG SZ	C:\Users\IEUser\AppData\Roaming\Shareaza\Collections
CompletePath	REG SZ	C:\Users\IEUser\Downloads
ConnectThrottle	REG D...	0x0000012C (300)
FilterMask	REG D...	0xFFFFFFFF (4294967295)
FlushSD	REG D...	0x00000001 (1)
IncompletePath	REG SZ	C:\Users\IEUser\AppData\Local\Shareaza\Incomplete

Figure 9.31 – Shareaza path

You will also find the search terms inputted by the user in the **Search** subkey, as shown in the following screenshot:

Search.01	REG_SZ	charlie tuna
Search.02	REG_SZ	charlie
Search.03	REG_SZ	john
Search.04	REG_SZ	charlie chaplin

Figure 9.32 – Shareaza Search

In the `Data` folder, there is a file called `Library1.dat` that contains a list of shared folders, shared files, and a list of the partially downloaded files. There is also a backup of the file appropriately named `Library2.dat`, which is used if the first file is corrupted.

Cloud computing

What is cloud computing? Is it remote storage? Is it a remote server? Is it remote services? The answer to all the above is yes. Cloud-based services are becoming more popular for businesses and users every day. As a digital forensic investigator, you have to know of the potential for cloud-based evidence. We have already discussed some aspects of cloud-based artifacts in this chapter. Now, we will discuss some different elements of cloud-based computing. There are various service models of cloud-based computing you may encounter when conducting your digital forensic investigation. They are as follows:

- **Infrastructure as a Service (IaaS)**: The remote infrastructure is offered to the customer for use, while the provider maintains ownership and control of the hardware. The customer only pays for the hardware/service needed and gives the customer the flexibility to increase/decrease hardware requirements as required.

- **Software as a Service (SaaS)**: Applications are provided to the customer via the network. The customer pays a subscription fee to the vendor to use the software. The content and the user files are stored on the service provider's servers but can be used/shared with other members of the organization.

- **Platform as a Service (PaaS)**: The operating system of the client is provided to the customer via a cloud server. The user can then install their applications and maintain their settings of the software, while the provider manages the hardware and operating system. The client is responsible for the system administration within their network.

Another consideration is the deployment method of cloud resources. There are four to choose from:

- **Public cloud**: A cloud resource is made available to the public or specific members of an organization. Local government, university, or a sector of the community can offer a public cloud resource.

- **Private cloud**: A cloud resource made available to specific members. The user must have specific rights to access the resource. For example, an organization may maintain a private cloud resource for employees only.

- **Community cloud**: A cloud resource is similar to a private cloud, and is where the users comprise multiple organizations with a similar focus. For example, a cloud provider may restrict access to a cloud resource that's used by numerous law enforcement agencies to law enforcement only.

- **Hybrid cloud**: A cloud resource made up of two or more different deployment methods.

As you can see, the use of cloud computing can directly affect what artifacts you find or do not find on the local system. It is entirely possible that there will not be any artifacts relating to your investigation on the local system, which then leads to the question, where are the artifacts/evidence?

The answer to that question is, anywhere in the world. The data/artifact you may be looking for may be stored on a server located one mile away or several thousand miles away in another jurisdiction. Investigating when the hardware is not physically available creates significant issues for the digital forensic investigator. If you are law enforcement and you have a search warrant, is the search warrant valid for data maintained by the service provider outside of your jurisdiction? For the corporate investigator, a search warrant is not an option, but if the data is stored in a jurisdiction where the privacy expectations differ from where the investigation is based, you may also run into issues with accessing the data.

In the United States, this issue was in dispute until 2018 and would have been decided by the United States Supreme Court. Ultimately, the issue was resolved at the legislative level when Congress clarified the Stored Communications Act and now requires the service provider to provide the requested data if the information "is located within or outside of the United States."

For the corporate investigator, the **service-level agreement (SLA)** should spell out who may access the data and specify if there are to be any limitations when conducting a data acquisition in response to an investigation. The SLA should also address the geographical location of where the data may or may not be stored and address how legal conflicts should be resolved when the data is stored in different jurisdictions.

Different countries provide different protections regarding privacy issues and criminal and/or civil procedures. What may be a crime in one jurisdiction may not be in the jurisdiction where the server containing the data is located. In the **European Union (EU)**, EU citizens must be notified before their personal information is accessed, and they must give their consent.

Once you have been given access to the data that is needed for your digital forensic investigation, you still have to deal with the best practices in handling evidence. You may have chain of custody issues; how do you know if the provider used a forensically sound methodology to collect the evidence? Can you validate the methodology to show that they collected all relevant information? You do not want the opposition in judicial/administrative proceedings to make the allegation that exculpatory evidence was not collected and presented to the fact finder.

When conducting a digital forensic investigation, there are some artifacts you can examine that will show if the user has accessed any cloud-based applications. In this chapter, we have discussed the cache of web browsers and what happens if the user accesses the cloud-based applications with the web browser. In *Chapter 6, Windows Artifact Analysis,* we discussed examining the prefetch files. Remember that prefetch files are used to speed up the application's startup and will contain date/time stamps showing when the user last accessed that resource.

Dropbox and Google Drive are the most common cloud-based storage options available to the consumer. When the user installs the Dropbox or Google Drive application, the system will create a folder where the user can sync the data to the localhost and the cloud-based storage. As the user changes the local file, the system will then change the file maintained in the cloud-based storage. Alternatively, the user can upload/change a file via a web-based interface using a shared or public computer, and the system will then change the file or the uploaded file available on the user's personal device(s).

When using the Dropbox application, there will be two databases of interest to the digital forensic investigator:

- `config.dbx`: Contains the user ID, account email address, account username, and path for the `dropbox` folder.

- `filecache.dbx`: Contains the `file journal` table, which includes information about the files being synchronized between the localhost and the cloud-based storage. The table will consist of the filename, file path, and file size in the local host ID. The localhost ID is how we identify the host that placed the file into the Dropbox storage.

If you are investigating a user who is using the cloud-based storage Google Drive, the following databases may be of interest:

- `sync_config.db`: This will contain the path the Google Drive folder on the localhost, show if USB devices are being synced, and the email account associated with the Google Drive account.

- `snapshot.db`: The `local_entry` table will contain information about the files that have been synced between the localhost and the cloud-based storage. This will include the serial number of the volume, filename, modified date/time stamps, file size, and show if it is a file or a folder.

  The `cloud_entry` table will contain the filename, modified date/time stamps, file size, and if the user shares the file with other users.

- `device_db.db:`The `external_devices` table will contain the device ID, USB device label, upload date/time stamps, and if the user has synchronized the device to the cloud-based storage.

  The `device_files` table will contain the device ID of the USB device, the file name of the synced file, the file path, and the date/time stamp of when the file was synchronized to cloud-based storage.

Like most technology, cloud-based computing is rapidly evolving and changing. As the number of consumers who use cloud-based technology grows, so will the number of evidentiary artifacts you will have to examine when contacting your digital forensic investigation. You will always have to be mindful of the potential use of cloud-based computing when conducting your digital forensic investigations.

Summary

In this chapter, we have focused on what artifacts may be created by the user as they use a web browser. We covered different web browsers and looked at social media applications. We discussed the various social media and what artifacts they may leave behind. It is possible there may be minimal artifacts left on the user's system, but there may be additional artifacts in the user's mobile device or in the possession of the service provider. We also went into P2P file sharing and what artifacts they will leave on the user's system. You should now be able to understand and identify the different browsers and the artifacts that can be found, understand and identify the most popular social media applications and identify common locations where artifacts may be found, and understand the basic structure and operation of P2P file sharing networks and be familiar with typical P2P file sharing client applications and artifacts.

In the next chapter, we will be focusing on report writing. You may be able to find every possible artifact indicating the guilt or innocence of the subject, but if you cannot create a report that is easily understood by technical and non-technical readers, then you will lose the ability to make the reader understand. If the reader cannot understand what is in your report, they will never know what user activities you uncovered during your investigation.

Questions

1. Google Chrome saves bookmarks in what kind of file?

   a. JSON

   b. Text

   c. URL

   d. XML

2. What file type is the Google Chrome history file?

   a. Word doc

   b. JPEG

   c. SQLite database

   d. XML database

3. Internet Explorer/Edge will save typed URLs in which hive file?

   a. SOFTWARE

   b. SYSTEM

   c. SECURITY

   d. NTUSER.DAT

4. What is the cache?

   a. A bunch of files

   b. A bunch of pictures

   c. Files stored by a web browser

   d. Files stored by the user

5. What are cookies?

   a. A tasty afternoon delight

   b. A text file

   c. Something a Girl Scout sells

   d. A small file created when you send an email

6. P2P applications typically use what kind of server scheme?

   a. Centralized

   b. Decentralized

   c. IMAP server

   d, SQL server

7. Which P2P application uses the `ShareH.net` and `ShareL.dat` files?

   a. eMule

   b. Shareaza

   c. Ares

   d. eDonkey

Further reading

Casey, E. (2017). *Digital evidence and computer crime: forensic science, computers, and the internet. Vancouver, B.C.: Langara College.* Available at `https://www.amazon.com/Digital-Evidence-Computer-Crime-Computers/dp/0123742684`.

Section 3: Reporting

Even with the best examination in the world, if the investigator writes a weak report or is unable to communicate their findings, they will not be successful as an investigator. An investigator must be able to clearly and distinctly translate complex ideas into simple language for a non-technical user, and do so while maintaining the ethical principles of the profession.

This section contains the following chapters:

10
Report Writing

I have worked with examiners who loved getting down to the bits and bytes of investigation. No one worked harder as they examined the digital evidence, tracking the digital breadcrumbs until they had the evidence they needed. They were smart and brilliant, and if I had committed a digital crime, I would not want them to investigate it. It had nothing to do with their ability to investigate and everything to do with their ability to write a report. To say their report was lacking is a massive understatement.

Report writing is one of the hardest things you can do as a digital forensic investigator. You have to take a very technical subject and explain it in a manner that a non-technical person will understand, while not making any assumptions about the potential user or the digital evidence.

We'll be covering the following topics in this chapter:

- Effective note taking
- Writing the report

Effective note taking

Your ability to take notes will directly impact your ability to write an effective report on your digital forensic investigation. Your notes will be the foundation of your reporting. A simple phrase that has impacted me as I conduct my exams is *if you do not write it down, it did not happen*. One of your examinations may take days or months; you will simply not be able to remember what exactly you did on day 14 of your examination.

The fundamental elements of notetaking should include the following:

- When you did something
- What you did
- What you saw
- Why you did something

Your notetaking starts when you get the notification, and you have to respond to the scene. This includes the date/time when you are notified, who notified you, and when you arrived at the scene. Document any actions you take; if you collected volatile data, RAM from the system in question, did you alter the digital evidence? The answer will be *yes*. This is where the *why* is essential. *Why* did you alter the digital evidence? Here, the answer is simple – because the evidence would be lost if it was not collected at that time.

Another example if you are responding to a commercial business is whether the digital evidence is contained in a server environment. You cannot (in most cases) shut down the server to create a whole disk forensic image; you will have to create a logical forensic image of the files in question. Once again, the question of *why* may be asked, and you will have to explain.

If the matter you are investigating goes to trial, the opposing counsel will have access to the same digital evidence and the notes that were taken during the investigation. They will use your notes and your report to recreate your examination of the digital evidence. They are attempting to see whether they can get a different result or reach a different conclusion based on your actions.

How detailed should your notes be? The format of your notes is typically personalized to each digital forensic investigator. The baseline consideration should be, if the matter goes to trial years later, can you remember the details of the investigation?

There is no note standard, but you should include the following information:

- Suspect details.
- Victim details.
- Location of the digital evidence at the scene.

- Specifics of the digital evidence, make, model, the serial number of the system, any identifying marks (also include damage – there have been claims made that I damaged the system after it was seized. If you document the condition of the systems at the time of seizure, this will remove the effectiveness of those complaints).

- Condition of evidence bags/seals – if there is damage or broken seals.

- Details about the forensic hardware that was used, such as firmware/serial number.

- Details about the forensic software that was used, such as version number.

- Any findings that support or do not support your hypothesis about what occurred.

As a minimum, that is the information you should include in your notetaking. Can you incorporate more? Absolutely!

What medium should you use to take notes? I prefer handwriting at the scene and then transferring the notes into the digital medium. My handwriting is not the easiest to decipher, which is why that is my method. Also, digital photos are a medium for notetaking. When documenting the condition of the system or the storage device, it is straightforward to take a digital image and then refer to the image when completing your report.

Each organization/examiner will have their own standards about what information needs to be recorded, as well as the method to use to record information. No matter which method you use, it is crucial that you are organized and consistent throughout the entire investigation.

As you can see, notetaking is the foundation for writing the report, which is our next topic.

Writing the report

The purpose of your report is to document the results of your forensic examination and may support additional investigative endeavors. The report may also be used in criminal court proceedings, civil court proceedings, or administrative proceedings. Others can use your findings to support a probable cause hearing, grand jury proceeding, or as a basis for an administrative sanction in the corporate environment.

Your report will be the first step in providing testimony regarding the matter you are investigating. The opposition will scrutinize your report and if they call you to testify, expect to be questioned about the content of the report you created.

As you prepare to draft a report, identify who will be your audience. If you are writing the report for the Chief of Information, the IT security section, or any technology-based group, your report should go into much greater technical detail than the report directed toward lawyers, judges, or juries. If you go into minute detail about every artifact you found, you will lose your non-technical audience. While the technical audience will want those types of specific details and may feel insulted if you explain the details in a non-technical manner, it is possible to draft a report that addresses the technical and non-technical audience. The following is a general template you can follow:

- Administrative information
- Executive summary
- Narrative
- Exhibits/technical details
- Glossary

The administrative section will contain information about your investigation, such as the following:

- The name of the agency, the case number(s), and the participants in the investigation. This will include information about the investigators, the victim(s), and the suspect(s). If the investigation started with another agency, you would also include the administrative information from that organization. Include a brief history of the investigation.

- When was the investigation started and what events transpired before you were assigned to the investigation? This could be who was interviewed or interrogated, or any search warrants prepared and served. You are providing a synopsis of the investigation before your involvement. Include the search authority you have in order to investigate/examine the evidence. Include what you are investigating, that is, the scope of the search, and who authorized the search. If the digital forensic examination is being conducted pursuant to a search warrant, include the search warrant and the affidavit used as an exhibit in the *Exhibit/technical details* section.

The executive summary is a section that summarizes the report. The narrative of the report will go into much greater detail than the executive summary. When the reader is finished reading the executive summary, they should have a high-level view of what occurred in the investigation. The executive summary should follow the following guidelines:

- Should be only 10 percent of the report

- Written in short, clear, concise paragraphs

- Should follow the same timeline as the narrative

- Should not include any information not included in the narrative

- Should contain your findings/conclusions

This allows for the non-technical user to understand what actions you took during the investigation without going into technical detail. For example, if you found illicit images within the user's picture folder on a Windows 10-based operating system, you could report that fact in the executive summary like so:

```
During the computer forensic exam, I found 10 images, whose
content depicted what appears to be a male and female juvenile
engaged in illicit activities.  The images were located in the
Pictures Folder of the user account.
```

Your non-technical audience will understand exactly what you intended. Most consumers are familiar with the Windows operating system and how the `Pictures` folder of the user's account is accessed and used. In the narrative section, you can include a more detailed explanation, such as the following:

```
I conducted by exam on evidence tag 2016 - 001, which is an
Asus laptop serial number ABC 00 DEF. I identified one user
account "bad guy 27" which had an RID of "1005". In the folder
labeled "Pictures," I found the following images: 001.jpg, 002.
jpg, and 003.jpg , which depicted what appears to be a male and
female juvenile engaged in illicit acts in violation of state
law NRS 200.481. The folder and the pictures had ownership
properties associated with RID 1005, "bad guy 27". Additional
technical details about the image(s) are contained in exhibit
#1 in the technical details section of this report.
```

Clarity is one goal you seek to achieve as you draft the narrative. You do not want the reader to have questions or be unclear about your report. This can be difficult as you are combining the technical and non-technical aspects of the investigation. You also do not want to overwhelm the reader with technical details and acronyms. If you are in the criminal justice environment and the prosecuting attorney will read your report, you will most likely educate them on the technical aspect. Define the technical terms and concepts within the detailed narrative. How detailed does the narrative need to be?

There is not an easy answer. You should detail the narrative enough to inform the reader about the investigation, so if you are not available to answer questions, it should suffice for a judge, jury, or lawyer. Can your investigation be recreated based on the details in your narrative? The opposing counsel will have the ability to review the evidence and your report. If there is not enough detail for them to recreate your actions, it gives them the ability to question your results. Remember, it is possible that the judicial proceeding will take place months or years later. Your report will be the official memory of your organization for what occurred during that investigation.

You also want to ensure that the narrative is not biased. Your goal is to report the facts without overstating/understating their importance. One of the hardest things during the investigation is identifying the physical person behind the keyboard. You will base your identification on the digital identification of the user account. You are correlating the user account with the physical person operating the keyboard, using additional sources of digital evidence.

The narrative should contains various subsections, all of which we will go over now.

Evidence analyzed

In this section, you will include all the evidence you have examined, including the make/model, serial numbers, and so on. If it is a desktop/laptop, you should include the hard drives as a separate but related item.

The following is an example of the evidence that could be examined:

Item Name	Tag Number	Description
Compaq Presario	Tag1	Compaq Presario Laptop Computer
Toshiba HD	Tag1 HD001	256 GB Toshiba SATA Hard Drive from the Compaq Presario Laptop Computer
SanDisk Cruzer	Tag1 TD001	128 GB SanDisk Cruzer Glide Thumb drive

In this example, the specific item has been identified and assigned the organizational identification number. I have assigned the Compaq laptop the organizational identification number "Tag1."Any storage devices found in the computer will also contain the same tag number. There was a Toshiba hard drive storage device located inside the laptop, so it has the organizational identification number of "Tag1 HD001." HD is an abbreviation for hard disk. If the laptop had two hard drives, the second drive would have the organizational identification number of "Tag1 HD002." If, when the laptop was seized, a thumb drive was found in a USB port, the thumb drive will have the organizational identification number of "Tag1 TD001." TD stands for thumb drive. You can also include the serial number of the item (if it has one) in the description field.

Acquisition details

In this section, you will describe the acquisition process of creating the forensic image(s). Identify the hardware or software used in the process and include the serial/version numbers. You should also include the date the hardware/software was verified. Your narrative should include a step-by-step analysis of how the forensic image(s) was created. Include descriptions of what steps were performed as expected, and also include what did not function as expected. If the forensic image hash value was not verified, include that fact in your report and what steps you took to troubleshoot the issue. You must understand if there was an issue with the creation of the forensic image(s). Failing to identify these issues can call into question the totality of your investigation and the analysis of the forensic image(s).

Analysis details

This section will comprise a large part of your narrative. Your analysis cannot be a printout of pages of files you deemed pertinent to the investigation. You have to analyze the artifact(s) and explain why it is relevant to the investigation to the reader. Include screenshots to help reference the reader to your explanation. Including a screenshot does not remove the requirement to explain what the screenshot is depicting. Tell the reader why the screenshot is important and explain the relevance to the investigation. Do not assume the reader can determine what information in a screenshot is important.
There are several different ways to present your analysis. You can do this chronologically, by device, or by the suspect. There is no right or wrong way to write this section. My preference is to create the report chronologically and by subject. For a storage device that was the system drive for a desktop/laptop, I would start by establishing ownership and usage of the device. Then, I would move on to the specific artifacts of the incident being investigated. Be careful not to get too far into the weeds and being overly technical with your technical descriptions. For the technical descriptions, I would include that information with the specific exhibit you are describing in the Exhibits/technical details section.

For example, if the date/timestamp of an artifact is pertinent, in the narrative, you can state that the user accessed the application on X X day at X X time. In the next section, you could go into more detail about the byte offset for the date/timestamps in the file record in the MFT.

Be careful when dealing with absolute statements or using unnecessary adjectives. I once read a report that described the user's Google searches as disturbing. You do not want to categorize the behavior/actions you find while doing your digital forensic exam. Your duty is to provide the facts to the fact finder, that is, the judge/jury, and allow them to make that determination.

At the end of the narrative is the time to present your conclusions/findings. This is where you offer your opinions on the subject's culpability in your digital forensic investigation. Keep it short and straightforward – for example, *based on my examination of the following evidence (list the items you examined in the course of your digital forensic examination), it is my opinion…* – and then lay out the facts based on the artifacts you analyzed. You want to make sure you avoid any inflammatory/descriptive language and remain unbiased and professional.

Exhibits/technical details

As you create the narrative in the *Analysis* section, you will reference specific artifacts. The screenshots of those artifacts should be placed in the Exhibits/technical details section. This will also include the output reports of the forensic tool(s) you used in the exam process. If you reference the artifact in the narrative, you must include it in the Exhibits/technical detail section; likewise, if you have an exhibit in that section, you must reference it in your narrative. I find it helpful to organize the exhibits and technical details in the same order I referenced them in the narrative. It helps the reader comprehend the content of the report if they view the exhibits after reading the narrative, and they are in the same order.

In the following example, I have included the owner information of the operating system, along with the install date/timestamps, time zone, and last shutdown date/timestamp:

Compaq Presario (Tag1 HD001)	
Product Name	Windows 10
Computer Name	BadGuy Laptop
Registered Owner	BadGuy27
Install Date	August 13, 2018, 08:52:58 (Local)
Last Shutdown	October 12, 2018, 23:44:11 (Local)
Time Zone	Pacific Standard Time

An appropriate narrative of the information would be as follows:

```
The system stores the operating system information in the
SYSTEM hive of the operating system.  The data was located in
the CurrentVersion sub-key.  The fields "Computer Name" and
"Registered Owner" are user inputted values.
The operating system was installed on August 13, 2018 at
08:52:58 PST. The registered owner information is BadGuy27 and
the System name is BadGuy Laptop.
```

The description is concise, factual, and unbiased, which is the goal of the report.

The final portion of this section will be a table of software/hardware used. You want to include the version numbers of the software/firmware so that others can repeat your examination. You also want to make sure that the organization licenses for your software are authentic. This can be a simple list, as shown here:

- FTK Imager 3.0.0.1443
- X-Ways Forensics 19.7
- Paladin 7.05
- Recon 3.14.1.12

There have been issues in the past where an organization has used unlicensed/pirated software in the exam process. This is not recommended and can result in negative sanctions against you and your agency. The use of unlicensed/pirated software can call the validity of your findings into question.

I cannot stress enough how important it is for you to proofread your report. You will not create a perfect report the first time round (or the second time). You will have grammar, spelling, and content errors in the report. You should always have a second person proofread the report after you have made the first draft. The second person will find mistakes you missed and help to determine how the report flows from one section to the next. You already have an idea in your head of what I say; the second proofreader will help determine if this is effective. The second proofreader will also bring a different insight to the report's presentation and help ensure that your conclusions are logical and without bias. Whenever I proofread a colleague's report, I would look at it from the opposition's point of view. My goal was to find any inconsistencies or gaps that could be exploited if the matter went to trial.

What format should your report be in when it is disseminated to the stakeholders? My preference was to deliver my reports in a digitally signed PDF. That way, if the report is altered, it will break the digital signature. Some digital forensic investigators will create an HTML-based report and burn it onto an optical disk, while others will use the reporting function of their forensic tool. There are many options you can use in the report's presentation; you will want to make sure you can authenticate its contents if you have to testify in a judicial/administrative proceeding. A PDF will allow you to authenticate with a digital signature while saving the report and related data to an optical disk, which will enable you to create a hash value to ensure that no one has changed the contents.

Summary

In this chapter, we have discussed notetaking and how important it is to take quality notes. You learned that notetaking is the fundamental building block in creating your report. You understood the makeup of a digital forensic examination report and what information it should include. We also discussed that technical and non-technical readers may read your report and that you have to draft your report with that in mind. With that, you are able to take effective notes and prepare a clear and concise report.

In the next chapter, we will discuss the culmination of your investigation and report writing; that is, taking the stand as a witness.

Questions

1. You should start taking notes _____?

    a. When you receive notification

    b. When you get to the scene

    c. When you start the exam

    d. When you start the report

2. What information should you include in your notes?

    a. What you had for breakfast

    b. The shoe size of the suspect

    c. Location of the digital evidence at the scene

    d. Weather conditions

3. There is a national standard for notetaking.

    a. True

    b. False

4. When drafting the report, who should you keep in mind?

    a. Supervisor

    b. Chief of police

    c. District attorney

    d. The reader

5. What information is not contained in the *Administrative Information* section?

    a. Your birthday

    b. Agency name

    c. Suspect information

    d. Witness information

6. The Executive Summary should not exceed 25 percent of your report.

    a. True

    b. False

7. What should your draft report be?

    a. Detailed

    b. Brief

    c. Clear

    d. Efficient

The answers can be found at the back of this book.

Further reading

For more information, you can refer to *Forensic Examination of Digital Evidence.*

A Guide for Law Enforcement, from `https://www.ncjrs.gov/pdffiles1/ nij/199408.pdf.`

11
Expert Witness Ethics

This is the final step in your digital forensic investigation: you, as the investigator, have received a subpoena to testify in a judicial or administrative hearing. Now, it is time for you to explain your actions and findings to an unbiased third party, that is, the jury. It does not matter how good or strong the evidence you found during your digital forensic investigation is if you cannot testify effectively. You must be able to testify and authenticate the evidence in your actions.

I know some digital forensic investigators who hate to testify. They love the collection of evidence; they love doing the exam and finding the relevant artifacts, but to get them into a judicial/administrative proceeding is very difficult. The first time you walk into a courtroom, it can be an intimidating environment. You may not know the rules, the procedures, and you may be afraid of making mistakes. To overcome those issues, you will need to prepare yourself.

We'll be covering the following topics in this chapter:

- Understanding the types of proceedings
- Beginning the preparation phase
- Understanding the curriculum vitae

- Understanding testimony and evidence
- Understanding the importance of ethical behavior

So, let's jump in and start talking about how to prepare to testify in a judicial/administrative proceeding.

Understanding the types of proceedings

There are a variety of proceedings where you may be called to testify or to present evidence. We will discuss some of the more common proceedings that you may encounter (The following are US-based proceedings; your jurisdiction may differ.):

- **Grand jury**: A grand jury is a panel of citizens empowered to investigate potential criminal conduct and to determine whether the conduct requires criminal charges. A grand jury will have subpoena powers that could include compelling testimony or requesting physical evidence.

- **Arraignment**: This is the formal reading of a criminal complaint. The accused is present and informed of the charges. At this hearing, the accused will plead guilty/not guilty.

- **Detention hearing**: This is a proceeding before a judge to determine whether the accused is to be detained/released while the matter is progressing in the criminal justice system.

- **Evidentiary hearing**: This is a hearing before a judge to examine the potential evidence that will be presented to the jury. The judge can exclude or limit the evidence that may be offered.

- **Trial**: This could be a criminal or civil matter. Here, both sides present evidence to the fact-finder (judge/jury), and you may be called to testify during the case in chief, as well as the sentencing portion.

- **Deposition**: This is a sworn testimony that occurs outside of the confines of the court and is commonly used in civil litigation proceedings. Typically, there will not be a judge present, only the attorneys and the witness.

As you can see, there are several occasions where you may be called to testify or to take part. Treat every avenue as if you are taking part in a jury trial. Ultimately, it should not matter in which aspect of the system you will be testifying. You will still need to prepare in the same manner.

There are many moving parts within the courtroom. Let's discuss some participants you may encounter as a digital forensic investigator:

- **Judge**: This is the supreme being overseeing the matter. The judge will determine all motions during the trial.

- **Court reporter**: A court officer responsible for creating the official record of proceedings.

- **Court clerk**: A court officer responsible for administrative issues within the courtroom.

- **Bailiff**: A court officer responsible for maintaining order and dignity in the courtroom.

- **Prosecutor**: A representative of the sovereign who will present the government's case against the accused.

- **Defense attorney**: Represents the accused in the matter being presented in the courtroom.

- **Plaintiff**: In civil proceedings, this is the party that is claiming that the actions of the defendant have harmed them.

- **Defendant**: The accused in a criminal/civil matter.

- **Jury**: A panel of citizens who will determine the guilt/innocence of the defendant.

- **Witnesses**: Individuals who have knowledge of the incident in question and can present evidence in the matter.

As a digital forensic investigator, your role may be that of an expert witness. Being called to testify can be stressful; remember that your ability to reduce this stress lies in your preparation. Part of your preparation will be becoming familiar with the process and its participants. The more knowledge you have of your jurisdiction's criminal and civil procedures, the more comfortable you will be as you navigate through the process.

In a criminal matter, the process begins when the accused is arrested, or a warrant is issued. The accused is taken before a judge (after being arrested) and is arraigned. A preliminary hearing is held, where the judge decides whether probable cause exists to go forward with a trial. Alternatively, the matter could go before a grand jury, where they will determine whether an indictment is warranted.

There will be several hearings before the matter is presented at a trial. Once the matter goes to trial, the prosecution representing the sovereign will present their case through the presentation of evidence and witnesses. The defense will be able to cross-examine each witness immediately after the prosecution has conducted its direct examination.

Once the government rests their case, the defense has the option of presenting a case, or if they feel that the government did not present enough evidence to overcome reasonable doubt, then they may rest also.

Once both parties have rested, then the judge will give the jury instructions on how they must proceed in their deliberations.

Before you get to the proceedings where you may testify, you must be ready. This is not something you can walk into without preparing.

Beginning the preparation phase

As a digital forensic investigator, your role in a judicial/administrative proceeding can be defined in two ways:

- **Witness (also referred to as a lay or fact witness)**: You will testify about events you observed. You are just presenting facts that you have personal knowledge of, such as where the evidence was found.

- **Expert witness**: You can testify to everything a lay/fact witness can, but now you may offer your opinion. You form your opinions based on your training and experience as a digital forensic investigator. It is your ability to provide an opinion that makes you an expert witness.

Your preparation starts with your participation in the investigation. You should treat every investigation as if it will go to trial and you will have to testify. No matter which side you are on in the judicial/administrative proceeding, start communicating with the attorney at the very beginning. Discuss what they need for a successful outcome. You want to learn everything you can about the participants, that is, the suspects, victims, and attorneys of the proceeding. Educate yourself about the points of dispute of the proceeding.

For example, if the point of dispute is the willful and knowing possession of illicit images, what artifacts show/do not show that the subject willingly and knowingly possessed the illicit images? As you work to answer this question, you have the responsibility to inform the attorney when you find information that proves or disapproves the point of contention.

I can almost guarantee there will be an expert witness on the opposition team. You will want to learn about them. You will want to review their curriculum vitae, learn about their experience, their education, and their certifications. If possible, review their prior testimony.

I remember one incident where I was called to testify as an expert witness in a motion hearing. During the hearing, I was on the stand over 4 hours being questioned by the prosecution, the defense, and the judge. Once my testimony had been completed, the opposition's expert witness was called to the stand. One of the first questions asked by the judge was, *"You have heard Mr. Oettinger's testimony, is there anything you disagree with about his opinions on the state of the evidence?"* The opposing expert witness thought for a moment and replied, *"No."* I will say that it was a powerful moment for me. Having another professional in my field validate my findings and opinions during a contested trial is something I strive for.

As you are preparing for your testimony, you are trying to answer the following questions:

- What is the theory of the case?

- Does my theory fit within the facts of the case?

- What facts are central to my testimony?

- What facts can I confirm or cannot confirm?

I cannot emphasize this enough: review your report and your notes before you take the stand and testify in the proceeding. Practice answering questions. Key to the preparation phase is working with the attorney so that you both have a clear understanding of the state of the evidence and your interpretation of the evidence. Before you can be appointed as an expert witness in a matter, you will have to be approved by the judge.

To begin the review process, you will have to submit a curriculum vitae, which is the next topic.

Understanding the curriculum vitae

A **curriculum vitae** (also known as a **CV**) is a document you create that outlines your education and experience, as well as your certifications and membership and professional organizations. The court and attorneys who determine your qualifications as an expert witness will use your CV to make that determination. The contents of your CV will contain a synopsis of *what* makes you an expert; it will highlight all your experiences that make you an expert in your field.

There is no a specific format you have to use when creating your CV, but all of them will contain the same content as it is the history of your professional life.

At the top of the CV will be your name and contact information. This ensures that your name is spelled correctly throughout the proceeding and when added to the witness list. You will also want to identify the field you are an expert in. If the attorney, judge, or court clerk is dealing with multiple experts in a matter, this helps to identify the area of testimony that you may be asked to speak about. You will also want to include a contact number, email address, and physical address. This allows for all parties to contact you. Also, your CV may be shared with other attorneys in different matters, and they will use that information to solicit you for additional opportunities.

> **Note**
>
> A note about the address used on your CV. You should not include your home address. You may testify in a matter that could deal with physical violence or the potential for incarceration. It does not matter which side you testify on; someone will likely be unhappy with the results. If you are working for an organization, use the organization's address. If you are working for yourself, I recommend getting a PO Box or a private mailbox.

You will then create a summary of your biography. This will include a synopsis of your career, education, and experience.

Next is the bulk of your CV, where you list your formal education and work history. You can use the following categories to organize the information being presented:

- **Formal education**: Degrees, certificates awarded.

- **Employment history**: As it relates to the field.

- **Teaching experience**: This will cross over with your employment history. Keep it relevant to the field you will testify about in the proceeding.

- **Licensing/professional membership**: List the relevant professional organizations you belong to. If the government requires licensure, be sure to include that as well.

- **Publication**: If you have authored a book, white paper, an article, or a blog, identify the publisher's name and address, as well as when the item was printed.

- **Awards**: If you have received an award for your work in the field, please list it.

- **Previous testimony**: You should list the previous cases where they have appointed you as an expert. This does not have to include a summary of the matter; instead, the use of a simple *US v Smith (2015)* will suffice.

Do not get caught up and overthink the CV by including *everything*. You will want to keep the content pertinent to the specific matter and what subjects will come into play during your testimony. You want to stay focused on the field-specific items; whether you graduated high school or worked at a fast-food restaurant during college isn't relevant. You are only providing the information needed for the judge/attorneys to determine whether your education and experiences qualify you as an expert witness.

When drafting your CV, I cannot emphasize enough that you refrain from adding information that is not true and accurate. I can understand wanting to *pad* the document to make it appear you are the best candidate, but if you lie about your CV and continue to lie after being appointed as an expert and testify, you could face severe repercussions when the lie is discovered.

Note

In 2016, The government arrested Chester Kwitowski after he provided false information about his education, experience, and credentials. At the time of his arrest, defense teams had hired him for five additional pending matters. Historically, he also provided expert testimony in state and federal court over 50 times. The prosecutors determined that the educational degrees Kwitowski claimed to have received did not exist, nor was there any record he had completed the professional certifications he claimed. Kwitowski claims to have worked with NASA, but the organization denied any involvement or work history with Kwitowski. Kwitowski also had a criminal history dating back nearly 20 years that included charges of battery, domestic violence, and aggravated battery with a deadly weapon.

At the time of writing this book, in 2020, Kwitowski is pending prosecution for two counts of giving false statements during the prosecution of a capital felony and three counts of perjury.

After you are requested to be an expert in the matter and you have submitted your CV, there may be a hearing to determine your qualifications as an expert. The bailiff will swear you under oath and you will take your seat on the witness stand. Each counsel will ask you questions in order to assess your qualifications to be an expert in the matter at hand. In some jurisdictions, the judge may also ask you questions. The judge will make a ruling to either approve or disapprove you acting as an expert.

If the judge approves you, then you will work closely with the attorney that requested you and work with them to determine the pros and cons of the matter. On the day of the trial, the attorney may call you as a witness in the matter and you will have to testify. We will cover this in the next section.

Understanding testimony and evidence

You are at the point in the trial where you are asked to take an oath and promise to tell the truth. You then take your seat, and the focus of the room is on you. You may have the judge sitting next to you at an elevated position. Across from you, you may see two tables. One table will be hosting the prosecution, which could be one or more attorneys. At the next table will be the defense, which can also comprise more than one attorney and the subject of the trial. There could also be a jury box that could contain 12 or more citizens whose job is to determine the guilt or innocence of the accused. Every single one of them is now watching you. This can be a little stress-inducing. Take a deep breath and focus on the questions that are being asked of you.

Your testimony will comprise technical details and your expert opinion. The technical information will include you explaining complex technical issues in simple terms. This enables the non-technical audience, that is, the judge and the jury, to understand what occurred and how it is being described.

You will want to speak in a slow, deliberate manner. This ensures your audience, including the jury and the court reporter, can understand the concepts you are relaying. You also want to add analogies to help explain the complex technical subject.

I remember a trial I was part of a few years back. I was the defense's expert in a matter that dealt with digital evidence and the possession of illicit images. While reviewing the reports, there were issues in the method that was used in the seizure of digital evidence. Based on the information in the reports, the computer systems were not seized in the method that would conform to best practices at that time. I informed the lead attorney about these issues as he was preparing to cross-examine the lead agent who was responsible for the seizure. The lead agent did not have a significant amount of experience testifying. During the cross-examination, the agent was not testifying as effectively as they could have. When the subject of the seizure of the digital evidence was started, the agent admitted to violating the "prime directive" of seizing digital evidence.

I asked myself the same question that is going through your mind: *What is the prime directive?* My only reference for the prime directive is watching episodes of the TV show Star Trek. What occurred is that the attorney conflated best practices with the prime directive, which the agent agreed he violated.

Once the trial was complete, I had coffee with the agent, and I asked him why he answered that he violated the prime directive. He stated that he had just been worn down by the questions of the defense attorney and did not want to appear stupid in front of the jury or his peers. I can understand that. Let's now talk about how to prevent that.

If the lawyers ask you a question you do not understand, it is perfectly acceptable to answer *"I am not sure what you are asking, could you rephrase the question"* or *"I do not know."* All are very valid answers. You may also be asked a question outside your expertise. Answer that question as *"that is beyond the scope of my expertise"* or *"that was not part of the investigation."*

Lawyers love to ask exceedingly complex questions; you have the right – if not the duty – to ask for clarification for any question you do not understand. Sometimes, lawyers will ask you a question that requires a narrative answer but wants a firm *yes* or *no* answer. Your answer should be "that is not a *yes* or *no* question, but one that requires a more detailed response."

Your words are not the only thing your audience is using to grade your credibility. Your physical appearance, your tone, and your posture conveys your attitude to your audience. If you take the stand in a rumpled suit, tie undone, and shirttail untucked, you will not be as effective as if you are wearing a freshly pressed suit, properly tied tie, and looking and answering questions like a professional. The following are some guidelines to consider when testifying:

- **Do not argue with the attorney**: You are an unbiased professional. You need to answer the questions to the best of your ability. If you get into an argument with the attorney, it does not help the audience understand the evidence. In fact, they may discount your testimony because of the appearance of bias.

- **Speak clearly and slowly**: If your audience cannot understand what you are saying, you are not as effective as a witness.

- **Avoid slang and acronyms**: Remember that you are translating a technical topic for a non-technical audience.

- **Do not be a comedian**: Do not make a joke; this is a serious situation. Someone's freedom could be at stake; it is not the place to be humorous.

- **Listen to the entire question**: Do not interrupt the attorney and try to answer what you think the question is. Only answer the question that was asked.

Remember, you are an unbiased advocate. Your job is to assist the fact-finder in determining what occurred based on the evidence.

Digital evidence caused some issues with the rules of evidence when it was first used in a judicial proceeding. You will want to follow all the best practices in the collection of digital evidence to ensure its integrity. By being able to demonstrate your efforts to ensure the integrity of the digital evidence, you will reduce the likelihood of the judge excluding the digital evidence.

All evidence must be authenticated. This means there must be a witness to testify about their knowledge of the evidence being presented. If a photo is being presented as evidence, the photographer must attest that they took the photo.

With digital evidence, the digital forensic investigator must testify that the evidence being presented is based on an exact and true copy of the original. Remember, we do not want to conduct our digital forensic examination on the original evidence. Digital evidence is very fragile, so we need to create an exact and true copy that can be validated using hashing.

For the evidence to be admitted in court, it must be reliable and credible, relevant to the facts of the matter, and material to an issue that is being questioned. If the evidence was collected in a manner the court determines to be illegal, then that evidence is tainted and can be excluded.

When you (or someone in your organization) collects the digital evidence, you want to make sure that the original evidence was preserved in the state that it was found. If you collected volatile data, explain to the court your reasoning for doing so. The collection of volatile data will cause changes to the system and alter the original state of the evidence.

As you can see, this process can be overwhelming. While conducting your digital forensic investigation, you may find yourself in a situation in which you question what the *right* thing to do is. This is an ethical dilemma, which leads us to our next topic.

Understanding the importance of ethical behavior

You have the responsibility to conduct due diligence, be truthful, and be objective during your digital forensic investigation. Your personal and professional ethics determine the baseline of your behavior. Failure to act ethically during your digital forensic investigation can cause the evidence to be excluded and/or result in you facing professional repercussions.

As a digital forensic investigator, you have specialized knowledge that has the potential for misuse. Failure to follow up on potential leads you discovered during your forensic examination is an ethical lapse that could have repercussions on you, a third party, or your organization.

What is the definition of ethics? It is the moral principles that govern the behavior of an individual or activity. It is not a distinct standard; it will depend on your culture to determine what is acceptable and what is not. In a professional setting, an organization may declare a professional set of ethics.

The **International Association of Computer Investigative Specialists (IACIS)** is an organization I belong to, and because of my membership, I agree to follow their Code of Ethics.

The following Code of Ethics is taken from `https://www.iacis.com/wp-content/uploads/2018/02/IACIS-Code-of-Ethics-and-Professional-Conduct-2017-V-1.3.pdf`:

IACIS personnel will advise and provide assistance to other IACIS personnel within the scope of their legal authority.

IACIS personnel will be honest and ethical when dealing with each other.

IACIS personnel must respect the rights and authorities of the directors, fellow members, and individuals encountered as a result of their membership in IACIS or in connection with IACIS sponsored or sanctioned activities.

IACIS personnel's actions, when representing or acting on behalf of IACIS, must be free from discrimination, libel, slander or harassment. Each person must be accorded equal opportunity, regardless of age, race, sex, sexual preference, color, creed, religion, national origin, marital status, veteran's status, handicap, or disability.

IACIS personnel may not misrepresent their credentials, employment, education, training and experience, or membership status; nor may they misrepresent the credentials, employment, education, training and experience, or membership status of any other member of IACIS.

IACIS personnel may not issue public statements that appear to represent the position of IACIS without specific written authority from the Board of Directors.

IACIS personnel must not commit any act of professional dishonesty.

IACIS personnel may not knowingly submit, aid, or abet the submission of plagiarized or any non-uniquely authored piece of work during any phase of an IACIS certification process or test. To do so will be considered to have been a dishonest act.

IACIS personnel have an obligation to report acts or suspected acts of dishonesty committed by IACIS personnel. Failure to report acts or suspected acts of dishonesty will be considered to have been a dishonest act.

IACIS personnel's criminal convictions are a serious affront to the ideals of IACIS and, as such, are not tolerated.

IACIS personnel have an obligation to fully and honestly cooperate with any investigation or inquiry conducted at the direction of the IACIS Ethics Committee or members of an IACIS Investigative Team.

Does that code of ethics apply to all digital forensic investigators? No. The ethics of an organization apply specifically to that organization. You can take that framework and use it in your professional and personal environments. You will notice that the only portion dealing with a digital forensic investigation is the one that states that IACIS personnel must not commit any act of professional dishonesty.

That is a broad statement. It is not a clear line in the sand of what is allowed or not allowed. Determine what is ethical as you perform your duties as a digital forensic investigator.

The **International Society of Forensic Computer Examiners (ISFCE)** has a much more specific code of ethics regarding professional behavior during a digital forensic investigation.

The following Code of Ethics has been taken from `https://www.isfce.com/ethics2.htm` for your reference:

Demonstrate commitment and diligence in the performance of assigned duties.

Demonstrate integrity in completing professional assignments.

Maintain the utmost objectivity in all forensic examinations and accurately present findings.

Conduct examinations based on established, validated procedures.

Abide by the highest moral and ethical standards and abide by the Code of the ISFCE.

Testify truthfully in all matters before any board, court, or proceeding.

Avoid any action that would knowingly present a conflict of interest.

Comply with all legal orders of the courts.

Thoroughly examine all evidence within the scope of the engagement.

This code of ethics contains definitive language about what is allowed or not allowed by members of their organization who have certified as a **Certified Computer Examiner (CCE)**. Members and non-members alike should use this code of conduct whenever they are conducting a digital forensic examination.

Maintaining a code of ethics in your professional life allows you to keep your objectivity during the investigation. If you cannot be impartial, you should not be a party to the investigation. I recently took part in a motion hearing to determine whether they should appoint me as an expert. After they questioned me about my qualifications, education, and experience, I was asked my opinion about the state of the evidence I have reviewed. On cross-examination, the prosecution told me, "Your duty as an expert is to find things wrong in the evidence." My reply was that as an expert, my job was to see whether I could recreate the examination and achieve the same results and conclusion. If the information I found was detrimental to the theory supported by the defense or the prosecution, I would disclose it no matter which side of the matter I was appointed to represent. With digital forensics, the data is the data; there is not a lot of interpretation about what the data means.

As you gain training and experience, I recommend that you achieve industry-specific certifications. The possession of certifications does not guarantee or make you an exceptional digital forensic investigator. A certification states that you have met the minimum standards of that organization. It does not mean you cannot make a mistake or come to the wrong conclusion. It also ensures that you are keeping current with the changes in the field. What was acceptable 5 years ago may not be acceptable now because of changes in technology or the law. Your training never stops as you pursue a career in this field.

Ethics is doing the right thing when no one is looking. If you compromise your ethics, you can negatively affect your career and investigation. Remember that your goal is to be unbiased and present the facts of the matter to the fact-finder. You are not an advocate for either side of the matter and you now have the knowledge to accomplish that goal.

Summary

During this chapter, you learned how to prepare to give testimony in an administrative or judicial proceeding. You can now identify the different proceedings and the participants. You can also create a CV and differentiate one from a resume. You also have the skills to ensure that you conduct your digital forensic investigation and exam while maintaining your objectivity and impartiality through the use of a code of ethics.

Thank you for your efforts and for working through my book! I am confident that you can use the skills you've learned here and apply them to a real-world setting.

Questions

1. An expert witness can offer _____.

   a. Testimony

   b. Facts

   c. Opinion

   d. Hearsay evidence

2. Preparation starts _____.

   a. When you receive a subpoena

   b. When your supervisor tells you to begin

   c. When the judge calls you

   d. When you start the investigation

3. Which court officer represents the sovereign?

   a. The judge

   b. The prosecutor

   c. The court reporter

   d. The bailiff

4. In a trial, the fact finder will be who?

   a. The jury

   b. The grand jury

   c. The judge

   d. The attorney

5. Which of the following should you NOT include on a CV?

   a. Formal education

   b. Teaching experience

   c. Professional memberships

   d. Salary

6. Which of the following is an appropriate answer to a question you do not understand?

   a. I do not know.

   b. You should try and guess.

   c. Ask to repeat the question.

   d. Look to the judge for help.

7. Why should you adhere to a code of ethics?

   a. To maintain your impartiality

   b. To make sure the correct side wins

   c. To ensure the accused is found guilty

   d. To keep your certification

The answers can be found at the back of this book.

Further reading

Refer to the following sources for more information:

- Smith, F. C., and Bace, R. G. (2003). *A guide to forensic testimony: the art and practice of presenting testimony as an expert technical witness*. Boston, MA: Addison-Wesley (available at https://www.amazon.com/Guide-Forensic-Testimony-Presenting-Technical/dp/0201752794)

- Poynter, D. (2012). *Expert witness handbook: tips and techniques for the litigation consultant*. Santa Barbara, CA: Para Pub (available at https://www.amazon.com/Expert-Witness-Handbook-Techniques-Litigations/dp/1568601522)

Assessments

Chapter 01

1. False
2. D
3. True
4. D
5. B
6. B
7. A

Chapter 02

1. D
2. False
3. D
4. A
5. A
6. D
7. C

Chapter 03

1. A
2. C
3. True
4. C
5. True
6. B
7. B

Chapter 04

1. B
2. C
3. False
4. False
5. C
6. False
7. B

Chapter 05

1. True
2. C
3. C
4. B
5. A
6. A
7. True

Chapter 06

1. A
2. C
3. C
4. C
5. False
6. False
7. C

Chapter 07

1. A and B
2. C
3. C
4. C
5. B
6. B
7. C

Chapter 08

1. A
2. D
3. B
4. C
5. D
6. C
7. B

Chapter 09

1. A
2. C
3. D
4. C
5. B
6. B
7. C

Chapter 10

1. A
2. C
3. B
4. D
5. A
6. B
7. C

Chapter 11

1. C
2. D
3. B
4. A
5. D
6. A, C
7. A

Other Books You May Enjoy

If you enjoyed this book, you may be interested in these other books by Packt:

Digital Forensics and Incident Response - Second Edition

Gerard Johansen

ISBN: 978-1-83864-900-5

- Create and deploy an incident response capability within your own organization
- Perform proper evidence acquisition and handling
- Analyze the evidence collected and determine the root cause of a security incident
- Become well-versed with memory and log analysis
- Integrate digital forensic techniques and procedures into the overall incident response process
- Understand the different techniques for threat hunting
- Write effective incident reports that document the key findings of your analysis

Digital Forensics with Kali Linux

Shiva V. N. Parasram

ISBN: 978-1-83864-080-4

- Get up and running with powerful Kali Linux tools for digital investigation and analysis
- Perform internet and memory forensics with Volatility and Xplico
- Understand filesystems, storage, and data fundamentals
- Become well-versed with incident response procedures and best practices
- Perform ransomware analysis using labs involving actual ransomware
- Carry out network forensics and analysis using NetworkMiner and other tools

Leave a review - let other readers know what you think

Please share your thoughts on this book with others by leaving a review on the site that you bought it from. If you purchased the book from Amazon, please leave us an honest review on this book's Amazon page. This is vital so that other potential readers can see and use your unbiased opinion to make purchasing decisions, we can understand what our customers think about our products, and our authors can see your feedback on the title that they have worked with Packt to create. It will only take a few minutes of your time, but is valuable to other potential customers, our authors, and Packt. Thank you!

Index

Symbols

342